ROBERT MITCHUM

"All the rest of us were so intimidated by what the studio said . . . but not him. That was his charm, that not caring."

—Janet Gaynor

"Hollywood's longest-running bad boy . . . he has managed consistently to offend more people than any other legitimate movie star."

—*Publishers Weekly*

"Mitchum's biography is full of anecdotes. His burly image is, if anything, enhanced. Mitchum is a man with a diverse personality: rebellious, infuriating and, certainly, unpredictable."

—*South Bend Tribune*

Robert Mitchum

A Biography
GEORGE EELLS

A JOVE BOOK

ROBERT MITCHUM

A Jove Book/published by arrangement with
Franklin Watts

PRINTING HISTORY
Franklin Watts edition published 1984
Jove edition/July 1985

ISBN: 0-515-08213-9

Jove books are published by The Berkley Publishing Group,
200 Madison Avenue, New York, N.Y. 10016.
The words "A JOVE BOOK" and the "J" with sunburst
are trademarks belonging to Jove Publications, Inc.

PRINTED IN THE UNITED STATES OF AMERICA

For
Natalie Schafer

Acknowledgments

Grateful acknowledgment is made to the following: Lillian Gish, Julie Mitchum Sater, Elliot Sater, John Mitchum, Ann Mitchum Morris, Sylvia Miles, Arlene Francis, Walter Kane, Vi Coulter, Carroll Righter, Lizbeth Scott, Henny Backus, Jim Backus, Allan Davis, Don Raye, Bill Thomas, George Leigh, David Dortort, Jane Greer, Mary Beth Hughes, Richard Egan, Jack Lemmon, Pat Rooney, Jack Webb, Eddie Jaffe, Fran Belleli, Mervyn LeRoy, Ella Raines, Lee Silvian, Barbara Hale, Bill Williams, Jerry Devine, Sarah Miles, Laraine Day, Ray Daum, Ted Montague, Steve Brodie, Kemp Niver, Mrs. Josephine Bruttig, Richard Segel, Paul Gregory, Janet Gaynor, Frank Liberman, Phil Berg, Grainger Hines, Liz Smith, Michael Hamilburg, George Givot, Tony Caruso, Tonia Caruso, Laura Killingsworth, Kay Gardella, Don Reed, Robert Renfrow, Henry Hathaway, Eleanor Corrigan, Phyllis Diller, Boyd Cabeen, Alvista Perkins, Barry Rehfeld, Jim Dougherty, Else Lanchester, Tom Miller, Karl Matzinger, Betty Matzinger, Don Shepherd, Robert Slatzer, Vincent Price, Norma Pearson, Tommy Rettig, Doug Warren, Martha Knowles, Yvonne Hemsey, Janet Sartin, Cheryl Lavin, Mel Lashley, Don Defore, David Chierachetti.

Special thanks to: Doug McClelland for use of research and photos related to Mitchum; Dr. Robert Knutson, Special Collections, Doheny Library, University of Southern California; the staff of the Library, Academy of Motion Picture Arts and Sciences; the staff of the theater collection, Lincoln Center Library for the Performing Arts; Tom Clapp and Stanley Musgrove for editorial advice; Liz Hock, a most sensitive editor; and, both first and last, my agent, Gloria Safier.

PROLOGUE

The time was a little past midnight, September 1, 1948. For the past two hours narcotics officers A. M. Barr and J. B. McKinnon had been lurking outside the ramshackle, three-room bungalow that sat on a hill fifty feet back from the road at 8334 Ridpath Drive. It was a warm, moonlit night, which from the officers' point of view, was both good and bad.

The heat had caused the occupants to raise the windows in hopes of cooling down the house, making it easier for the two police officers to overhear everything that was being said inside.

But the bright moonlight presented a problem: it forced the policemen to keep close to the darker sides of the little bungalow, or hidden in the shadows cast by the shrubbery and cactus plants that helped screen the house from the view of neighbors.

It was the eighth month of surveillance of a number of members of the film colony and their hangers-on, and the officers were optimistic that tonight their persistence was going to pay off. They were confident that the girls who had moved into the house only a couple of weeks before would be giving another of their frequent and noisy parties. They had had a tip that a bobby-sox idol would be on hand. If not, they would settle for twenty-year-old Lila Leeds, a Lana Turner look-alike.

Lila was not established enough to garner the big headlines. She had spent six months under contract at Metro-Goldwyn-Mayer and her option had not been exercised. Then her agent, Louis Shurr, had placed her with Warner Brothers for another six months, but as studio head Jack Warner told a friend, "We had great hopes for the kid. But she just kind of went to seed before we could find a good role for her."

Warner Brothers had dropped her, and in the interest of economy Lila had rented the bungalow with the peeling paint on Ridpath in Laurel Canyon where hip members of Hollywood tended to gravitate. Her new roommate was a twenty-five-year-old dancer named Vicki Evans, who aspired to chorus work in films and nightclubs.

That two members of the Narcotics Division of the Los Angeles Police Department should have spent three-quarters of a year to come up with two such small-time users of marijuana seems incredible in 1984.

Transpose the last two numerals and step back to 1948. In that year Commissioner of the United States Treasury's Bureau of Narcotics Harry J. Anslinger was America's czar of drug enforcement, and he had brainwashed both ordinary citizens and law enforcement officers to believe that marijuana was "the killer weed" whose use led inevitably to hard drugs—and probably death.

As Barr and McKinnon slipped from the living room windows to the one in the bedroom wall and back again their hopes rose and fell. The girls' plans for the evening seemed to be in a state of flux. To pass time the officers made friends with the young boxer dogs Lila had purchased to guard the premises.*

During Barr and McKinnon's vigil they took special interest in a series of calls about whether or not two men were going to drop by. From bits of information they pieced together, they had reason to believe that the appearance of these men would make their patience worthwhile.

---

*When Lila learned that her boxers had failed to warn her and had made friends with the cops, she quipped, "They must be police dogs in disguise."

They also knew that the expected visitors had been delayed because one of them had been sent a script to read, after which he wanted to go directly to dinner. His friend who kept calling back, the officers believed, was trying to lure him to Ridpath Drive. Finally there came a call announcing that the two had downed a fifth of Scotch and were on their way. "The boys are at the bottom of the hill and lost," Lila told Vicki after still another call, "but they're loaded."

Not long after she imparted this information a 1948 Buick, which Barr and McKinnon had no trouble recognizing, wheeled to a stop in front of 8334 Ridpath Drive.

Out stepped a broad-shouldered giant of a man whose distinctive walk was due chiefly to the thrust of his barrel chest. He was dressed in a brown jacket, a red and white checked shirt and tan slacks. He wore no hat, and his unruly hair easily would have identified him to millions of movie fans as Robert Mitchum. For Barr and McKinnon, who had recently given up keeping him under surveillance, only a glance was necessary for them to realize that they had their man, a man whose fans included men, women and teenagers—some of the latter had formed a fan club called "The Bob Mitchum Droolettes"—a man whose arrest would earn headlines. Their months of tailing Bob Mitchum to bars, parties and late-night gathering places where the hip crowd hung out had finally paid off.

The other man, who would have been totally unknown to moviegoers, was even more familiar to the narcotics officers. Robin "Danny" Ford, a fringe character, had had a number of encounters with the narcotics squad. Originally Barr and McKinnon had planned to wait for a large party to get underway. Now they were tempted to spring.

Bob and Ford made their way up the path and climbed the steep flight of steps leading to the house. They were enthusiastically welcomed by Lila, who looked fetching in white shorts and a blue bathrobe, and Vicki, who was somewhat more formally clad.

The officers could hear Lila urging the visitors to notice how she had redone the house, but they saw Bob flop down on the sofa indifferently and demand that the lights be dimmed because they hurt his eyes, even though he was wearing dark glasses. He tossed a package of cigarettes on the coffee table and, Barr claimed, Lila picked it up. After examining its contents, she exclaimed, "Oh, you've got brown ones and white ones, too," referring to the color of the cigarette papers the joints were rolled in. "I want some of the white ones."

She extracted a couple of joints from the package, lit them and extended one to Bob, who accepted it. Shortly, he jumped up and ran to the window. When his friends inquired what was wrong, he said he'd seen two faces peering in. Lila laughed and advised him to stop mixing booze and grass, but he insisted he had seen window peepers. Vicki assured him it was only "those damn puppies" who were always trying to get into the house.

Barr and McKinnon swiftly moved to the porch where they let out the dogs. Then they cautiously tried the kitchen door. Finding it locked, they scratched at it in imitation of the dogs. Vicki, who said she assumed it was the boxers wanting in, threw open the door to find herself face to face with two men, guns drawn. They flashed their badges and pushed their way into the living room where Lila, Bob and Ford were caught with glowing joints between their lips or in their hands. Vicki was the only one who had not lit up. Bob instantly removed his cigarette from his lips, crumpled it and tossed it into an ashtray. Ford quickly followed suit. Barr leaped forward to retrieve the two joints, burning his fingers in the process. When he held out his hand to take two partly smoked joints from Lila, she responded by reaching into the pocket of her blue robe and handing him a newspaper-wrapped package containing three joints and eight benzedrine pills.

Picking up the cigarette package Bob had tossed on the coffee table, Barr recovered fifteen additional sticks of marijuana, then picked up the telephone and called headquarters, requesting additional officers.

"I'm ruined," Bob said.

"Danny" Ford echoed those sentiments, although just how he was ruined he did not make clear. Bob identified Ford to reporters as an insurance and real estate salesman. Later, in a more forthright statement, the star described Ford as "one of the hangers-on who attached himself to me after I got out of the service." In fact, Ford worked mostly as a bartender.

Bob's mood, meanwhile, swung from one extreme to the other. Even before he was requested to, he thrust out his arms to receive the handcuffs. But in the squad car on the way to the jail he bitterly announced that he supposed he was "all washed up in pictures."

At Lincoln Heights jail, where policewoman Eleanor Whitney took Lila and Vicki, curiously enough the girls echoed the same sentiments the boys had expressed. Lila even confessed a certain relief at her arrest. She confided that she had had a premonition of trouble. "About ten o'clock last night I wondered if the police were to come in, could I get to the bathroom with the marijuana before they got in. This is it. I'm glad it's over. I'm ruined."

Vicki, who had not been caught smoking, suggested to police officers that they take her instead of Bob and Lila because, she said, "They have so much more to lose. I'm unemployed." Yet when the police arrested everyone, Vicki joined the chorus, announcing, "I'm ruined!"

At the Los Angeles County Jail newspaper reporters and photographers were on hand, jostling one another for position to get quotes and photos from the $3,000-a-week movie star, who greeted them with, "Yes, boys, I was smoking a marijuana cigarette when they came in." Then, almost as an afterthought, he said, "I knew I'd get caught sooner or later." He obligingly posed for the photographers as he speculated that his wife Dorothy, who had gone east two months before after telling acquaintances that her husband had "gone Hollywood and was hanging out with undesirables," would never reconcile now. "Not with her temper," he observed. "She's a very resolute woman."

When booked, Bob gave his age as "thirty-one."

His address?

"Thirty-three seventy-two Oak Glen Drive."

His occupation?

"Former actor."

Had he any identifying marks?

"Yes." He rolled up a shirtsleeve and pointed to a tiny tattoo. "An obscene word," he confided.

Had he ever been arrested before?

"Only for speeding, drunkenness and disorderly conduct," he smilingly informed the police. As an afterthought, he commented, "It's ridiculous. We'd been in that house seven minutes. We just stopped by before going for a bite to eat in the San Fernando Valley."

At about the same time, Sergeant Barr summoned the press corps to make a statement that would send shudders through the Hollywood establishment: "Many big shots—stars and other top names—do not patronize small street-corner peddlers for fear of a shakedown. However, we have reason to believe there is an 'inside ring' of perhaps no more than three persons right inside the film industry, who are supplying large numbers of narcotics users. Most prevalent use is of marijuana, but we know other drugs are being used. And we're going to clean the dope and the narcotics users out of Hollywood! And we don't care who we're going to have to arrest. . . . This is only the beginning of a Hollywood clean-up!"

In spite of Barr's warning, Bob spent the predawn hours talking compulsively, mixing hip putdowns with feelings of despair as he sparred with the press. Indicating the prison garb issued him, he flippantly told photographers, "Sorry my new outfit doesn't appeal to you, fellows. It doesn't appeal to me either." He complained about McKinnon and Barr's rudeness in causing him to miss his dinner, noting that he hadn't even been offered a cup of coffee since being brought in.

During booking, he said, they had stripped him, shackled him and left him stark naked to be questioned by a psychiatrist, who after an exchange of platitudes, asked if Bob went to parties.

Bob allowed that he did.

What, the psychiatrist wanted to know, did he do?

"I get drunk, follow pretty broads, make a fool of myself and stagger home," Bob said he told the psychiatrist.

The psychiatrist wanted to know whether he ever went to parties with men.

Bob did.

What, asked the doctor, did he do at those gatherings?

"Talk dirty, play poker, get drunk."

The doctor was curious whether his subject liked pretty girls. Bob said he did.

Did he ever go out with them?

"No," Bob said.

"Why not?"

"Because my wife won't let me."

Ruth Waterbury, who was there representing *Modern Screen*, said that Bob clearly enjoyed the shocked laughter which greeted his little anecdote. He loved shocking people, in Waterbury's opinion. When she inquired what he would do if the public turned on him, she said he looked her straight in the eye and defied her. "I'll never forget his answer," she recalled. "He said, 'I think I'll go in the religion business. Can you imagine the kind of hit I'd be with my personality out selling religion!'"

Cautioned by attorney Grant Cooper, who had turned up at the jail, to be careful not to damage his case, Bob's mood changed visibly. He said he was afraid he had already done that, and he appeared sincerely regretful when he revealed that he had had to bow out of his speaking engagement scheduled for that morning on the steps of City Hall celebrating National Youth Day. He sighed and announced, "Well, this is the bitter end of everything—my career, my home, my marriage."

The reporters, sensing his switch of mood, pressed him. Didn't he foresee the trouble he was getting himself into? That question appeared to change his mood once again. He looked the assemblage in the eye and informed them that he didn't give a damn. He was still ahead. He'd lived in a boxcar during the depression, had nothing to eat but cold, raw potatoes. He warmed to the subject, reminiscing, "It got worse. When I was thrown off a train it was ten degrees below. I was freezing until I put newspapers inside my clothing to keep warm. Then some creep set my pants on fire, almost burned them off. When you've stood naked from the waist down under a street light in Idaho looking for a clothesline from which to steal frozen pants to thaw out in the local depot—from that moment on everything else is up."

A few hours later, attorney Jerry Giesler, who had successfully defended a parade of other prominent citizens in trouble, was retained to defend Bob. After a talk with Giesler the star clammed up. Both Howard Hughes's RKO and David O. Selznick's Vanguard, who shared Bob's contract, asked the public to withhold judgment until he was adjudged guilty or innocent. Selznick went even further in special pleading, infuriating the star by describing him as "a very sick man in need of medical treatment instead of a lawbreaker."

Bail was set at one thousand dollars each for the four defendants, and a habeas corpus hearing was scheduled for the following week. Upon release, Bob immediately went into seclusion in a small cottage on North Palm Avenue occupied by his mother and stepfather. A few select friends rushed to his side. On hand, too, were representatives of the industry, intent upon salvaging, if possible, the five million dollars' worth of investments tied up in Bob's unreleased films, including *Rachel and the Stranger* with Loretta Young, *Blood on the Moon* with Barbara Bel Geddes, and at Republic, *The Red Pony* with Myrna Loy.

Bob refused to discuss anything about his troubles with family or friends, and retreated to a screened porch. Behind closed doors he paced up and down, arrogantly refusing sympathy or advice, telling off the establishment, the movie industry, the city and all of its inhabitants in a voice that carried to the street. He remained there, cursing his fate until the arrival of Churchill Ross, a blond, college-type comedian of late 1920s films, whose glasses and slightly stiff neck were his comic trademarks but whose career had ended tragically when the stiff neck developed into arthritis of the spine which bent him into a grotesque figure.

Ross, who had become a Bahái convert, had been trying for almost a decade to convert the Mitchums to that faith. Bob was not interested, but Ross's caustic wit amused him, and a close friendship developed between the two. He now surprised everyone by motioning Ross to join him on the porch.

Ross was taken aback by Bob's hostile attitude toward the world in general and his bitter conviction that he was finished in pictures. But both were outraged by the Selznick release referring to Bob as "a sick man." As he paced, Bob told his visitor what Hollywood could do to itself and where it could take his career and shove it, in the pungent patter (as he called it) that he spoke so creatively. He insisted that he didn't give a fuck whether he continued in pictures or not. He'd arrived in Southern California on a freight train with a dollar and twenty-nine cents in his jeans, and he would be happy to leave the same way. His wife and children would never return to him now.

Ross interrupted, trying to reason with the angry figure who continued to pace the length of the porch. He was totally unsuccessful. Finally, losing patience, Ross told Bob to knock it off. Without referring to the physical disability that had cut short his own career, he reminded his friend that worse things had happened to others. "You've got a lot at stake," he later told friends he had said, "and you're going to have to show a little humility to salvage what you have." Carefully feeling his way, he managed to break down Bob's defenses. Bob grew silent, stopped pacing and stared out of the window. When he finally spoke, he poured out his regrets. He was convinced he had destroyed his mother's respect for him. This meant more to him than his career, and more importantly, he was convinced in his heart of hearts that if Dorothy refused to return, as he was now certain she would, he would simply go out of control. "You don't know how scared I am," Ross quoted him as saying. "Scared shitless." He turned away and stared out toward the street. His shoulders began to shake, and Ross knew that one of the screen's preeminent, don't-give-a-damn he-men was silently weeping.

CHAPTER 1

By any standard Robert Charles Duran Mitchum's childhood had only one continuing source from which he could draw a reassuring sense of stability. His mother, Ann, a determined, forward-looking woman, believed that young children were capable of early achievement and that relying on conventional education stultified a child's natural impulse to investigate and understand the world around him. Like her other children, Bob, through Ann's efforts, was able to read and write by the age of three. Had circumstances been different, this remarkable woman would have seen to it that Bob and her other children received every advantage; due to events beyond her control, however, this was not to be.

At the age of nine, Ann Gunderson emigrated with her family from her native Oslo, Norway, to the United States in 1903. By 1910 they had settled in Bridgeport, Connecticut, and she had grown into a chestnut-haired beauty of studious bent. She was a hard-working, spiritual, somewhat shy girl, so it came as a distinct shock to her family and friends when she developed a romantic interest in a young serviceman stationed in New London, Connecticut.

11

James Mitchum, who was Scotch-Irish on his father's side and pure-blooded Blackfoot Indian on his mother's, hailed from Lane, South Carolina (roughly forty miles north of Charleston). He was a small, handsome man, but Ann's family was apprehensive about his reputation as a brawler—one of those men who experience physical pleasure in fighting for fighting's sake. His standing challenge to take on "any three men" in the Bridgeport–New London area was well known. It is understandable that Ann's family was anxious about her involvement with him: Should the couple marry, her family feared, any children they might have would inherit his pugnacity.

Marry him Ann did in 1911. For a time the newlyweds led a life typical of young marrieds in military service. The Army transferred Jimmy Mitchum to the Charleston area where little Annette, better known as Julie, was born in 1914. Then he was transferred back to Connecticut where Robert Charles Duran Mitchum arrived on August 6, 1917.

Shortly, Jimmy was mustered out of the service, and since jobs were scarce around Bridgeport and New London, he took his little brood back to South Carolina where he found civilian employment in the Charleston Navy Yard.

It was a happy time for the young couple and their children. Jimmy's salary was good, and the Mitchums made frequent weekend jaunts to such places as Savannah, Georgia, or Tampa, Florida, where Jimmy happily shepherded the family to public beaches, amusement parks and a zoo where he made his eighteen-month-old son laugh aloud at such antics as feeding an orange to an ostrich. The elder Mitchum's joy was increased by the discovery that Ann was once again pregnant, since they both dreamed of a large, close-knit family.

But their happiness was not to last. After the signing of the Armistice ending World War I in 1919, railroad workers went on strike. Inexperienced workers, among them Jimmy, were called upon to keep the trains running. Jimmy drew an assignment as a brakeman, an arduous and difficult task under any circumstances. Since neither he nor his coworkers were sufficiently prepared, what happened to Jimmy is not altogether clear. Either he gave the wrong signal or the neophyte engineer misinterpreted his instructions, but the engineer backed up instead of moving forward. Taken unaware, Jimmy was caught between the couplings of two freight cars. Forty-five minutes after the accident the young husband and father died of internal injuries, leaving Ann with two small children to support and a third on the way.

Hours after learning of her husband's death, the grief-stricken young widow boarded a train bound for Bridgeport with her two bewildered children. Julie, at four, was able to comprehend what had occurred. Eighteen-month-old Bob, who could only sense the feelings of agitation and grief, responded by crying fitfully throughout the trip.

Upon arriving in Bridgeport, Ann settled her impressionable children into her mother and father's household. Her father, Gustav Olaf Gunderson, was a 265-pound behemoth of a man, blessed with what was to become known as "the Mitchum build"—beefy shoulders, a barrel chest tapering to slim hips and long, strong legs. Possessed of the strength of Hercules, he could sweep up a barrel of potatoes on each shoulder or a bull calf and carry it from barnyard to pasture because it was "yist too veak to valk."

By trade he was a sailing man, albeit one who shunned the responsibility of captaining a vessel, settling instead for filling the position of first mate because he lacked the moral courage to assume responsibility for running a ship. According to members of his family, he was to bequeath both his physical strength and lack of courage to his most illustrious grandchild.

Gustav's other notable weakness was his wife, Petrina, a petite, teacup-fragile woman with a darting glance and a waspish tongue who ruled him as if he were a mastiff with a ring in his nose. A vivid personality, she often asserted her independence by packing up, and, without asking leave, journeying back to her native Norway. Gustav put his foot down only when Petrina, a would-be actress, proposed joining a touring dramatic company (as their son, who could pick up and instantly play any instrument with strings, had done), or going to New York where she would try to break into silent films. During this first and subsequent visits of her grandchildren, Petrina took them to "the movies," always comparing herself (to her advantage) with the featured character actress. If Gustav bequeathed his build, strength, natural baritone voice and lack of moral courage to his grandson, Petrina, during his childhood, may have planted the notion he could act.

After closing the flat in Charleston and arranging for the furniture to be shipped to Bridgeport, Ann accompanied the casket containing her young husband's body to that city for burial. There she rented quarters for herself and the children on Logan Street. Then for a brief time before her pregnancy began to show she took a job at a photography shop in order to conserve the settlement the government had made in recompense for her husband's death.

During this period a good-natured young neighbor, Rose Resenia, looked after Julie and Bob. Rose, who did not attend school or work, quickly made herself so indispensable that when what was then considered public decency required Ann to quit her job, Ann arranged for Rose to work as a hired girl when "her time came."

Weak and dispirited, Ann waited until she had regained some strength before she and Rose packed up the family and journeyed to North Brattleboro, Massachusetts, where they stayed on a farm with one of Ann's married sisters until Ann felt strong enough to go back to work.

A problem remained. The small compensation check she received from the government plus her salary did not add up to enough for her to hire Rose full time. Julie was not a problem, but Bob and baby John needed continuous attention. This time another sister, Jenny, and her husband, John—known affectionately as "Aunt Yenny and Uncle Yon" because of his accent—volunteered to take the boys. John adapted easily, but there had been too many changes in the past year for Bob. The pillar-to-post existence forced upon the family by his father's death had changed a happy, sweet-natured boy into a withdrawn, lonely child. He ate poorly and lost weight, becoming, in his own phrase, "skinny and ferret-faced."

He became so unhappy that Ann decided to bring him back to Bridgeport after several months. Though the boy was not yet five, his original puckish sense of humor was now often laced with resentment and cruelty directed specifically at his sister and mother.

A definite sibling rivalry grew between him and Julie. While the boys had been gone Julie had taken to rounding up neighborhood children and seating them on the front steps. "I would appear from behind the hedge—sing, dance and say witty things," she recalled sixty years later. "One day a passerby patted me on the head and said, 'Young lady, you should be on the stage.'" Julie had only a vague idea of what "the stage" was, but she ran into the house, stamped her foot and told her mother, "I am going on the stage or I'm not going to eat my dinner." Her mother looked at her calmly and said she didn't know anything about "the stage," but she did know that people sang songs. "Songs have words, and words have meaning. You want to communicate," she informed her agitated daughter.

"With that statement she established me as a noncommercial performer," Julie says. "Because anytime a bit of commercialization crept in she would get it out fast."

Ann responded to Julie's impulses to entertain by offering the six-year-old a choice between piano and dancing lessons. Her slim budget would not accommodate both. Julie chose the latter because it provided a chance to go downtown, have an ice cream soda and wear a dance costume.

Sometime later Ann heard of the weekly amateur contests being held at the Park Theater. She took Julie down to visit the manager, who looked the child over and asked if she also sang. She did. He was concerned whether patrons would be able to hear her in the last rows. Ann motioned Julie to the stage, then took the manager into the lobby and closed the doors. They heard Julie loud and clear, and he put her in the next contest.

Julie collected first prize, fifteen dollars—a sizable sum to her *and* to her mother. Frequently, thereafter, Julie competed in amateur shows, earning a formidable reputation as a contestant, which in turn led to her debut as a semiprofessional around the Bridgeport area.

Sibling rivalry, then, was perhaps inevitable. Anything Bob's older sister did, Bob wanted to do too. Soon he was pestering to go to dancing school. Ann acquiesced, but the undertaking was not a success. He could only manage a single-footed time step; the other foot never seemed to keep up. Although he may have been the best one-footed tap dancer in Bridgeport, classes and practice bored him. After his first public appearance he announced his retirement.

Soon, it seems, he was heard spinning fantasies about his life, some positive, some negative. Other reports of his described his "explorations," such as leaving the house without permission. Whatever he did, he drew the attention he craved. For instance, when he and John disobeyed and left the lawn after dark one evening, sometime later Bob came tearing into the house breathless and obviously terrified. "Mom! John's been hit by a car!" he shouted. "But he's not dead yet!"

Ann and Julie sprinted two blocks to find John had been knocked down by a car, and had arisen unhurt in the path of a second auto which caught him under the chin, breaking his jaw. The accident sent John to the hospital for a couple of weeks, but only temporarily curbed Bob's propensity for roaming.

During the same period Bob suffered an "accident" of his own. The family gathered to view an eclipse from Eagle Pass, a hill not far from where they lived. It was a bitter cold evening and Bob, who has never been able to tolerate cold weather, turned blue and shivered all the way back to the house. Since their home had no central heating, he rushed to an old-fashioned gas heater. Trying to jostle Julie and John out of the way so he could get all the warmth, he edged too close to the scorching heater guard and succeeded in branding himself with a bar and a circle beneath it. For weeks afterward he could sit with only one cheek on a seat; and for several years afterward the brand on his rear end made him particularly identifiable from behind!

Around this time Ann made a discovery that would transform Bob into a local celebrity. One morning while cleaning his and John's room, she removed a piece of crumpled paper that had been stuffed in the window to keep it from rattling. For some reason still unfathomable to her, she uncrumpled it, and with growing pride read a verse that her six-year-old son had composed. She was stunned by his facility with words and later often said she had told herself, "He's a writer! A writer!"

Henceforth she never discarded any scrap of paper without scrutinizing it for literary output. "I read more grocery lists than you'll ever know," she once confessed. But soon she had a collection of his work, including a short story titled *The*

Adventures of Sure-Shot Shorty, and a sheaf of poems including one of his earliest efforts, *A War Poem*.

By the time she had collected a body of his work, Ann had secured a position as a linotype operator at the *Bridgeport Post* (through a brief, disastrous marriage to an alcoholic newspaper reporter) and had struck up a slight acquaintance with a dashing and eccentric Englishman who was in charge of, among other things, the children's page of the paper. He was whispered to have been a circus bareback rider, a merchant seaman, a soldier of fortune and the third son of a baron. Rumor had it that he had first arrived in the United States as a "lookout" (a polite word for spy, he explained) for some member of the British government. Hugh Cunningham Morris was undeniably a great spinner of tales, an art, Ann felt, he inspired in both Bob and John. He talked especially eloquently about his experiences with Winston Churchill during the Boer War and World War I and enjoyed anyone's challenging him on his Churchill connection, which provided the opportunity to whip out an IOU for five pounds with Churchill's signature on it.

That in 1923 he had come to Bridgeport to preside over the children's page in a newspaper, while Churchill years earlier had emerged at the forefront of British journalists and then had gone into politics, probably says reams about their respective journalistic abilities. Yet Ann found him amiable, attractive and intelligent. He further won her over by promising to consider her son's poems as a basis of a feature article.

Morris not only printed some of the poems, he ran an interview and a picture of the young poet. Bob later said that everyone read some deep meaning into his creations except himself. "I was Bridgeport's answer to Nathalia Crane," he mockingly commented in reference to a now-forgotten child poet who once had been a literary rage.

Since the feature story drew attention to the economic struggle that the young widow was experiencing in supporting nine-year-old Julie, six-year-old Bob and four-year-old John, it may have marked the beginning of the movie-star-to-be's wariness of the press. It also has, apparently, made him wary about revealing his inner feelings through publication of his literary endeavors.

Following the publication of the feature, Ann and the Major, as Morris was nicknamed, began their courtship. The Major became a frequent dinner guest, much to the displeasure of Bob, who blamed the Major for the emphasis on the family's economic straits.

Even though the Major, a pilot, offered to take Bob flying, the boy persisted in his efforts at being almost impossible to win over. "We gave the old boy a pretty hard time until we grew old enough to appreciate him," he admitted to an interviewer years later.

The Major agreed with Ann that most children were indoctrinated *not* to think for themselves. Like her, he encouraged them to question authority of teachers, relatives, parents and even himself. They were encouraged to counter with *Why?*

That *Why?* caused especially severe problems for Bob when he reached the lower middle grades of McKinley Grammar School. If Ann had no ready answer to a question, she would go with the child to look up the information at the public library. In this way the Mitchum children came into possession of some fairly esoteric facts, and they, especially Bob, were not shy about challenging teachers.

Such intellectual dissent from preteenagers drew the wrath of the faculty. That, combined with the children's united opposition to Ann's marriage to the Major in 1927, prompted her decision to remove them from what she considered an oppressive environment.

The previous year her father had bought a farm in Felton, Delaware. "He was tired of his wife's spur-of-the-moment trips to Norway, and felt that if she had a farm to oversee, she wouldn't be moving around so often," John Mitchum explained in 1982. To Ann, sending the children to stay with her mother seemed a solution to several problems. They would benefit from a healthier environment, there would be less opportunity to get into trouble, and they would receive closer supervision than she was able to provide because of her job. If she was reluctant to be separated from them—and she was—her ambivalence vanished when she heard that Bob had been taking John to sing on downtown street corners for coins tossed in a hat. Usually the donations were pennies, but on one occasion a passerby tossed "the little urchins" a half dollar. When Bob took the money for himself, John "sang" to his mother, including the "little urchins" quote rendering Ann's decision to send them to Delaware unwavering.

Actually, the responsibility for the children fell more on Willie Tetrault than on the boys' grandmother, Petrina. Willie, who was Petrina and Gustav's son-in-law, and the children's uncle, had been a professional wrestler until the Gundersons acquired a farm. But he willingly gave up the spotlight, not only to accommodate his in-laws but also because he had sworn on Jimmy Mitchum's grave that by all the gods in heaven so long as he was alive Jimmy's little ones would never suffer. He was delighted to have Ann send the children to the farm.

Julie and Bob attended a one-room country school. Both loved the novelty of rural life, and still reminisce about their jaunts across the fields in the fall gathering Spanish needles in their cotton stockings, and experiencing the sensual puckering caused by eating green persimmons they picked from trees along the way.

Occasionally the mischievous Bob would amuse fellow students by catching a big bullfrog and slipping it into the teacher's desk drawer, only to have it leap out into her face at some unexpected moment during the morning.

He was at an age when he took delight in devilment, especially tormenting his older sister. One ritual, which remained vividly with Julie for half a century, was his trick of suddenly leaping out from behind a tree, appearing from behind a fence or scaling a rooftop to flick tiny pebbles at her until she gave chase. "I had the Mitchum rib cage, but got cheated on the legs. Very sturdy and very short," she says. "Bob would run like a deer, leaping over things and leaving me far behind. One day he went into the barn, up into the hayloft with me right after him. He jumped down the hay hole, just missing a pitchfork sticking up the wrong way. So did I. Then onto the manger he went and jumped over it to the back of the stall. He made it. I didn't—and he purposedly hadn't cleaned the stalls that day."

Julie remained in Felton only a few months before going to Philadelphia where more theatrical opportunities awaited. Bob and John stayed on with their grandparents and the Tetraults.

By far the strongest influence on Bob was his Uncle Willie, whom the brothers came to regard as a surrogate father. Willie reciprocated to the point that although he would slap the fire out of his own children, he never would lay a hand on the Mitchums, even when they got into trouble.

Bob, ever eager to please Willie, was not always successful. On a mission to chop firewood, "Brother Robert, intrepid as always, grabs a double-bitted axe and heads for the woods with me trailing," John remembers. "There he surveys the loftiest pine in the entire forty acres. This particular specimen shot up eighty feet in the air, and Bob took to hacking and whacking it with gusto."

Meanwhile, Willie grew impatient and set out to find what was taking his nephews so long. As he entered the stand of trees he heard a great swishing sound, then a crash as the pine hit the ground. "He came close to breaking his vow never to lay a hand on us." John laughs. "Bob had felled a prize specimen that Uncle Willie had already sold to the telephone company for a pole. Now he would have to give back the forty dollars he'd received for it."

In Felton, despite the attention he received from his relatives and the frequent visits of his mother, Bob began to exhibit an antisocial strain of behavior. How deeply he was affected by his father's death (many psychologists contend small children misinterpret a parent's sudden unexplainable absence as desertion) and by the exile forced on him by his mother's having to work, only Bob knows. And since he has always shied away from revealing his inner feelings, scuttling such discussions by fabricating improbable adventures or making jokes to derail serious conversation, he has never said. And whether these traumas produced a feeling of abandonment and loneliness that has haunted him all his life is also something only Bob knows.

Ann, fully aware of how much the boys—especially Bob— missed her, visited as frequently as she could afford to. In 1928, after she became pregnant and was forced to give up her proofreading job at the *Post*, she moved to her parents' farm to await the birth of her baby.

Reporting and editing positions were scarce, so the Major remained in Bridgeport, visiting the farm on weekends. There, his eccentricities made him a popular figure, although sportsmen were on one occasion annoyed by his insistence that his collie, Bosun, be allowed to run with the hounds on a fox hunt. Bosun, fleet of foot, handily outran the pack, caught up with the fox, ran around it a couple of times, then turned and headed for home. When the hounds reached the point where the scent had been carried in divergent directions, confusion developed. Many of the hounds whirled and led their masters to the Gunderson farmyard and Bosun.

The next week the Major lent Bob the fine English saddle he owned, and Bob borrowed a fast-moving red mule from a friend to ride in the hunt. Serious sportsmen felt the Major and his stepson were making a mockery of the hunt and tightened qualifying rules for participation.

Being banned from fox hunting was of no consequence to Bob, but he was heartbroken by his Uncle Willie's refusal to allow him to use the Major's gun or to have one of his own on the grounds that in unskilled hands it spelled danger. His yearning for one increased immeasurably when his friends Benny and Solly Markowitz obtained an old Bernard. That it frequently misfired did not diminish its desirability in Bob's view. He unsuccessfully tried to trade some of his own possessions for part ownership. After the Markowitzes took him and John fish shooting, and he saw that the mere concussion caused by a bullet landing near a fish stunned it and brought it to the surface, nothing could deter him from acquiring a gun.

Reasoning that the Major wouldn't be using his fine English saddle to ride in the hunts, Bob traded it for a second-hand Winchester .22. For weeks after, he hid this prized possession in the weeds to prevent his uncle from discovering it. Every day the Mitchums and the Markowitzes went fish shooting until Benny Markowitz spotted a crow sitting in a tree and, fearing his old Bernard would misfire, asked Bob if he could borrow the Winchester. Bob hurriedly waded into the stream and handed Benny the gun, making sure no moisture got on it. Benny casually tossed his Bernard to Bob. As Bob caught it, it fired. A moment later Solly Markowitz put his hand to his shoulder, looked disbelievingly at it, and cried out that he had been shot. The others assumed he was joking until he pulled off his sweater and shirt and the blood gushed forth. Staunching the flow as best they could, the boys carried Solly to a neighbor's house, where a doctor was summoned. He rushed Solly to the nearest hospital. After a day on the critical list, Solly quickly improved—but not fast enough to prevent natives from labeling Bob and John "those two ornery Mitchum boys."

Public censure was nothing compared to their Uncle Willie's disappointment in them. He gathered his nephews at the kitchen table in the old farmhouse and gazed at them as tears welled in his eyes. Finally, as John remembers, he said, "I told you kids I didn't want no guns. Now, by jeez, you see I'm right. You could of killed somebody. Or yourselves. I swore by your father's grave I'd do everything right by you. I've worked myself to the bone. Done everything for you, and now you do this to me." The boys sat at the table, mute and miserable at their inability to utter an excuse or apology.

Automatically from then on, the Mitchums, especially Bob, could do no right in Felton. He was the number-one suspect when any trouble occurred at school. Publicly he assumed a don't-give-a-damn attitude, but in a letter to his mother in Bridgeport he vented his anger at always being the chief suspect by railing against a teacher recalled only as Mr. Petry. Bob wrote to his mother, calling Petry a coward, and vowing some day to come back to ruin the teacher as he said the teacher had ruined him. But, he lamented, it would be just his luck for Petry to be dead.

Bob's stay in Felton reached a turning point one morning when he dropped by the lower school to discuss some matter with John. The principal ordered him off the grounds, and when he failed to obey swiftly enough, the administrator called the police. A scuffle developed, pitting Bob against five grown males. John joined the fray, biting one before they succeeded in ejecting his brother. Upon hearing of the latest problem, Ann decided the time had come for her sons to leave Felton.

The next stop for Ann, Bob, John and half-sister Carol was Philadelphia with Julie, where her husband, a naval medical corpsman, was temporarily stationed. Shortly thereafter, Julie received an offer to join the "Six Connecticut Yankees," a vaudeville act featuring precision dancing. She accepted, and the family followed her to Manhattan, taking an apartment at Eighty-ninth Street and Columbus Avenue. The group was soon joined by the Major, who had been laid off by the *Bridgeport Post* and now was freelancing while searching for a steady job on a metropolitan newspaper.

Bob attended Haaren High at Fifty-ninth Street and Tenth Avenue. A natural leader, he avoided allying himself with any of the various ethnic and mutually hostile gangs. Although still "skinny and ferret-faced," there was something about him that attracted other loners, people who were surprised by their uncharacteristic and inexplicable fascination with him. Noting this, his mother remarked, "Robert doesn't have any friends, he has disciples."

Julie, who shared an empathy with him which made verbal communication all but unnecessary, elaborated on her mother's remark later. "For all his followers," she said, "Bob was and always will be a painfully, excruciatingly lonely person. Because he has chosen to hide the sensitive side of his nature and people can't become friends with someone they can't understand."

As a teenager Bob began to realize that insolence, truculence and crudity were protective traits behind which to hide a more fragile, vulnerable side. He cultivated a manner that suggested he could turn dangerously violent without warning, and repelled conventional people with foul language.

Yet his family and friends recognized this as a facade. As an example, Julie recalls arriving home one afternoon to find the apartment uncharacteristically quiet. Her mother sat in a rocking chair in a somber mood. In response to Julie's questions, her mother motioned toward Bob's bedroom. Julie went in. "He was butchered," she says. "He wasn't quite fourteen years old, but he'd come on a gang of roughs pushing John around, bouncing him from one to another. Bob waded into the circle, told John to get away and he stepped into his [John's] place. They kept knocking Bob down until he couldn't get up anymore. That's how he got his broken nose.*

---

*When he became a star, he would claim his nose had been repeatedly broken when he was a professional tanktown fighter in twenty-seven professional boxing matches. Appraised of this, his mother sniffed, "He may have had twenty-seven fights, but they weren't in a boxing ring. John was the boxer in the family."

Not that Bob was to take many such beatings. Very quickly he attracted disciples who insured him against such attacks. The first of these was a four-foot, one-inch, one-hundred-pound, gun-toting dapper Puerto Rican remembered only as "Pee wee." "Pee wee" was outraged by the attack and drove home his commitment to Bob and John by invading neighborhood tough Benny Callaghan's* territory, shoving a gun in Callaghan's belly and announcing, "I don't use chains, bottles, knives. For me, guns. So leave my friends alone." Word spread to other gangs, and the Mitchums could walk Eighty-ninth Street freely, courtesy of "Pee wee" and his associates.

That "Pee wee" was a fence amused Bob, who was developing a fascination for the criminal mind. "Pee wee's" apartment was a warehouse of improbable booty, including a submachine gun in a battered violin case. When Bob inquired who would buy such a rusty article, "Pee wee" allowed he'd give it to some "broken-down gangster and go halvsies."

Bob, stimulated by this thwarting of authority, later would manufacture largely imaginary stories of surviving a poverty-stricken childhood—the Mitchum-Morrises were poor, but hardly destitute—by rolling drunks.

"Yes, largely imaginary," says John, "although there was a bit of the con in brother Bob." He illustrates with an incident that occurred during the latter part of their stay in Manhattan. The great depression had cost everybody in the family but Julie their jobs. They were subsisting on her salary, which didn't cover luxuries. In fact, John's only pair of trousers were thirteen-button, bell-bottom sailor pants which had been donated to him by Julie's serviceman husband. They were not only a necessity, but a prized possession. One morning John awakened to find them missing. Enlisting Bob's help they searched fruitlessly. Finally Bob commented that John threw his clothes around so carelessly that when he undressed the previous night he must have accidentally tossed the bell-bottoms out the window. John borrowed Bob's extra pair of overalls and went on an unsuccessful search beneath his window.

While walking down Eighty-ninth Street that afternoon he

---

*The name of this individual has been changed.

met one of Bob's disciples whom he noted was wearing bell-bottoms. John inquired whether by chance Joey had found them on the street. "Naw," was the response, "your brudder sold 'em to me fer fifty cents."

As Bob began cultivating the tough-guy stance, it protected him on the streets, but kept him in scrapes at Haaren High. When he was caught zinging a teacher with a pea shooter, the principal expelled him.

Bob accepted his expulsion without protest, but his mother, feeling the punishment was extreme, went before the school board to plead his case. Her eloquence moved a member of the board to inquire whether some extracurricular activity might keep Bob out of trouble. Sports, perhaps. Bob rejected the suggestion. Even though he had pitched on the junior high team in Felton, racking up twenty-four strikeouts, he had never developed an interest in team sports. Having proved himself in that one game, he lost interest.

"Music," Ann piped up. Bob assented, saying he had always wanted to play a C-melody saxophone. The board instructed the principal to provide one, along with weekly instruction. Ann considered the lessons too infrequent. Although she had never touched a sax, she purchased a book and together she and her son mastered the instrument in a short time.

Too short, perhaps. While Bob's deportment improved during the time he was learning to play the instrument, once he earned a seat in the school band boredom set in. He was expelled from school for the final time, he claims, after he dropped a firecracker into a brass horn during a rendition of the "Poet and Peasant Overture."

No longer a student, he went looking for a job. The widening depression had cut off the Major's free-lance sales, and Julie's salary barely provided for essentials. That December, Bob was grateful to be helping behind the lunch counter of the drugstore located in the Astor Hotel. For both his Christmas and New Year's dinners he feasted on hamburgers and chocolate sodas.

When 1932 dawned to grimmer prospects than 1931, Bob decided not to burden his family further. As he tells it, he hitchhiked to Fall River, Massachusetts, where he applied at the Fall River Line, falsifying his age as eighteen, and signed up as deckhand on a salvage vessel. His dream of voyages to "the South Seas and Tahiti and all that," he was to tell interviewers, was jettisoned when the owners discovered his age and unceremoniously dumped him ashore fearing prosecution under child labor laws.

Asked about Bob's days at sea, his mother laughs and says, "Bob's seagoing days were all spent in the harbor. He had no adventures at sea because he never left port." In fact, the Major had heard the owners needed someone on their ship while it was inactive because, according to Maritime Law, if no one is aboard a commercial sailing vessel, anyone can board and claim it.

The job was ideally suited to Bob's temperament. A loner since early childhood, he enjoyed isolation and took full advantage of the long sequestered hours to read voraciously and to write poetry expressing his feelings of alienation. Luckily, the owners provided a supply of canned food, fresh fish and shrimp. Whenever he finished a meal he tossed the dishes overboard. When the dishes ran out, so did Bob.

Out of work and reluctant to go home, he was captivated by and considered joining the mysterious, slightly seedy, highly romantic figures who waved at the world from atop freight trains as they rattled into the tantalizing unknown. Instead he hitchhiked to Rising Sun, Delaware, where his family had moved. But employment was not to be had, so as his fifteenth birthday approached Bob prepared a bindle and explained to his mother that he was going off to learn what lay beyond the horizon. His mother forbade it, but relented after they agreed on selected post offices along the route where he could expect money orders awaiting him at the general delivery window.

There were to be many such leave-takings, the little tableau of the family gathered on the porch, and Bob, one pants leg up and the other down, his bindle swinging jauntily over his shoulder, backing away from them, waving and admonishing, "No tears now! No tears!"

"Before he left the first time he took Daddy outside and seriously asked him to look over the family," Julie recalls. "He was very protective, family-oriented. And do you know one of the reasons behind those trips besides boyish curiosity? He was so uneasy and embarrassed about accepting gifts. He didn't know how to respond gracefully. That's why the first trips always occurred just before his birthday or as Christmas drew near."

In 1933, rivalry with his older sister sent him on what was planned as his first transcontinental trek. Hearing that the Navy was transferring her husband to Long Beach, California, and that Julie and her infant son were joining him, Bob set out to beat her to the West Coast. Aware that Julie was stopping off in Kansas to show her child to her husband's parents, Bob decided to detour through southeastern Georgia to see the Oke-fenokee Swamp, which had caught his imagination during his voluminous reading. He was certain he could do this and still turn up at the apartment Julie's husband had rented at Olive and Alamitos streets in Long Beach before she arrived.

In this first major step in investigating the world, his luck quickly ran out. According to him, he had got off a freight on the edge of Savannah, Georgia, and was making his way to the post office when he was picked up and jailed on what he thought was a vagrancy charge. Since it was Friday he assumed he would be held until Monday, be credited for time served and freed. Instead, to his astonishment he heard the judge charge him with robbing a local shoe store. Bob sometimes claims to have spoken up to point out that if the judge would consult his sheet, he'd find Bob had already been in a Savannah jail on that date. At other times he says he spoke up to plead not guilty on the grounds that he was serving time on a vagrancy rap in another city. In a third variation he says he was charged because he was carrying thirty-eight dollars in his pocket—and the assumption was that he must have stolen it. In yet another he told of a police officer, "a big sumbitch" who konked him over the head with a blackjack and ran him in. He was held over the weekend, and sentenced to 5, 90, 180 days or an indeterminate sentence on the Chatham/Brown County farm chain gang—depending upon to whom he tells the story, and when.

About landing on the chain gang, he explains, "They did that all the time. That was a cheap way of keeping their roads repaired."

Julie's version is simpler, less a storyteller's story. She says Bob was on his way to the Savannah post office to pick up his mother's money order, was stopped by a police officer, found to have only a few cents in his pocket and was sentenced to a seven-day term on the chain gang on a vagrancy charge.

Moved by his experience on the gang, Mitchum wrote on a postal card to his mother:

> *Trouble lies in pools along the barren road I've taken*
> *Sightless windows stare the empty street.*
> *No love beckons me save that I've forsaken*
> *The anguish of my solitude is sweet.*

(Many years later, having failed to shock Helen Lawrenson, who was doing a profile of him for *Esquire*, with assaults of scatological humor, assorted profanities and obscenities, Bob suddenly changed tactics and recited the poem.)

Bob claims that on the gang he was shackled to a six-foot, eight-inch Creole murderer who became a close friend. Together they shook down newcomers for a quarter to insure assignment of a desirable bed. Beds actually were assigned automatically, but the massive Creole's threatening manner discouraged victims from attempting to regain their quarters or beat up the con artists.

The chain gang experience obviously stimulated Bob's imagination; he has also said that a group of bad-ass murderers serving long sentences protected him because they realized he was not yet fifteen. (After a fanciful rendition of the chain gang story a reporter from *Rolling Stone* inquired whether Bob identified with the criminal mind. Bob thought it over and said no, but his associations with criminals had helped him understand the workings of their minds.)

His descriptions of his departure also have as many variations as those of his arrival. Sometimes he has said he and the Creole mutinied and fled into the forest. At others, that he conked a guard over the head with his shovel, took the guard's key, unlocked his shackles and escaped amidst gunfire. "If they didn't hit you, they wouldn't bother to chase you," he explains.

His family confirms that he actually did escape—probably

at night when the shackles had been removed to relieve pressure on the ulcer that they had caused on his leg. Confused about directions, Bob got lost and crawled and swam through the edge of a swamp, somehow avoiding copperheads, water moccasins and alligators. The next morning he was befriended by three backwoods sisters who took him to their parents' home where they fed, bathed and gave him clothes and let him rest before going on his way.

Sometimes he joins some buddies in Alexandria, West Virginia—or was it Cleveland?—where his friends had commandeered an empty house and were running a kind of dognapping ring. One day, he asserts, his leg began paining him and he asked a policeman for aid. (The irony that a chain gang escapee should seek help from a lawman is fully appreciated by Mitchum.) The policeman rushed him to a hospital where it was discovered gangrene had developed, and the doctors began discussing how much of his limb should be amputated. He seized the first opportunity to escape and rode home to Delaware in the back end of a truck. Once there, his mother cured him. In the inevitable second version, he hitchhiked back to Rising Sun, picked up on the final lap by two doctors who delivered him to the house where his family lived. The doctors helped him to the door where they told his mother that if she loved her son, she would take him to a surgeon at once and arrange for an amputation. She thanked them and gently ushered them out. Then she went looking for Bob, who was delirious and trying to escape from the house.

"He was like a frightened animal," she recalls. She soothed him and put him to bed, assuring him that his leg would be saved. Then she took a basket and went into the fields and gathered a basketful of foxglove. For three days and nights she poulticed his leg with the weed, which she dimly recalled had been used medically in Norway, and prayed for help. As the shoots wilted she would apply a new batch. She left Bob only to go out and gather more. Gradually the foxglove broke the infection, the leg drained, the swelling went down and the leg was saved.

In detailing the variations Bob works on his recollections; it becomes apparent that like Sherwood Anderson he is by nature a storyteller. In his memoirs, Anderson recounts going on a fishing trip with a half dozen men, and having the proprietor of the lodge where they stayed catch his fancy. Strange things happened. Anderson began inventing speeches for the man. Later at a dinner in Chicago, he began repeating the incidents. Suddenly one of the fishing party, whom Anderson had forgotten was in attendance, stood up and denounced the tale-teller as "the champion liar of the world." Before leaving, he bowed and said, "Go ahead, you liar. Don't let me stop you. Don't let the truth get in your way."

Anderson reports this in detail, then says: "... Just the same, I swear that although I may have been inventing some, I had really got the quality of our host at the fishing camp. If he had not said some of the things I made him say, he should have said them."

He then adds: "What I am here trying to do comes to the same thing. I believe in imagination, its importance. ... Besides, men do not exist as facts. They exist in dreams."

Bob might have expressed those sentiments. Certainly he lives by them.

CHAPTER 2

After his recovery from the gangrene, Bob hopped a freight and headed directly for Long Beach where he worked at a series of menial jobs—dishwasher, truck driver, quarry man, stevedore—anything to make a little money. "I was a bouncer in a bar, but the customers bounced me so often the boss finally bounced me permanently," he once said. Unable to secure work, he spent several weeks lying on the beach, later claiming he rolled drunks for spending money, explaining to writer Bill Davidson, "I didn't know any better."

Even though he was willing to try almost anything, steady work was impossible to obtain. Bob also began getting itchy feet as he saw the freight trains roll by. He confided that riding through the night, feeling the wind blowing through his hair and sharing the camaraderie of hobo jungles gave him a sense of freedom. "I speak pungent patter on occasion," he once noted. "For the most part, that's to show I'm a free-and-easy guy, ready to be friendly to all." He said he learned when he was on the road that if he spoke as he had been taught, the other hoboes had a tendency to shut him out. "You can discuss almost anything, even philosophy and psychology, and fre-

31

quently learn a surprising lot around the jungles and on the clanking boxcars, but you've got to do it in a common tongue," he said.

Hobo jungles were not his only option for a place to spend the night while bumming around. As was the custom of penniless wanderers during the 1930s, he would frequently approach the village marshal in some small town and ask to be put up in jail overnight. In return for the hospitality, the next morning he and other volunteer guests would sweep up the empty cells and take out the garbage. For years afterward he retained a fraternal feeling for down-and-outers, and he amused interviewers by maintaining that in many jails the food was better than in the studio commissaries.

But his stays were not always voluntary. Once in Texas he claims to have received a five-day vagrancy sentence and when he became obstreperous, claiming it was no crime to be poor, his jailers tossed him into solitary confinement. "It wasn't the worst thing that ever happened to me. I *liked* it. Well, *like* is a little strong," he says. "*Appreciated* might be a better word. It wasn't half as rough as being on the chain gang."

Another time in Pennsylvania, a woman beguiled by his charm provided him with the necessities and arranged a job for him in her brother's coal mine. Sent into the pit, Bob felt the walls closing in on him and realized he suffered from claustrophobia. He attempted to quit, but the foreman threatened him with a huge hammer, thereby persuading him to stay. Unable to eat and weak with fear, Bob stuck it out until he received his first paycheck. After paying off his benefactor for room and board, he sneaked to the railroad yards and hopped a freight headed toward Delaware.

While in Rising Sun Bob was to meet a girl who eventually would play a pivotal part in his life. There had been lots of girls in his life, and sex was a casual thing to him. But as a man/boy who divided women into madonna/easy-lay categories, they had meant little to him. Dorothy Spence was a special girl.

Dorothy, who was thirteen, had previously had a few "dates" with John Mitchum. Although only thirteen himself, John was dating several girls, and even though he thought Dorothy "pretty, charming and delightful," he found her a little more reserved and ladylike than he preferred.

Bob, on the other hand, was deeply smitten by the tall, trim, brunette beauty who seemed wrapped in serenity. He found it helped curb his loneliness and spiritual homelessness to be around her, though she gave him little encouragement. In view of Bob's later reputation for being catnip to women, it is amusing that Dorothy initially didn't respond to him. He struck her as uncouth and overbearing. "To be perfectly honest," she once confided, "I didn't like him. He was a wise guy. He never thought of paying a compliment like other boys, preferring to tease."

One night, while Dorothy and a friend waited for their dates, Bob and a boy who owned a car came along and invited them to go joyriding. After waiting for a half hour, the girls decided they had been stood up and went out with Bob and his friend. It was that evening that Dorothy apparently perceived that beneath his brash exterior Bob hid an interesting mind and an imaginative outlook. There was a complexity about him that made her other young suitors seem dull by comparison. She resisted the attraction she was beginning to feel toward him, but Bob, sensing her ambivalence, focused his special charm on her alone.

Dorothy lived in Camden, Delaware, a small town about three miles from Rising Sun. This presented something of a problem since Bob owned no car and was bored walking over and back alone. He solved his dilemma by insisting John accompany him. "I had to wait around while he courted Dorothy," John says. "We'd rollerskate over. Then I'd sit like a bump on a log while they sparked. When it got time to leave, Bob and I would put on our skates and back we'd go to Rising Sun. Bob eventually got a wife out of it, and I got to be a pretty good skater."

The Spences were far from pleased about their daughter's involvement with the part-time hobo whose formal education was scant and whose attitude cheeky. Aware of this, Bob made attempts to tone up his background. Noting that he still favored the leg which had had gangrene when he became tired, Mrs. Spence inquired how he had injured himself. In a valiant attempt to make the cause of his handicap seem more respectable, he omitted mentioning his stint on the chain gang, and informed her he had hurt it jumping off a freight train.

Such a faux pas reinforced the Spences' conclusion that he was no companion for their daughter. They forbade Dorothy to date him, but she went anyway, even though Bob was prone to get into fights over her. "No other boy in town would go out with me," she told writer Thyra Samter Winslow. "Then Bob left town. So there I was—all by myself. Lonely, too."

Once again Bob's destination was Southern California, but this time he decided to take John with him. "He took me out by the woodpile and seriously talked about the burden we were on Mother and the Major," John says. "Of course, I was all for going. But you know, he abandoned me in Louisiana. We jungled up for the night right out of Lake Charles. In the morning there was a great big freight making up, and brother Robert strolled over and got on. I went to the water tower to get a drink of water. When I looked up from the hose I had a .45 at my right temple and a .38 at the left. The town constable and a railroad detective had their guns right on me, and Bob yells, 'Come on! They won't shoot!' When I didn't move and the train began pulling away, he waved and yelled, 'I'll see you.'"

Not before John got lost, wandered through five states and got picked up in Los Angeles for "evading railroad fare"—a polite way of labeling him an unwelcome bum. Since the city had no juvenile hall, John spent three days in Lincoln Heights jail. When he arrived at Julie's home in Long Beach a week late, Bob looked up from the book he was reading and casually inquired where John had been. "Trying to find California," his younger brother replied. "Hell, all you had to do was head west," Bob informed him as he turned back to his reading.

The Morrises arrived close behind John, hoping for a brighter future in the West. While hunting for a place to live, the Major spotted a three-room cottage at 314 Wisconsin Street, which two men were refurbishing for rental. He rushed home and brought his family back to inspect the place which belonged to Emmet and Earl Sullivan, who turned out to be cousins of Broadway columnist Ed Sullivan. Bob quickly spotted in the backyard a shack which had originally served as a storage room before being turned into a chicken coop. He suggested that he renovate it for use as a bedroom, an idea that pleased the Sullivans. In fact, everything about their new tenants pleased the Sullivans, except the renters' inability to pay their rent on time. "It was purely a matter of economics," Bob later told Ed Sullivan. "We didn't have any money."

To stave off eviction, the family entertained their landlords. One evening, for instance, Julie played the piano, John played the guitar and sang, and Bob performed a scene from Shakespeare and then crooned popular songs.

Such tactics were not effective indefinitely. One day Earl Sullivan arrived, determined to collect some payment on overdue rent. How much cash did Bob have in his pocket? Bob had eight dollars, but to keep a reserve, he said six dollars. Earl demanded it be applied to their debt, but the ever-ingenious Bob counterproposed that they place it on a racehorse named Joe Schenck (for the movie executive). After perusing the racing form, Earl insisted on betting on another horse. Schenck won, paying a handsome return. "So I told Earl that from then on we didn't owe any rent because he'd touted me off a longshot winner," Bob told Ed Sullivan. "'You are right,'" he said, quoting Earl, "'but don't tell Emmet.'"

That fall John attended Long Beach High School, and Bob hired himself out for whatever odd jobs turned up. But work was scarce, so he spent the greater part of his time lying on the beach with newfound buddies. One of these was Frederick Fast, whose father owned a factory in Toledo, Ohio. Fast was fascinated with Bob's tales of hobo life, and before returning to Ohio he issued an invitation to Bob to drop by the Fast residence if he ever passed through Toledo.

Much to Fast's surprise, late in the fall of 1935 Bob called him from a city-run mission for boys in downtown Toledo. Fast hurried down and brought Bob to his home, and after some resistance from his conservative father, Fast persuaded the older man to hire his scruffy-looking friend to operate a punch press in their factory. Bob was in no position to turn down employment, but was humiliated by the elder Fast's criticism, and retaliated by dressing more sloppily than necessary and refusing to wear socks even in subzero weather.

His employer would have been even more upset had he known that Bob was experimenting with marijuana—then assumed as inevitably leading to hard-drug addiction—during early 1936. Although Bob maintained his experimentation was limited to "an occasional, isolated instance in Toledo," at least one long-time acquaintance scoffs at this. In any case, the clash between Fast's and Bob's personalities resulted in Bob's being fired.

With a few dollars in savings Bob had only one thought in mind—to get to Camden, Delaware, to visit his beloved Dorothy. Upon arrival he was taken aback to find she was working in Philadelphia as a secretary for a life insurance company. In Camden he had been able to scare off potential suitors with his threatening physical presence, but Philadelphia was too large for such a technique; he now had to woo Dorothy in a more conventional fashion. However, she was receptive, and they agreed that they would marry as soon as he had established himself.

So it was back to Long Beach, hopping freights and hitch-hiking, landing a job, getting laid off, lying on the beach, horsing around with other beach rats, strutting about to show off his filled-out body with the inherited barrel chest, slim waist and long, strong legs, and chasing girls and catching them without it interfering in the least with his feelings for Dorothy.

Possessed of a well-muscled frame, Bob was disdainful of the dedicated body builders who worked out on the beach. One eager youngster boasted he had gone from hoisting 60 to 180 pounds, which elicited only a raised eyebrow and an uninterested "No shit" from Bob. Stung, the boy placed the barbells in Bob's line of vision and managed to get the 180 pounds above his head. Through clenched teeth, he exulted, "See!" Bob gazed at him beneath lazy eyelids and drawled, "Now you've got it up, what're you going to do with it?"

The Mitchum family had arrived in Long Beach not long after Elias and Oranne Truitt Day were hired to guide the Players Guild of Long Beach. The Days represented a coup for the little theater. Elias was a former Broadway actor who had toured

Europe and North America as a monologist and impersonator. He had also produced Broadway hits on the Chautauqua circuit throughout Canada and for eight years prior to coming to Long Beach had been dean of the Drama Department of the Bush Conservatory in Chicago. He boasted he had done everything on stage "except blackface," and he possessed the stature, experience, contacts and drive to turn the struggling group into a first-rate little theater.

Julie was quick to sense that the Days could help her refine her technique and began appearing in productions. She also obtained engagements in local nightclubs, working as a sophisticated chanteuse in the tradition exemplified by Hildegarde. Sensing that Bob was interested in developing creatively beyond the poetry he was writing, she suggested he join the Players Guild. He curtly dismissed the suggestion, but when the Sunset Oil Company announced that it was sponsoring a contest to choose a popular singer for their radio program, he agreed to compete. Should he win, he rationalized, he could use the money to go east and claim Dorothy. Julie helped him choose the number and coached him.

On the night of the contest a supremely confident nineteen-year-old strode onto the stage and launched into "Would You?", a popular ballad of the era. "He seemed to have no stage fright, but I was backstage having kittens watching my baby brother make his stage debut," Julie recalls. "I was dying—the stage mother supreme. And that night in Long Beach in 1936, the women spontaneously did what press agents later encouraged them to do for Sinatra several years later." For the girls Bob always had such appeal, but his magnetism was apparently too sexually oriented for that time and place. He didn't win.

No commercial offers materialized from his appearance, but Bob had experienced his first encounter with the limelight, and he had enjoyed performing.

Julie again suggested that he try out for a role in one of the Players Guild productions, but he was reluctant—even after she informed him that the girls outnumbered the men five to one. The latter information was sufficiently intriguing, however, that he persuaded John to join him in building and moving scenery. The brothers shared strong sex drives which they in-

dulged in casual encounters, and which, according to John, in
no way denigrated Bob's almost obsessive love for Dorothy.
They were, he remembers, very active roosters in the Players
Guild henhouse.

Both Bob's mother and sister kept urging him to take advantage of this opportunity to acquire acting experience. As
his mother pointed out, acting was a possible way to earn large
amounts of money that otherwise would probably never come
to him. Still Bob resisted. Privately the two women concluded
that secretly he wanted to act, but like his grandfather Gunderson he lacked the courage to face tryouts. John thinks Bob
felt there was something unmanly about acting. During the
1937 season Julie read a script called *Rebound* that Elias Day
was to direct. "There was a character in it named Johnny Cole,
a gauche young man—slightly clumsy, delightful in an un-
formed way," she says. "Bob had a natural leonine grace, but
no technique. Mother and I decided that natural grace combined
with Bob's lack of stagecraft would create the quality the 'Johnny
Cole' part called for. But we knew there was no point in saying,
'Go down for the tryouts.' Instead we waited until the night,
and while we were having dinner I said to Mother, 'They're
having tryouts at the Guild. Let's all go down and see what
those cornballs are doing.'"

Around seven the family strolled down to the old Union
Pacific Depot at First and Alamitos streets. The train station
had been transformed into the Depot Playhouse. Julie and her
mother lingered in the lobby gossiping with acquaintances,
leaving John to select a seat that would put Bob on the aisle.
When the women came in Julie maneuvered it so that she
occupied the seat directly behind Bob. Periodically she whispered humorous comments about the proceedings in her brother's ear to keep him amused and interested. Then, when director
Day asked those who desired to read for "Johnny Cole" to step
forward, Julie reached through the space between the back of
the chair and its seat and gave Bob a sharp pinch. He leaped
up, and she shoved him down the incline toward the director's
table.

Day's welcome made it awkward for him to retreat, so Bob
accepted the playbook, read over the scene to get the sense of

it and easily outclassed the competition for the role. According to the family he looked and sounded exactly right for the character, and his lack of stage technique produced the winning awkwardness they had envisioned to enhance the character.

Day and his wife, Oranne, who also directed, were impressed with Bob's potential as an actor and a writer. They encouraged him to write plays and songs, as well as his poetry, and planned to use him in future productions.

He responded by writing and directing two children's plays, one of which, *Trumpet in the Dark*, contained a starring role tailored to the talents of his half-sister, Carol, and a lesser one for John. That Bob did not appear in subsequent Day productions was due chiefly to the opposition of the casting committee, and especially to the objections of the Players Guild president and administrative business manager, Mrs. Walter Case, a civic and social leader who was offended by the vulgarisms which he mischievously uttered whenever she was within earshot.

Day, who had migrated to California after suffering five bouts of pneumonia while living in Chicago, succumbed to his various respiratory illnesses on January 13, 1938. One of those chosen to step in for him was a former protégé, Larry Johns, who arrived from Broadway with the rights to his friends George S. Kaufman and Edna Ferber's *Stage Door*. This represented a coup, for the play had not yet been released to stock companies and little-theater groups. Johns also extracted a firm agreement that he was to have a free hand—unhampered by the casting committee's considerations of long service or loyalty to the group—in choosing the most suitable performers from among the hundred-odd auditioners.

Johns chose Bob for the role of the young playwright. In the *Long Beach Press-Telegram*, drama critic Marjorie Moorehead's Sunday piece gave Bob a sentence in a separate paragraph located well up in the review: "Robert Mitchum is ideally cast as the egotistical young playwright who 'goes Hollywood' and loses Terry [the leading lady] by doing so."

In 1982 Johns recalled that although Bob was innocent of almost any previous experience or technique, his instinct was correct. "He was just born to it," Johns observed. "As a director, I found he needed only the merest hint and he could find his way from there. In little theater it is sometimes necessary to give players line readings. Never with him. All I had to do was help him heighten and shade what was already implicit in his conception of the role. He didn't own a dinner jacket, and I loaned him mine. He used to josh me that loaning him that tuxedo was my greatest directorial contribution to his performance."

One of Bob's beach friends was young Anthony Caruso, the only one of his buddies who was making his living as an actor. At that time an under-canvas stock company, the Harvey and Ruby Hart Players, had pitched their tent in Long Beach for an open-end engagement, and Caruso had landed a job playing juvenile leads. "Bob was doing all kinds of odd jobs to help support the family, but sometimes the going got so rough he'd come around the tent to bum a quarter or so. His ambition was to be a writer, and he was a good one. So I was surprised when he got into *Stage Door*. I went to see him and from the first he was a pro without actually being one. He was just a natural actor. From the time he opened his mouth he was so good nothing could stop him."

Robert Renfrow, who later acted at the Players Guild before going to Broadway, met Bob and John Mitchum during Bob's last season at the Depot Theater. "He was a magnificent guy!" Renfrow says. "Oh, what a wild son-of-a-bitch. He was willing to let it all hang out. If you didn't want the answer, you'd better not ask the question. You see, he had no hangups. That was one of the things that made him such a magnificent actor."

When Renfrow got to know him better, Bob would drop by his house to find out whether Renfrow had any joints; if Renfrow did, he would share one with his visitor. "If I didn't have any, he'd always have one or two tucked away. But he wanted to save his and use yours. He used grass as kids do today— as a recreational thing."

Bob's next appearance in 1938 was as Duke Mantee in Robert Sherwood's *The Petrified Forest*. Once again he astonished his acquaintances and coworkers with the ease he exhibited on the stage. Speaking of his work, they agree that he intuitively gave performances far beyond what his technical capacity and experience equipped him for. "I loved Bogart in the film," Julie said years later, "but he couldn't touch Bob in the part. Bob didn't have Bogart's stagecraft, but only after a couple of roles at the Guild Bob managed to take the other two players and unite himself with them in a perfect triangle from the audience's point of view. And that's magic."

In 1939 Larry Johns cast Bob in an English comedy, *Ghost Train*, and Bob revealed another facet of his talent which would serve him well later in his career: His ear was so acute that he could reproduce his stepfather's British accent with such accuracy that even Mrs. Case was convinced that should he ever choose to apply himself, he was a young man with a future in theater or films.

Even before Bob was lured to the audition of *Rebound* in 1937, the Morris-Mitchum household reminded many of their friends of the zany one portrayed by Kaufman and Hart in *You Can't Take It With You*. The driving force was unquestionably Ann Mitchum Morris, who was as charming as she was unflappable. Opera singers, tap dancers, torch singers, chanteuses, actors, instrumentalists of all kinds, painters, writers, mystics, and, in addition, such friends as Tony Caruso and Elmer Ellsworth Jones, whom Bob always insisted upon introducing as Elmer Ellsworth Swami Mother Have You Met Miss Jones—all were welcomed to the Wisconsin Street home where the door was always open to anyone creative and sufficiently original and eccentric.

Many came as friends of her children and remained to become friends with Ann. Dean Martin's uncle, Leonard Frye, a dancer, showed up early in the morning at least once a week. As he sat at the breakfast table chatting with Ann, he made a disturbing noise with his fingers on the table. Finally Bob, who was always a light sleeper if he wasn't suffering from insomnia, got up one morning to ask what Frye was doing pounding on the table. Pounding on the table? Frye was outraged. He was simply working out new routines.

Larry Johns also became a frequent visitor. He found the Mitchums and the Major, their ebullient stepfather who cursed only in Arabic, every bit as amusing as any of the characters

Kaufman and Hart ever wrote. The Major had by this time won over Ann's three children, as well as almost everyone else who heard him spin his picaresque tales of adventure in the British Empire.

The *You Can't Take It With You* analogy may have struck Larry Johns as particularly apt. John owned eleven pet reptiles, including a five-foot-long gopher snake. "It was a constrictor," John says, "but not strong enough to hurt an adult. Most of the other ten were rattlers, and I kept them locked up in cages. I did have a great rapport with them—especially this one red-rock rattler who would never strike anybody. It seems stupid as I look back on it, but I'd pick him up and let him crawl around my arms. He'd never bite. I had great confidence in that.

"Brother Robert didn't. So one night I found out he had a date with this girl I was interested in. I waited until he was in the bathtub—buck naked. Then I tossed the snake in the bathroom. It settled down between him and the door, looking at him. He wouldn't get out of the tub, and I took out the girl."

Ann took the snakes in stride, as she did everything else. On nights when six were expected for dinner, Bob invariably would arrive with three extra guests at the last minute. His mother would cry. "Oh, isn't it wonderful to see you!", and then slice the meat a bit thinner. Although the Major earned only a small salary as managing director of the Long Beach Yacht Club, having not yet established himself as a stringer with the *Post-Telegram*, the rest of the family did odd jobs and contributed to the support of the household. And no one was disturbed on evenings when a dozen or more friends converged on the three-room cottage after dinner.

Looking back on those lean but fun-filled years, John says, "Mother was a miracle. Just a miracle. Amidst it all, she'd get out her easel and paint and talk and accept everything with bland serenity."

CHAPTER 3

By mid-1939 Julie's marriage had broken up and she had moved into an apartment in Hollywood where she was working as a chanteuse in nightclubs. Bob, who was dabbing in writing special material for her, soon found that his services were in demand by other struggling performers. Even though most of them were slow to pay, he optimistically moved in with Julie to share expenses. When it was necessary for him to be in Long Beach for the Players Guild he commuted by rail on the famous old Red Car. Gradually he placed numbers with female impersonator Ray Bourbon. He also sold material to ex-Ziegfeld beauty Peggy Fears and to risqué songstresses Nan Blackstone and Belle Barth. Whether he was ever paid for them is unclear. But the only real money he made was from vaudevillian Benny Rubin. Rubin hired him to turn out a routine overnight for a hundred dollars, and upon receiving the material sent him a check for three hundred. That year Bob also wrote an oratorio which was performed at the Hollywood Bowl by Orson Welles for the Jewish Refugee Fund.

He also claimed to have written numbers for Noel Coward and to have devised a format for Arlene Francis's *Calling All*

Girls. However, Francis failed to recall his involvement in her project, and when asked about Mitchum's claim, Noel Coward replied, "I have the pleasure of knowing Mr. Mitchum, but I am not aware he ever wrote any material for me."

Despite his talent for interlocking rhymes, kaleidoscopic meter and felicitous images, he was unable to turn out enough material to support himself. (Some entertainers avoided paying at all.) So Bob supplemented his earnings by taking a job as a driver and general handyman for the famous costume designer Orry-Kelly.

"When we shared the apartment a lot of Hollywood people got some weird ideas about us," Julie says, "because I wasn't dating anyone—wanted nothing to do with men—and Bob didn't go out with other girls. He picked me up at the club almost every night and nobody asked us why.

"I was just out of a divorce and wanted no part of males, and he was trying to save money so he could go back to Delaware and ask Dorothy to marry him. But we were so close we seemed to communicate without having to verbalize what we were thinking, and that gave rise to a lot of Hollywood poppycock."

As time went on Bob began developing new friends and hanging out at Victor's, a restaurant on Sunset Boulevard near Fairfax Avenue. The clientele was a mixture of fallen stars, extras, party girls, stuntmen, starlets, hookers, hustlers, johns and dealers. It was said to be a place where anything could be had for a price—if not in the restaurant itself, then in the alley that adjoined it.

After a while Bob began to renege on his part of the agreement with Julie that he would carry out the trash, wash the dishes and tidy up the apartment if she had to hurry off for an audition or other appointment. He often failed to perform his tasks, but never failed to leave a rhymed apology, signing his communications in such fanciful ways as: "The-good-for-nothing brother of a nightclub daisy."

Where his puckish sense of humor couldn't take him, Bob's hypnotic tales could. Late one evening as they sat in a diner having coffee, Julie was amazed to hear Bob entertain the waitress with stories about his experiences at sea. "Which were so much strudel," Julie says. "But before long he had tears streaming down the poor girl's face with his description of how he had lost his right arm in the anchor chain. Mind you, he was sitting right before her with a coffee cup in one hand and a cigarette in the other, but she was weeping up a storm of sympathy."

From the beginning of his career Bob's ability to make such incredible stories believable has been responsible for much of the nonsense that has appeared about him. In speaking of his early days in Hollywood, for example, he has claimed that he and his friends shared a community overcoat complete with hidden pockets in which to secrete stolen items. He says whoever was responsible for the food supply that day donned the coat, went to market and gathered supplies. (Why they were wearing such a heavy coat in warm weather he never has bothered to explain.) "If we'd lost the coat, we'd have starved," he told one reporter. At other times he has said that anyone who was broke survived by running up a tab at Victor's. He also has claimed to have turned down a $500-a-week guarantee from a literary agency to write special material for performers, instead taking a job at Lockheed paying $29.11 a week because he believed that "unless you were carrying a lunch pail, you weren't working."

Even when perpetrating an elaborate put-on Bob has always brought the actor's true belief to his tall tales. Nor has it ever prevented him from varying details of the same yarn for different audiences in order to produce the emotional impact he wants.

In late 1939 astrologer Caroll Righter hired Bob as a general assistant on his tour of East Coast resorts. Bob's duties included driving Righter's Ford, running errands and, after Righter's public lectures, pitching personal astrological charts to the audiences. Bob was delighted at the prospect of the trip, a steady salary, and most of all, the opportunity to visit Dorothy.

He and Righter set out from Los Angeles for Palm Beach by way of New Orleans. Outside Rayne, Louisiana, an incident occurred which, surprisingly, Bob has never mentioned to the press. A wind of hurricane magnitude seized the Ford he was driving, slammed it against the side of a bridge and then into a telephone pole with such force that the pole snapped off, barely missing the car, which spun around twice before plunging into the bayou, where it swiftly began to sink. A typewriter stashed in the back seat hit the back of Righter's neck and momentarily stunned him.

"Bob leaped out his side, got around to my side of the car which was smashed," Righter recalled forty-three years later. "He managed to pry open my door and get me out onto safe ground. He literally saved my life. But he has never mentioned it, much less bragged about it."

Bob ran to a bridge and scrambled up one of its girders to the highway to flag down a car. Wet, muddy and disheveled, he couldn't get anybody to help, so in desperation he stood directly in the path of an oncoming car and forced the driver to stop. Together they got Righter up the girder and, by the time they reached Rayne, Righter was feeling well enough to forgo a doctor and check into a hotel. Three days later a fire truck hauled the Ford back onto the highway and towed it into town where the firemen turned a hose on it. When they opened the doors to clean the inside, eels, fish and all sorts of marine life emerged. Amazingly the car started and, after minor repairs to the right door, Bob covered the seats with several thicknesses of heavy brown paper to protect Righter and himself from dampness as they proceeded to Florida. There Righter delivered his first lecture, and Bob surprised his employer with his adeptness at luring audience members into making appointments for personal charts. The new team went on to work every posh resort on the Eastern seaboard between Palm Beach, Florida, and Newport, Rhode Island.

"Then we went to Philadelphia where Bob and Dorothy decided to marry," Righter says. "I came back to Hollywood. After the wedding he called and said it was cold in the East and he was unhappy. I invited them to come to stay with me on Whitley Avenue in Hollywood, which they did."

Naturally Bob remembers it differently. At times he has said that he won $2300 in a crap game and quit working for Righter after a quarrel because Righter warned him that his sign, Leo, was incompatible with Dorothy's Taurus, and that a subsequent serious conflict would cause the marriage to destruct swiftly. On other occasions Bob has claimed that a butler in one of the mansions in which Righter was lecturing caught him purloining seven bottles of Scotch, and he vanished into the night to spare Righter embarrassment and himself possible arrest. On hearing these stories, Righter smiles benignly and sighs, "Oh yes, Bob is a romantic Leo. They can't resist embellishment of facts."

In any case, Bob, who claimed he had insured Dorothy's interest and loyalty by sending her menacing photos and notes warning her not to become serious about any other man, left Righter's employ and swept Dorothy away from her desk at the Philadelphia insurance firm. The couple then traveled from the Quaker City to Dover, Delaware, where they obtained a marriage license. Dorothy, who had developed into a slim, attractive, endearingly shy young woman, went shopping for a dress in which to be married, while Bob and their friend, Charlie Thompson, went in search of a single gold wedding band. Unable to recall her ring size, they borrowed the jeweler's sample and set out to find Dorothy. Having forgotten the store at which they left her, they wandered up and down the street looking for her until she spotted them and rushed out of the store, wearing the dress she was trying on. They measured her finger, and she rushed back into the store, worried the management might conclude she was making off with their merchandise.

Meanwhile, Dorothy's parents were anguished at the idea that their daughter intended to marry this likable ne'er-do-well who appeared without hope of a future. They nagged, pleaded and did everything in their power to dissuade her, but Dorothy was a young woman who knew her own mind. She coolly informed them that she was fully aware of Bob's faults, and recalls asking them, "When there is love, who needs perfection?"

On Friday evening, March 16, 1940, Dorothy, Bob and Charlie Thompson rode around until they spotted a Methodist parsonage in Dover. They went to the door, rang the bell and, when the door was opened, Bob and Dorothy requested to be married. The minister inquired whether they preferred the old or the new ceremony—a matter of indifference to Bob, but

Dorothy thought the old sounded more romantic. In that case, their host replied, all of them had better adjourn from the unheated living room to the kitchen where it would be warmer for the long ceremony. He then disappeared to don a frock coat and summon his wife. Shortly thereafter, amidst air heavy with the aroma of cabbage being cooked for a New England boiled dinner and with Charlie and the minister's wife as witnesses, Dorothy Clement Spence became Mrs. Robert Mitchum.

The next day they took the one hundred dollars Dorothy had saved and the one hundred Carroll Righter had wired in response to Bob's urgent plea, and boarded a Greyhound bus for Los Angeles. (So much, it would seem, for Bob's claim of winning $2300 in a crap game before quitting his job.) The newlyweds treated the bus trip as their honeymoon, stopping off for a few days at the Pioneer Hotel in Amarillo, Texas, before proceeding to Hollywood, where they gratefully accepted Righter's hospitality.

Bob made fitful stabs at breaking in as a radio writer; pressed for funds, however, he began turning out formula-ridden, suggestive songs for small-time nightclub entertainers which earned him ready cash but which left him virtually no time to pursue his real goal. To make matters worse, some of the entertainers welched on payment for his material.

When Dorothy suggested she look for a secretarial job so that they could rent an apartment and stop imposing on Righter, Bob approached his parents in Long Beach. Six people were already living in the three-room house, so he could hardly expect to move in there. Instead what he asked for was the chicken coop he had remodeled, and kitchen privileges. His request was granted.

Embarrassed by having to impose, Bob felt obliged to assume some of the responsibilities his stepfather was unable to fulfill. He decided to give up the uncertainties of becoming a writer for factory work. With World War II already raging in Europe, defense plants were hiring large numbers of employees for the first time since the great depression. Hearing that Lockheed was taking on people, he applied and was hired in April 1941.

The job could not have come at a more fortuitous time.

Having just learned he was to become a father, he had gone out, frightened yet elated, to blot out his apprehensions about the future and celebrate his coming fatherhood. When he sobered up he found he had depleted the small amount of money he had planned to use until payday.

But a man of Bob's amiability and charm never finds himself without friends willing to advance him small amounts of cash, and he borrowed enough to tide him over until he received his paycheck.

Instead of the day job he had expected Bob was assigned to the graveyard shift—midnight until eight a.m.—serving as helper to a man named James Dougherty, who operated a shaper machine. A shaper is actually a wood-cutting instrument, but at Lockheed it had been adapted for use on aluminum. The metal was placed on a pattern, then a wheel at the bottom of the machine ran around the pattern, cutting the metal in the same design.

Since he had drawn the night shift, Bob accepted a good role in a Players Guild production. On opening night, May 8, 1941, while he was in the dressing room applying his makeup, Dorothy arrived to tell him she was going into labor and would be unable to sit through the performance. He leaped up, brushed aside the suggestion that someone else take her to the hospital and in a borrowed car rushed her to the emergency room, arriving back at the theater with just enough time to finish dressing before his appearance in the opening scene. He even managed to call Lockheed to inform them that he would be taking off from work that night. After the final curtain and still in his makeup, he hurried back to the hospital to await the birth of the baby, a boy whom Bob and Dorothy named James after Bob's father.

Bob claims that he was one of the most inept factory workers ever employed. Jim Dougherty remembers him as efficient, citing the fact that he was soon promoted from helper to operator of a shaper, turning out smaller pieces, and was rewarded with a raise. Bob says he was miserable and constantly concerned about his safety on the job. Dougherty remembers him as a "real comedian who kept us laughing all the time. He was a real nice guy." For his part, Bob has vivid memories of

Dougherty's beautiful blonde wife, Norma Jean. He claims that Dougherty carried in his wallet a photo—which he had taken—of her wearing nothing but a skimpy apron. It was the first seminude photo of Marilyn Monroe—though she had yet to take that name.

The Doughertys were a fun-loving couple according to Bob, who particularly enjoyed Norma Jean's sly humor. He especially remembers an evening at the Palladium for Lockheed workers and their spouses. According to Bob, he had not started thinking about an acting career and Norma Jean hadn't started modeling and certainly hadn't thought of changing her name. They simply had a good time dancing to Tommy Dorsey's orchestra, which featured a young band singer named Frank Sinatra.

Dougherty is bemused by these recollections so many years later. "Bob has a good memory, but it's too good," he comments. "We never socialized with the Mitchums. I never met his wife. I don't recall taking my ex-wife to the Palladium. I don't remember hearing Sinatra or seeing him before he became famous. I've been to the Palladium lots of times. I went there to dance to Lawrence Welk's Champagne Music."

Bob was still running a shaper when Dougherty left to go into the service. Before Dougherty was released Bob had made his first major film. "I saw a movie, and there he was on the deck of an aircraft carrier. I don't remember the name of it—I was so surprised I said to the guy I was with, 'Gee, I used to work with him.' I never did see Bob after I got out of the service. I tried to get in touch with him through a friend, but whether he got my message, I don't know. I just wanted to say hello. We're both getting up there and I just thought we could reminisce a little bit."

Bob, who had always been able to hop a freight when pressure mounted, now found the responsibilities of marriage and a son and the monotony of a factory job bearing down on him. Nor did he adapt well to the graveyard shift at Lockheed. To break the boredom he accepted a role in another production at the Players Guild, but this increased rather than relieved the pressures. He ingested so much No-Doze and chewed so much tobacco laced with Tabasco sauce that he had real difficulty in sleeping. No matter how long he lay in bed, four hours was the maximum amount of sleep he could manage, and even that was not uninterrupted. He lost weight and developed such a severe case of chronic insomnia that in one seventy-two-hour stretch he slept only fifteen minutes. Constantly exhausted and irritable, he quarreled with his family and worried about meeting his financial responsibilities. Suggestions that he have a checkup or seek psychiatric help drove him into such fits of temper that well-meaning friends and family members stopped making them.

Even his vision had begun to bother him, and one morning at Lockheed where he was now operating a drophammer, it failed. "I just suddenly went temporarily blind," he explained. Extensive tests uncovered no medical cause for his loss of sight. After further examination and tests, his doctors informed him that his blindness was psychologically induced by hatred for the job and other deep anxieties. "They advised me to quit," he has said. "I told them I couldn't. I had a family to support. They told me to blow the job or blow my mind." Faced with those alternatives, Bob left Lockheed and began looking for other employment.

Soon after, he and a friend from the Long Beach Players Guild, Jack Shay, were looking through the *Los Angeles Times*'s help wanted ads. Shay, a wild Irish dreamer, asked why they should restrict themselves to nine-to-five jobs. Why not work as movie extras? Given the developing manpower shortage because of the war, studios welcomed whomever they could get for crowd scenes. Bob agreed.

Their greatest handicap was that each owned only one suit. Bob's was a shiny blue serge which Orry-Kelly had bought him while he was employed as Kelly's driver. The seat of the pants had split sometime before, but Dorothy had cleverly mended and reinforced it with strips of adhesive tape.

Nevertheless, Bob and Shay registered with central casting and soon began working in low budget films. In one, during one scene which required him to move swiftly along a city street, Bob felt a draft in unfamiliar parts. The tape had given way, and his career seemingly had come to a halt.

Not so. Shay proved his loyalty by insisting that they share his suit on alternate days. "Whoever had the suit that day took the job," Bob told writer Eleanor Harris. "The directors weren't casting us anyway. They were casting the suit."

In May of 1942 Bob finally got a break. He was taken to the old California Studios on Gower where Harry "Pop" Sherman was turning out the *Hopalong Cassidy* series. The official version of the story is that agent Paul Wilkins made the introduction. Unofficially some old-timers insist that Pop's daughter Teddy, who was writing *Hoppy* scripts for her father, arranged his employment. They say she was driving along Sunset Boulevard on her way to the studio when she spotted a neat, handsome young fellow thumbing a ride. Impulsively she stopped and picked him up. When he inquired how far she was going, she told him to California Studios. He asked whether she could get him on the lot. She not only took him along to the lot, but also introduced him to her father.

Harry "Pop" Sherman was producer and financier of the *Hopalong* series, a big man in small-time pictures. "My pictures are for the rabble, the little people," he used to say. Of course, they were formula westerns, but in each there was some important scene designed by Sherman to insure the film's success, and he insisted on being on the set to back up the director in handling it. Should the director prove incapable of getting the most out of this or any other scene, Sherman would step in. "He was a good journeyman director," George Givot, who worked for him occasionally, says, "and that is meant as higher praise than it may sound."

At the time of his introduction to Sherman, Bob was six feet two, blessed with an extraordinary frame on which 180 pounds were distributed so well that he had a twenty-eight-inch waist. His hair was light brown, and his hazel eyes remained half-hidden by lazy lids. Those lids, plus a scar beneath his left eyebrow and a nose that had been broken and imperfectly reset, could add up to a menacing appearance. "I could look mean and my hair was down to my cleavage," Bob once said. "'Pop' Sherman spotted that and told me not to have my hair cut if I wanted to be in his next picture. I had a bit as one of the outlaw gang in *The Last Frontier*. They paid me fifty bucks and all the horseshit I could sell. I had to borrow fifty on my grandmother's coffin fund to pay my initiation fee into the union. I just broke even."

On the bus between San Bernardino and Kernville, California, Bob boasted that he had formerly been a cowpuncher in Laredo, the sort of claim most drugstore cowboys were moved to make. Consequently, the stuntmen saw to it that he was assigned an outlaw horse. When Bob attempted to mount him, many of the other members of the company, including star Bill Boyd, hid out to watch the action. On Bob's first try the horse threw him before he was astride. He stood up gamely and mounted. Again, the horse threw him. This time Bob pulled himself to his feet, limped over to the horse, looked it in the eye, then pulled back and slugged the animal in the nose. "It's you or me," he grunted, staring into the startled horse's eyes. After a moment he moved and swung himself into the saddle. He stayed on, too. "I had to stick on," he told writer Ruth Waterbury, "because Dorothy was pregnant again. She had to quit her job, and money was scarce around the house."

His determination won him Bill Boyd and "Pop" Sherman's admiration; whenever a *Hoppy* film was being cast there was always a part for Bob if he wanted one. During the eight *Hoppy* films he made during 1942 and 1943, he went from an unbilled member of a posse to the romantic lead in *Bar 20* and back to villains, gaining not only much needed earnings but also valuable experience in front of the camera.

In *The Leather Burners* Bob's part consisted mostly of getting roughed up by Bill Boyd. But George Givot, who was in the cast, recalls that he was surprised at the way the neophyte actor came across on the screen. "He was a handsome guy, but he photographed better than he appeared on the set. He had photographic charisma that few people seem to have, and if they have that, they don't need much else. That's the secret of screen success—to have that certain something that makes people look at you when you're doing nothing, watch you, remember you and wait for you to come back when you're off screen," Givot says. "Even in small parts in cheapie productions, he had that."

Dorothy Mitchum may have sensed that same magnetism would make Bob a star after seeing him on screen with Boyd in a preview of *Hoppy Serves a Writ*. (In 1983 Bob facetiously told Gene Shalit on the *Today* show that this is his favorite film.) He had almost no lines, but when the audience saw him they "went mad—immediately." He had never taken acting lessons, and it was obvious he never would have to. The only adjustments he would make would be a minor correction to his broken nose and to learn to raise the pitch of his voice an octave from its natural bass.

Nineteen hundred and forty-three proved to be a break-through year for Bob. He appeared in two pictures for MGM, five for Universal, one for 20th Century–Fox, one for Republic, two for Columbia (of which one was released in 1944), plus two for Pine-Thomas distributed by Paramount, and seven *Hopalong Cassidy* films distributed by United Artists.

On the whole, the twenty parts he played were of short to medium length. At Metro-Goldwyn-Mayer he had a brief touching moment as a soldier who died in the arms of Ella Raines in *Cry Havoc*, a moment which did not fail to catch the attention of audiences and casting directors. But the best opportunity presented itself early in 1943 in *The Human Comedy*, based on William Saroyan's sentimental best-seller. Directed by the illustrious Clarence Brown, the movie had a huge cast headed by Metro's top box-office star, Mickey Rooney, and such other stalwarts as Frank Morgan, Van Johnson, James Craig, Fay Bainter, Marsha Hunt, "Butch" Jenkins, Darryl Hickman, S. Z. Sakall and Carl "Alfalfa" Switzer, among others. Bob, Barry Nelson and Don DeFore played lonely soldiers who pick up a couple of town girls, Donna Reed and Dorothy Morris. Since Nelson was under contract to MGM he drew most of the best lines in the soldiers' scenes. But Bob created the most original character by dint of sheer personality, bringing to an undefined part a combination of humor, cockiness, sentimentality and alienation that foreshadowed the antiheroes later popularized by Brando, Clift and Dean—and he did it before screenwriters were creating that type of character.

Excellent though his work in that big-budget picture may have been, such was the freedom of the free-lance actor in the early 1940s that later he could be sold for two unbilled roles in adventure features without damaging his future. Bob's agent,

Paul Wilkins, committed him for two films, *Aerial Gunner* and *Minesweeper*, which Pine-Thomas was making back to back. Bill Thomas and Bill Pine, former publicity and promotion men known as "The Two Dollar Bills," specialized in low budget action features. Neither of them spotted anything significant about Bob's work; to them he was just another $75-a-day actor. However, after Bob Gilman, who was in charge of Paramount's east coast publicity, and Russell Hohlman, head of casting in New York, saw *Minesweeper* they wired Thomas urging his company to sign "the fellow who played the sergeant." "I thought, jeez I don't even know how to get hold of him," Thomas recalls. "I had a secretary track down his agent's name. He wasn't anybody of importance. So I called him and tried to appear a little offhand about what I wanted. I said, 'That guy you sent us, the one we paid seventy-five dollars a day for *Aerial Gunner* and *Minesweeper*. Maybe we could talk some kind of a deal.' He cut me off with the news he had interest from two or maybe three other companies, but Mitchum wanted to free-lance."

By remaining free, Bob had the chance to play a hapless shakedown artist who attempted to blackmail two operators of the Arthur Hurry School of Dancing, run by Stan Laurel and Oliver Hardy. Although this 20th Century–Fox production of *The Dancing Masters* was one of the team's lesser efforts, it gave Bob the opportunity to observe the renowned comic geniuses at work, and not so incidentally, provided much needed money to run the Mitchum household.

One of the contract offers Bob spurned came from Columbia Pictures, yet Paul Wilkins obtained a two-picture commitment for him at the studio later that year. In *Doughboys in Ireland* he was cast as a buddy of leading man Kenny Baker. Jeff Donnell, who played the female lead, found Bob an amusing, kind-hearted fellow. "I don't remember much else from 1943, but I do remember his saying his wife was pregnant and already had the older boy to look after. So he insisted she stay in bed and rest while he slipped out at five a.m. But he complained that this other actor who gave him a ride to our location brought along a thermos of coffee every morning. I remember him saying, 'We sit in the car and drink it, and it's the worst coffee

I've ever tasted.' I asked why he didn't tell the guy. He just looked and said, 'No way. How can you tell a man his wife makes the world's worst coffee?' Which I thought showed a very sweet side of him."

During the filming he confided to Donnell that Columbia wanted to put him under contract at $350 a week. She said she had accepted a similar offer in order to support her child. He replied his situation was similar to hers, and she advised him to take the security. She could see he was undecided, and he did turn down the offer eventually. "Now it was his decision. It wasn't any agent's or anybody else's. He had this inkling" she says. "And a few months later he got the Bill Wellman show, *The Story of G.I. Joe*. But If that hadn't come along, I'm sure he wouldn't have regretted his decision. He has this quality—I'm me and this is it. And whatever happens, I don't give a damn."

What happened was so good for his career that many of his 1943 pictures were rereleased. *We've Never Been Licked*, in which he originally got eighth billing, was reissued with his name above the title. *False Colors*, in which he had rated only seventh billing, was reissued with his name set in bigger type *above* the film's leading actor, Bill Boyd. And in two movies starring Randolph Scott, *Corvette K-225* and *Gung Ho!*, in which Bob rated fifteenth and ninth billing, he received costar billing in rerelease. He was definitely on his way.

CHAPTER 4

In Hollywood where multiple marriages and divorces always have been indigenous to the film industry, a handicapper might have given one-hundred-to-one odds against the survival of Bob and Dorothy's marriage past the first six or twelve months.

If all aspects of such a union, as understood by those involved, were fed into a computer, it is probable that as many reasons for failure as success could be compiled. Yet by 1942, the year they moved to Hollywood, the two of them had weathered economic problems which had necessitated sharing quarters with his family; they had made adjustments to the arrival of their first-born with all the responsibilities it entailed; and they had weathered the strain imposed when Bob suffered psychosomatic blindness induced by the boring factory work and the necessity for Dorothy to secure a job.

In many ways their backgrounds also made their marriage's survival improbable. Dorothy had been a sheltered, slightly spoiled, willful daughter of overprotective parents, a girl with little experience in the outside world. Although she had spent a brief time in Philadelphia, she still clung to small-town values such as being well groomed—something that never crossed her husband's consciousness. Although strong, she was diffident. She was also a somewhat aloof young woman who found it difficult to relax socially until she had had a couple of cocktails.

Bob, on the other hand, was witty, multitalented and at ease in the ways of the world. Basically gentle, thoughtful and a "street intellectual" (a friend's description), when drunk he became almost a caricature of an extrovert. Among other out-of-work actors who congregated around Schwab's drugstore at Sunset and Crescent Heights, he affected the forward-swaying shoulders and rough-speaking mannerisms of a 1940s elemental male. Down the street at the notorious Victor's he consumed quantities of alcohol which made him unpredictable, obstreperous—and open to experimentation with the latest far-out kicks devised by the habitués of Victor's hipster hangout.

Who could have guessed that beneath the public persona lurked a loner who since his early teens had read voraciously to educate himself? When Bob was a preteenager, Joseph Conrad was his favorite author and he had read most of Conrad's novels before quitting school. But his taste was catholic, embracing everything from comic strips (*Our Boarding House* and *Li'l Iodine*) to esoteric poetry (e. e. cummings) plus a special fondness for William Wordsworth. Eugene O'Neill and Aldous Huxley were favorites, and he read and reread Thomas Wolfe.

Not only did he read and appreciate these writers, he was able to commit to memory those paragraphs that appealed to him. Years later he surprised the usually acerbic Helen Lawrenson during a series of interviews for an *Esquire* piece by quoting extensively from most of the above-mentioned writers. In an unmistakably admiring profile, Lawrenson reports being startled by the breadth of his knowledge—for a movie star. Bob's taste was not impeccable, though. He was an unshakable enthusiast of the novels of a now largely forgotten popular writer, Mary Austin, who when asked how it felt to achieve the peak of artistry replied quite seriously, "Lonely."

Bob also spent solitary hours writing poetry and composing songs. Presumably because they represent his private self, only snatches of the poetry and a couple of the songs have ever been published.

A play he wrote called *Fellow Traveler* may or may not have been optioned by the Theatre Guild. Friends are inclined to believe he wrote such a play, but doubt that the New York producing organization optioned it. On occasion Bob has explained he gave it up after receiving a complimentary note about the script from Eugene O'Neill, accompanied by O'Neill's dictated notes, which ran longer than the play, for suggested revisions.

Necessity caused the Mitchums in the early days of their marriage to practice role reversal, though of course they did not use that term to describe what they were doing. When employed, Bob was still unable to support his dependents, so once again Dorothy secured a secretarial position with an insurance company. Her salary of $80 a month proved inadequate even though in 1942 their rent was $32.50, gasoline for their 1927 mustard-colored Whippet was eighteen cents a gallon, and milk for the baby they had named James Robin (nicknamed Josh) was fourteen cents a quart. Supplemented by Bob's sporadic earnings, however, it enabled them to just get by.

Bob proved to be a surprisingly adept homemaker. In one important area—cooking—he already outshone her. When they were first married, Dorothy knew nothing about preparing the simplest recipes. Bob, on the other hand, had acquired the rudiments of cooking in hobo jungles, had expanded his skill in Long Beach under the tutelage of his mother, and had further increased his expertise while sharing an apartment with Julie in Hollywood. For Dorothy's birthday the first year in the bungalow he baked a cake, and frosted and inscribed it with a shocking-pink message: "Happy Birthday, Darling!"

The years of adversity may have forged an unbreakable bond between them. The question of who contributed what was irrelevant. Since she had to go to the office daily, any spare money for clothing went into cheap but attractive dresses to keep her looking presentable.

This was a matter of indifference to Bob. Casually dressed on the street, at home he wandered around barefoot in ragged jeans and a shirt he seldom bothered to tuck in. He publicly boasted of owning the smallest wardrobe of any actor in films; as he worked mainly in westerns, this was unimportant. If he was cast in a modern-dress picture which called for apparel he didn't own, he borrowed it from a friend. Bob and his friends, Steve Brodie and Johnny James, pooled their funds to buy a community dinner jacket. They commissioned Mattson Brothers, "Tailors to the Stars," to construct a breakaway tux which in forty-five minutes could be adjusted to fit whoever was to wear it. As a gift the store owners included both notched and shawl collars which could be attached in five minutes. Whatever else Bob needed he often borrowed from the wives of men in the service—which meant he could keep the garment indefinitely.

Bob had registered for the draft and eventually was classified 1-A. As a defense plant worker, husband, a father and a dutiful son who contributed to his mother and half-sister's support, he received a deferment.

Since the Mitchum bungalow was centrally located it gradually became a gathering place for a group of friends including Brodie, James, Jack Shay, Tony Shay and his wife, Leslie Brooks, Peter Cole, and Kay and Richard Crane among others. All were enthusiastic poker players. Bob was highly derisive of Dorothy's tactics, but when the final tally was done, she won and he lost—BIG!

Shortly after 1942 turned into 1943, he and Dorothy decided to move. His earnings had increased substantially, and she had discovered that another child was on the way. Their search brought them to 1022 North Palm Avenue and a two-bedroom, frame house with peeling white paint that the owner was willing to rent for fifty dollars a month. Despite its appearance the Mitchums were proud of it—even though he later described it as a "shanty" and said, "I could have picked it apart with my thumb."

Shortly after they moved in, Bob's mother, Carol, Julie and Julie's son found a house six doors down from Bob and Dorothy.

John and the Major had gone off to war. In fact, the Major had volunteered his services upon the outbreak of hostilities between England and the Axis. He had written his old friend Winston Churchill, only to have Churchill thank him for his spirit but reject him for being a bit long in the tooth. Enraged at the rejection, the Major subtracted ten years from his age and managed to sign on with an oil tanker. From there he became first mate on an unescorted spy ship which took him into the Pacific shortly after Pearl Harbor. When the United States entered the war the Major transferred to a large concrete barge used to transport fresh fruit and vegetables. Discovering an empty hatchway, the Major filled it with Hawaiian soil in which he planted radishes, guavas and tomatoes. All went well until the barge was strafed at Okinawa by Japanese planes. When the Major saw his radishes being uprooted and his near-ripe tomatoes demolished he was beside himself. According to Bob, he picked up an automatic rifle and started blasting away at the Japanese. When he awoke he found himself knocked two decks below with most of his teeth missing. The fall and the loss of his teeth he reportedly accepted as being part of the fortunes of war, but the loss of those burgeoning tomatoes was something for which he could never forgive the Japanese even after the armistice had been signed.

The Major's exploits provided much amusement in both houses on Palm Avenue, and the proximity of the houses proved a blessing when both Bob and Dorothy were working and someone was needed to look after Jim. In general, the family enjoyed one another, although there was a lack of closeness between Dorothy and Julie engendered, Dorothy sensed, by the close relationship Bob and his older sister had shared over the years.

By the time it became necessary for Dorothy to resign her position to await the birth of their second child, Bob's agent was managing to find frequent employment for him. When not acting Bob fixed up a bedroom for the children to share, and family and friends eagerly awaited the birth. With Jim a miniature replica of his father, many hoped that the second child would be a girl. But on October 16, 1943, another boy was born to the Mitchums. They named him Christopher.

Bob's agent, Paul Wilkins, often said timing was everything, and now he concluded that the moment had come for Bob to give up free-lancing, not only for economic reasons, but also for the grooming and promotional buildup the changed status would afford him.

Early in January 1944 Wilkins circumvented all intermediaries by calling in a favor owed him by a friend. The friend arranged an interview between Bob and director Mervyn LeRoy. Well connected to the movie industry by birth and his first marriage, LeRoy had the added advantage of having proved himself by directing some important artistic and economically successful films.

When Wilkins approached him he was preparing the film *Thirty Seconds Over Tokyo*, starring Van Johnson. Wilkins showed LeRoy some photos of Bob, and LeRoy scheduled a meeting. Bob's rugged presence and GI look appeared made to order for the project, and the director decided to test the young actor. Bob, never given to understatement, claims to have been "tested for no less than thirty roles" before LeRoy said, "You're either the lousiest actor in the world or the best. I can't make up my mind."

Apparently he never did make up his mind about how much star potential Bob possessed, but his response was positive; he cast Bob in the role of a crewman aboard the plane piloted by Johnson in the raid over Japan.

LeRoy encouraged Metro-Goldwyn-Mayer to place Bob under contract beginning February 2, 1944, only to discover when the company went on location that Bob was not the low-profile, malleable type the studio preferred. When the company moved by rail to Egland Field outside Pensacola, Florida, where they were to train with B-25s for the filming of the Doolittle raid, there was heavy drinking en route and several incidents in which Bob was involved.

At Egland Field Air Force regulars resented actors wearing officers' uniforms and living in the barracks. Some of the cast, including Bob, drew more than the usual dose of animosity because of their high visibility and civilian status. "Bob had taken quite a lot of pushing around without retaliating," says his friend Steve Brodie, who was also in the cast. "That's why I've always thought of him as 'The Gentle Giant.' But there was a limit to his patience."

It came one evening when Van Johnson, Robert Walker, Sr., William "Bill" Phillips, Brodie, Bob and several others were sitting in the barracks passing around a bottle. A drunken sergeant burst in, and as Brodie recalls it, sneered, "'Oh, here are the Hollywood fags all together. Suckin' out of the same bottle.' With that Mitch came off the deck. He grabbed that son-of-a-bitch and they went fifty feet to the front doors and down six steps before they got outside. Mitch took both doors off the hinges, and when we got to him he was throwing this guy in the air, and when he came down Mitch was clocking him again. It took three of us to stop it. Mitch just came unglued. Word of the fight spread, and about a week later this poor son-of-a-bitch came to apologize. Mitch said he didn't want his apology, but the sergeant said it was a command. Mitch asked if that meant it wasn't of his own free will, and the sergeant told him his executive officer had ordered him to do it. 'Forget it,' Mitch said. 'Send *him* the next time.'"

According to Brodie, Bob never backed off from anyone. "A bunch of us had a battle cry if trouble developed," he said. "It was, 'Redass.' Like 'Hey, Rube!' in circuses and carnivals. Yell 'Redass!' and we'd all converge. If you took Mitch unawares and yelled it today, he'd probably respond." Brodie paused. "It became his nickname, too. Because if he got real drunk he'd drop his pants and make it wink at the moon."

Bob was also a "practical joker," recalls Brodie. "During shooting on location at Egland, Mitch was banging a film executive's secretary. The executive finds out about it and he's furious. Now he calls all of us down on the lawn and says, 'I know someone here is having an affair with my secretary. She is not my girlfriend or anything of the sort, but it isn't proper for this to go on within the organization. Now I want the man involved to stand up and admit it.' Do you know what old 'Redass' did to me?" Brodie demands. "He stood and said, 'Brodie, I told you he was going to get you.'"

It was Bob's nature to rebel against authority. When the *Thirty Seconds Over Tokyo* company returned to MGM in Culver City, a stuffy executive spied Bob driving his battered old Chrysler. Word was passed to him that he should get a different car. He replied that none he could afford were available to him because of the wartime shortage, to which the executive replied that the alternative was for Bob to park off the lot. Bob expressed his disbelief at this stand but promised not to drive the Chrysler to work again. Next morning he had a nine a.m. call

but didn't arrive on the set until one-thirty in the afternoon.
LeRoy demanded to know where he had been, and Bob patiently explained how he had walked from his house to a bus
stop, boarded a bus, transferred, boarded another bus, and
transferred. Another cast member, Tom Murdock, confirmed
that he had seen Bob at a bus stop and had offered him a ride,
which Bob had refused, saying he was determined to get to
the studio on his own. Neither producer Sam Zimbalist nor the
executive who had ordered the ban could shake Bob's stand.
"You didn't find my car acceptable—fine. I'll ride buses," he
informed them. A standoff developed until late in the day when
the ban on the Chrysler was lifted. Next morning Bob was his
usual punctual self.

Nor was Bob threatened by the director in whose hands his
professional fate conceivably lay. At one point LeRoy decided
too many personal calls were being placed from the sound stage
and issued an edict that no one was to use the telephone on
the set. Bob protested that he had business to discuss with his
agent, and LeRoy responded that the agent would have to visit
him or Bob would have to locate a pay phone. A sign was
posted prohibiting any outgoing calls. After a couple of days
Bob sneaked a call through and someone snitched on him.
LeRoy dressed him down in front of the entire company, which
made Bob livid. A few minutes later the phone rang. Bob
rushed over, tore the box off the wall, ripped the wires out and
smilingly handed the phone to LeRoy, saying, "Here, Mervyn,
I think this is for you."

Despite these and other incidents LeRoy was so enthusiastic
about Bob's potential that he considered putting him under
personal contract if MGM failed to exercise their option. While
LeRoy felt there was a surfeit of experienced, talented and
easy-to-handle actors at Metro and that this maverick of a man
would not exactly blend into the decorous atmosphere there,
he was planning to direct *The Robe* and felt Bob would be
suitable for a major role.

Immediately after confirming that MGM was not going to
pick up the option, LeRoy called Bob's agent and urged that
Wilkins persuade Ben Piazza, head of talent at RKO, to speak
with Bob. Piazza did, and then suggested Wilkins try to stir

enthusiasm in Sid Rogell and Jack Gross, two producers who were making the type of films in which Bob was most likely to be cast. Gross was impressed with Bob and arranged for him to meet Gordon Douglas, who was directing *Girl Rush*. Douglas's enthusiastic report influenced RKO to sign a seven-year deal with Bob on May 25, 1944, commencing June 1. True, it was for the same amount Harry Cohn had offered at Columbia, and there was no guarantee Bob would escape westerns, but it did give him a shot at *The Robe*, which at that time was scheduled to be made by Leroy at MGM. Also, an arrangement was worked out for David O. Selznick's Vanguard to share the contract. The terms were promising: If at the end of twenty-six weeks the option was exercised, Bob's salary would rise to $400 a week for the next twenty-six weeks. Then, every twelve months, if the contract was renewed, he would receive raises to $500, $750, $1,000, $1,250, reaching $2,000 a week in the seventh and final year. The advantage of the Vanguard connection was that being a Selznick star would endow Bob with panache; Selznick's people would see to it that Bob appeared in sound, sleek vehicles whether under Selznick's aegis or on loan-out.

The deal, however, was almost called off by Bob before he went in front of the cameras. The studio wanted to change his name to John Mitchell, and Bob was all for tearing up the contract, but Wilkins sent him home and adroitly solved the problem by sending a memo to Ben Piazza:

Ordinarily I would not be too much concerned over the possibility of a name change for a client. However, I feel that in his case there are several points to be considered. In the first place, he is not the accepted pretty-boy type, therefore, the main consideration is that he should have a name that is as different as his personality. After all, in America people are called everything from O'Houlihan to Schmalz; what they are called has no bearing on their ability or achievement. Mitchum has made several pictures with featured billing under his own name, from which he receives fan mail from all over the world. Now that he has reached the point where his ability is being recognized, it doesn't seem advisable to start him over with another name. I have observed that the main reason for changing a name is to try to build someone up who hasn't made good under their previous name. This is certainly not Mitchum's case. He desires to cooperate in every way possible, but feels that his name is different, not like every other aspiring young actor's. For these reasons, we request that he be known on the screen as Robert Mitchum.

P.S. He has just finished 15 weeks in *30 Seconds Over Tokyo* and will be featured as Robert Mitchum. He has been billed under the name in *Love From A Stranger,** co-starred with Kim Hunter; *Gung Ho!*, *We've Never Been Licked* and several others for Universal.

Bob's first role under the new contract was hardly of Cary Grant caliber—or even that of a Grant reject. *Girl Rush* starred comics Wally Brown and Alan Carney, and Bob, who received fifth billing, played the romantic lead opposite Frances Langford. He didn't complain, but he did "thank" Piazza for "building" his career by getting him cast in a western musical where the villains were routed by Bob's persuading his cohorts to invade the bad men's hangout in drag!

His next two assignments were also westerns—but this time Zane Grey westerns. In *Nevada* Bob received star billing for the first time, and made his mark in such formula films, though he was later to complain that the only thing that changed was the leading lady. In *West of the Pecos* his leading lady was played by pretty and talented Barbara Hale, making her screen debut. This time a few alert reviewers saw beyond the formula and commented that Bob brought something special to the stock character he was assigned.

His complaints were so persistent about these assignments, however, that in July RKO granted him permission to test at International for a part in ice skater Sonja Henie's last picture. The result, as RKO must have anticipated, was that International executives took one look at the six-foot-two Mitchum and the diminutive skater and informed his home studio that

*Retitled *When Strangers Marry*.

Bob seemed "unsuitable for the part." His implied failure to measure up to the "different" kind of role he had been begging for enabled RKO to impress upon him that he didn't always know what was in his best interest.

Still, his services were in demand. One request came from independent producers Maurice and Frank King, who released their pictures through Monogram. In the late summer of 1944 the Kings wrote studio head Charles Koerner, claiming to have brought Bob to Ben Piazza's attention. In gratitude, they said, he had promised to try to arrange for Bob to be lent to them for two films at $7,500. Piazza indignantly denied this claim, and Koerner ignored them.

Nothing more was heard about it until November 1, 1946, when Maurice King wrote to the new head of RKO, Peter J. Rathvon, claming that in 1944 he and his brother Frank had cast Mitchum, then an unknown, as the lead in their film *When Strangers Marry*. He said Mitchum's screen presence "bespoke such promise" they tabbed him as a cinch for stardom, but their small company was unable to place him under contract. However, because they wanted to "retain a claim" on the young actor in the future, they approached Ben Piazza at RKO. Piazza, he said, set up a meeting at which Charles Koerner, Joseph Nolan, Steve Broidy, Trem Carr, Piazza and the Kings were present. Mitchum was put under contract to RKO, he maintained, with the understanding the Kings could use him in two pictures each year. While preparing *Dillinger*, King said they tried to exercise their option, but agreed not to do so when Piazza explained RKO did not want Mitchum associated with the production "because of the nature of that particular script." But in 1946, King said their company had three scripts ready to shoot and were "urgently in need of Mitchum." He concluded, "We right now request your earnest consideration of this matter, and trust that you will be able to facilitate this player's availability to us. Thanking you very much."

Piazza fired off a reply. "The bold-faced effrontery of Maurice King's letter to Mr. Rathvon, dated November 1st, is almost too silly to answer," he began, detailing the history of the negotiations. He pointed out that the King brothers' memories and records were faulty because Mitchum was already under contract to the studio when the Kings claimed to have ap-

proached him in August. Mitchum, Piazza said, actually worked
for the King brothers in *When Strangers Marry* from May 24
to June 3, "overlapping two days of RKO's contractual start,
June 1." He further said he had met the Kings only twice—
both times by accident. He had attended no meeting, had never
seen Steve Broidy and barely knew Trem Carr. On November
18 Peter Rathvon finally replied to Maurice King, going over
the claims and closing: "In my opinion it is very plain that you
have no right whatsoever to the services of Mr. Mitchum, and
we have no intention of making him available to you."

Lester Cowan's inquiry about Bob's availability to play the
lead in *The Story of G.I. Joe*, based on the World War II
communiqués of Ernie Pyle, received rather a different reception. Cowan had already signed William Wellman to direct and
was dickering with Fred Astaire to play Pyle. But Wellman
was urging Cowan to get Bob for the role of Lieutenant Walker,
feeling certain he could turn him into a major star as he had
done with several others, including Jimmy Cagney and Gary
Cooper.

RKO was interested, but unreceptive to Cowan's request
that he be given an option on Bob's services for one picture a
year. Finally Cowan decided on October 24 to leave the matter
open to negotiation and proceed immediately with the test.

The scene that Wellman chose to shoot had Mitchum writing
letters to mothers whose sons had been killed. A key scene in
the script, Wellman later wrote that using it for the test was a
big mistake. "Really, for I saw something so wonderful, so
compelling, that I was mad at myself for not having built the
set before so that I could have made the test the actual scene
that came out in the picture."

Although Bob steadfastly believed that in the end Cowan
and Wellman would use an established star, Cowan notified
RKO that Bob would begin work between November 14 and
18 and agreed to pay RKO $800 a week for five weeks, plus
pro-rata pay if the production ran over schedule. Burgess
Meredith, rather than Astaire, played Pyle, and the contract
contained a guarantee that only Meredith's name would precede
Bob's on all positive prints, paid advertising and publicity.

The script, the producer, the director, the company and the

billing were of such a satisfactory nature that even so chronic a complainer as Bob could find little to grouse about, beyond the fact that RKO was being reimbursed for his salary and pocketing a $450 weekly profit on his services.

Despite all subsequent statements in which he has disparaged taking acting seriously, he earnestly applied himself to creating a well-observed character. Once, in an unguarded moment, he granted an interview which probably represented his youthful, idealistic attitude toward his profession: "I like pictures. . . . But you've got to take them seriously—be a real actor or quit. . . . You've got to do a thing as well as you can in Hollywood. The time has passed for semi-professionals.

"There are too many pastel people—pastel characters—in Hollywood. They don't know how to portray a character. Some of them are just busy little people studying their lines. If they learned more about life, about people, about psychology, about acting and timing, their characterizations would be more believable, more truthful, easier to take."

There is the ring of authenticity to this quote; Bob had not yet concluded that films—with rare exceptions—were pieces of merchandise.

Later he would develop a cynical pay-me-and-I'll-show-up attitude toward his work. Defending his less-than-flattering view of acting in a discussion with Julie one time, he maintained that a good actor did not *feel* the part, he thought it. Acting, he insisted, was entirely intellectual, to which his sister recalls responding, "Really? Is that why you developed combat fatigue from those months on the set of *G.I. Joe*?" In recalling this exchange she said, "He did, you know. He actually developed combat fatigue. Crawled under a table—that's how deeply he got into the part." She believes he developed the macho image because it was commercial, and he was able to do it because acting was "not central to his being. It was not his central theme and didn't matter. In his writing he would not compromise. He remained true to himself. But that he shows no one, that's what he won't reveal."

On March 31, 1945, Bob received greetings from Uncle Sam; he was to report for active duty in the Army on April 11.

Although studio biographies later claimed that he repeatedly tried to enlist but had been rejected because of an old back injury, he laughed: "When they took me away, I still had the porch rail under my fingernails."

As usual, he has various versions of the event. In 1983, for instance, he told a *Rolling Stone* interviewer that he had been sitting on the front porch thinking about the sweetness of his life, "just having a drink, looking at the stars, smoking a Pall Mall" when a car slammed to a halt in front of his house, a man leaped out, raced up the sidewalk and jumped on his porch, blinding him with a flashlight in his face. Bob said he responded by leaping up and breaking the nose of his attacker, who turned out to be a Los Angeles policeman. The cop had come to the wrong address.

As Bob tells it, he was so outraged that he demanded to be arrested, leaping into the police car, "screaming, 'Let's go downtown right now, motherfuckers!'" This mistake earned him a painful beating in which his opponents used a billyclub, a gun, fists and knees. He says that on advice from a studio lawyer he pleaded guilty to assault, anticipating a ten-dollar fine. Instead the judge toyed with a 180-day sentence until informed that Bob was enlisting in the Army. Consequently the judge held him in jail over the weekend and then ordered he be led to the troop train in handcuffs. As Sherwood Anderson would have said, if that's not the way it happened, it should have.

Actually, on April 6 Bob was under stress because his draft number was up, his induction was imminent and both his wife and one of his sons were ill. He got drunk, and as usually happened when he was in that condition, a contretemps ensued. This time it was at his mother's house, and the issue—that he had been denied permission to speak to his wife and had been hung up on. A disturbance followed, and the police arrived. Although no one would press charges, Bob demanded to be taken to the Fairfax Station where he was charged with being in "an intoxicated condition on private property." Judge Cecil Holland fined him ten dollars and sentenced him to County Jail where he spent all of Saturday and part of Sunday, when he was released to prepare for induction into the Army on Wednesday, April 11.

He was assigned to Camp Roberts, and after completing infantry training was transferred to Fort MacArthur. In the early days he claimed he had been a drill sergeant and was later assigned as assistant to an orthopedic examiner. Later on a television show he puzzled the program's British host by amending "orthopedic examiner" to "keister police" in the interest of entertaining the audience. When that drew a startled response from the host and a laugh from the studio audience, Bob said, "A rectal inspector. A poop snooper." He then increased the laughter by inviting the host to assist him in a demonstration—by dropping his pants. "We used to line up nine hundred troops a day, tell them to drop their jeans [sic] and spread their cheeks," he asserted. By 1983 Bob had become a master of coarseness. He told the reporter from *Rolling Stone* that he had been assigned to the medics, his job being to look up "the asshole of every GI in America." Asked by the reporter what he had been looking for, he replied, "Piles, hemorrhoids, bananas, grapes, dope . . . you name it."

Luckily for Bob, *The Story of G.I. Joe* was highly regarded by the U.S. Army, and he devoted part of his eight months in the service to it. On April 25 Lester Cowan arranged for Bob to be released from basic training for one day to do retakes. In July Bob was given a working furlough of four to six weeks in which he was to promote the picture across the United States which in turn would bolster the war effort. Immediately Ben Piazza seized this opportunity to strengthen Bob's RKO connection. He contacted the New York office, informed them that Bob was staying at the Sherry-Netherland, and ordered that a man from the office be assigned to him. Rutgers Neilson went to see the soldier-actor and was favorably impressed with his cooperative attitude. Bob agreed to be interviewed for a piece to run in the Sunday supplement *Parade*, to appear on Paula Stone's top-rated radio interview show, and even attend a dinner at the Waldorf-Astoria in honor of the new Postmaster General, Robert Hannigan, without complaining. At the instigation of Neilson, "The Two Bobs" posed for a photograph which was widely syndicated. On every level Bob cooperated fully, and Neilson came away from the assignment not only convinced RKO had a star on its hands, but also, as he wrote Piazza, that Bob happened to be "a swell guy."

For all the glamorous accommodations and outings, Bob's financial position was far from adequate for a rising young celebrity with a family to support. He might dine at the Waldorf, 21, Sardi's and other chic spots, but his extended family was feeling a financial bind. Upon learning he was entitled to a bonus check, he quickly wrote the RKO accounting department and in his flamboyant style demanded that payment be made at once, ending the letter with the following riposte:

> My passionate love to everyone and my most humble gratitude to the boys in the "dark-paneled backroom."
> With deepest devotion always,
> Pvt. Robert Mitchum

The film opened the last week in July to huzzahs for everyone—Bob, Burgess Meredith, Freddie Steele, Wally Cassell, Wellman, Cowan and scriptwriters Leopold Atlas, Guy Endore and Philip Stevenson. *Time* magazine trumpeted that this was "far and away the least glamorous war picture ever made. It is a movie without a single false note. It is not 'entertainment' in the usual sense, but as General Eisenhower called it 'the greatest war picture I've ever seen.'"

At the year's close *The Story of G.I. Joe* was included on most of the "Ten Best Pictures" lists. When Academy Award nominations were announced, Bob was among those chosen for the Best Supporting Actor category. Characteristically he put down the whole idea by announcing that he had voted for James Dunn, and he refused to attend the ceremonies. Nevertheless, those close to him agree that he was deeply disappointed when he didn't win. Still, when queried about it, he sloughs it off with: "You notice the Academy hasn't messed with me since."

CHAPTER 5

On April 11, the day Mitchum was drafted, the Western Allied and Russian armies were already pushing across Germany. On April 25 they met, and it was but a matter of days until, on May 8, Germany unconditionally surrendered. Still, experts forecast that the war with Japan might drag on for who knew how many years. Then on August 6 the Enola Gay dropped the first atomic bomb on Hiroshima, leveling ninety percent of the city. Three days later a second nuclear blast devastated one-third of the city of Nagasaki, killing or injuring seventy-five thousand inhabitants. By September 1945 World War II had officially ended, leaving in its wake the loss of innocence. The Holocaust, resulting in the extermination of six million Jews, dimmed man's view of himself as a rational, humane creature. And with the dropping of the first atomic bomb, pragmatism (saving Allied lives) took precedence over the higher morality of refraining from snuffing out two hundred thousand civilians. A dark view of humanity replaced traditional optimism and the belief that society was evolving to an ever-improving state. Nihilism and, later, existentialism followed in the wake of world-wide grinding poverty and political instability. The conflicting interests of the USSR and the USA sowed the seeds of the Cold War. That the world had undergone a series of cataclysms and would face a series of crises which would produce a new moral code and new view of man was inescapable.

Mitchum, after serving eight uneventful months in the army, was released on a family-hardship claim on October 12, 1945, without ever having left the country or, to all appearances, having been affected personally by this turn of events. If anything, his rugged masculinity was now seasoned with a hint of sensitivity making him a new type of star—and one to be reckoned with. In prewar days the complicated mixture of good and evil that he projected might have doomed him to portrayals of villains, or limited him to character roles; but by the fall of 1945 a few studio heads, alive to shifting values, perceived that the social change would exceed what had followed in the wake of World War I and other major conflicts.

Given Mitchum's minimal involvement in the war effort, he needed no time to readjust to civilian life. On October 13, the day after he was mustered out of the service, he went before the cameras with two other Selznick stars, Dorothy McGuire and Guy Madison, and one of RKO's bright hopes, Bill Williams, in what was first called *They Dream of Home*, later titled *Till the End of Time*. In this sentimental tale of three ex-Marines' adjustment to the peacetime world, Madison, handsomer than most boys next door, was cast as the conventional leading man of prewar films—a character whose problems could be solved by meeting and winning the love of the right woman. In contrast, Bill Williams played a paraplegic who would have to learn to live with his tragedy, and Mitchum's character embodied the outsider, the flawed character as much at odds with himself as with society, the serviceman returning to civilian life. For this man, whose baggage included a steel plate in his head and a drinking problem, the question of what direction his life would take was problematical. His eventual adjustment was neither as inevitable nor as wholesome as Madison's, nor as bleak as amputee Williams's, whose dreams of a professional boxing career were irretrievably shattered.

It was Mitchum's triumph that he projected turmoil beneath the patina of cynical bravado. Fortunately, postwar audiences were receptive to less-than-perfect profiles, pronounced sensuality and complicated moral motivations. Following as it did his memorable portrait of the tough-yet-tender Lieutenant Walker in *The Story of G.I. Joe*, this performance confirmed that Mitchum was no nova but a real star.

As befitted a rising star, RKO lent Mitchum $5,000 for a down payment on a $12,500 two-story house at 3372 Oak Glen Drive, with the agreement that one hundred dollars be deducted from his weekly paycheck until the loan was repaid. He and his family were extremely happy with this arrangement, but they would have been even happier if Mitchum's agent had been able to persuade the studio to treat the loan as a bonus for Mitchum's signing a new seven-year deal in mid-1946.

That Selznick's Vanguard company shared RKO's optimism concerning Mitchum's future is confirmed by a stern memo which reprimanded the latter studio for taking full-page advertisements in *The Hollywood Reporter* and *Variety* identifying Mitchum as an "RKO STAR." Vanguard contended this was a blatant violation of the terms of their joint contract and warned that they would not tolerate it any more than RKO would allow him to be advertised as a "SELZNICK STAR."

The dailies of *Till the End of Time* stimulated Mitchum's employers into a whirlwind of creative deal-making on his behalf. In the first three weeks of March 1946 they accepted two offers from Metro-Goldwyn-Mayer for him to costar in a film with Katharine Hepburn and Robert Taylor, and another with Greer Garson and Robert Montgomery (later replaced by Richard Hart), which would introduce him to another segment of movie audiences—those who attended Metro's slickly produced, high-budget films. During the same period at RKO he was assigned to *What Nancy Wanted*, eventually released as *The Locket*, in which he played a leading role along with Laraine Day and Brian Aherne.

This sudden rise in fortunes was enough to turn anyone's head—but Mitchum was not anyone. He had known Laraine Day at the Players Guild in Long Beach before she became a Hollywood star. Soon after he moved to break into films he had encountered her in Schwab's Drugstore and got the impression she had "frosted" him. Furious, he vowed that one day he would play opposite her and would "wipe her off the screen." But now that he was playing one of her leading men, he hardly had the opportunity since it was her starring vehicle. Nor did he have the inclination to carry out his threat. Instead he contented himself with avoiding any contact with her that was not in the line of duty.

Day later said she thought he "was marvelous as the romantic painter. Very much like himself. Still, it wasn't. It *was* a performance and I thought next to *G.I. Joe* it was the most interesting work he had done so far. But off-camera there was always a little distance between us that shouldn't have been there, because we'd known each other so long." She said this in 1982 and had forgotten or had never been aware of the supposed snub at Schwab's. Then she added, "At one time I thought perhaps there might have been some kind of moral barricade, because I had a reputation as a strict Mormon. But in later years I learned he reacted that way to almost everyone. Deborah Kerr, Charles Laughton, David Lean, John Houston—all have gone on record how much they admire him. I wonder whether they aren't impressed *because* he's so aloof? Aren't people who can't be reached always the ones that intrigue you the most? Don't you find that especially when famous people run across someone who is not impressed with their fame, it's a very intriguing quality?"

Not in the case of Katharine Hepburn. In *Undercurrent* Mitchum played the mysterious, retiring brother of an evil and sadistic industrialist (Robert Taylor), who is married to the frumpy daughter (Hepburn) of a famous scientist. At first the daughter mistakes the character Mitchum plays for the handyman, but eventually falls in love with him and runs away with him to escape her murderous husband.

While the film was a prestigious undertaking, Mitchum's role was relatively small. Under the circumstances he grew bored waiting around and indulged himself with practical jokes and imitations of everyone, including Hepburn, until she read him off in front of the company. "You know you can't act. If you hadn't been good-looking, you would never have gotten a picture. I'm tired of playing with people who have nothing to offer." Mitchum accepted her dressing down with good grace and referred to the incident frequently afterward, embellishing it to the point where he had the two of them become such good buddies that she later grew concerned over the way Vincente Minnelli was directing one of his scenes, and warned, "Don't let them fuck you, Mr. Mitchum, darling." Sherwood Anderson, please write.

Before finishing retakes on *Undercurrent* and *The Locket*, Mitchum began work with Greer Garson on *Desire Me*.* He was set for seven weeks with the eighth week free, and was to receive co-star billing second only to Garson, who was at the height of her popularity and treated by most of her co-workers as if she were royalty. Mitchum immediately startled her by nicknaming her "Red." Whether out of ignorance or devilishness, he also consumed a hamburger with a slice of raw onion and a salad with roquefort dressing for lunch on a day when they were doing a love scene. "Her eyes would spin around and she'd offer me a Chiclet," he told friends. "I'd refuse. 'Gum?' No thanks. It didn't occur to me my breath was spinning her out. Horses didn't seem to mind."

Mitchum was as unhappy with the la-de-dah manners, as he called them, of Garson and director George Cukor as they were with him. Cukor had undertaken the project under protest because neither he nor anyone else seemed able to understand Zoe Aikens's screenplay. The plot was complicated and much of the dialogue so stilted that it might have served as a tongue-twisting exercise in a speech class.

Overworked and unhappy at having to juggle three parts on two separate lots, Mitchum went to studio manager Goldberg and asked for a dressing room on the ground floor. Goldberg's automatic response to any request was a refusal. "Will you let me explain?" asked Mitchum. "I'm bicycling back and forth between here and MGM. I need to make quick changes. The dressing room I have is so far up my nose bleeds everytime I go up there. And the doniker's down the hall. Neither Lawrence Tierney nor Bill Williams is working presently. Why can't I use one of the rooms assigned to them?" Goldberg's answer was still no. Mitchum pleaded, promising he would give up

*At various times it was titled *Carl and Anna*, *Karl and Anna*, *A Woman of My Own*, *Sacred and Profane*, and *As You Desire Me*.

the room as soon as its occupant came back to work, but Goldberg remained adamant.

On the RKO lot the buildings occupied by executives, producers and writers overlooked a small flower garden. About half an hour after his confrontation with the studio manager, Mitchum strode into the middle of the flower garden with a hose in one hand and a bar of soap in the other. He wore a towel around his middle, and as he soaped himself, yelled, "Hey, Goldberg!" Eventually his cries summoned almost everyone in the three buildings to the windows. Some of the secretaries were chanting, "Drop the towel! Drop the towel!" Finally, not only Goldberg but also studio head Charles Koerner appeared at their windows. Goldberg was too busy ordering Mitchum to stop to notice, and Mitchum was shouting, "Either I get the dressing room or I drop the towel!" Koerner wanted to know what was going on, in response to which Mitchum shouted out his request and was immediately granted a ground-floor dressing room. At the same time he substantially increased his reputation as a rebel.

By July 11 the company shooting *Desire Me* was demoralized by the unshootable script and the lack of rapport. Both Mitchum and his stand-in, Boyd Cabeen, who were drinking heavily, became irate when late in the day George Cukor announced there would be night shooting. Mitchum already was scheduled for nine a.m. retakes on *Undercurrent*. He and Cabeen, who were feeling no pain when the director dismissed them, headed for a nearby bar, proceeded to get roaring drunk and concocted a scheme to get even with both Cukor and Vincente Minnelli.

They drove back to the lot and told the lone gateman that Mitchum had left his wallet in his dressing room, which was located in the makeup building. As Mitchum later told a friend, they entered the building and proceeded to strip the place of head forms, mustaches, beards, brushes, sponges, scissors and all other items needed for the next day's shooting, including Lucille Ball's wig.

"Now he could have made it out with those things without any trouble, but he didn't," a friend says. "He was feeling guilty about it being late and him being drunk, and Dorothy at home alone with the kids again. So he spots a standing hair dryer—which was something she has always wanted. He up-ends it and lugs it to the car also. Then he and his stand-in got two more which they'll deliver to two girls. They get in the car and wave good-bye to the guard, who waves back and lets them go. They're just cracking up at how disrupted everything will be in the morning.

"So now it's six in the morning. These two makeup people come in and one is saying, 'Where is that beard I put out last night? The one for Louis Calhern.' And the other one is looking all over for Lucille Ball's wig. Then they notice the hair dryers are gone. They realize somebody has been in the place and cleaned it out.

"Eventually someone checks the list to see who'd come through the gate, and Bob Mitchum had. They wake up the guard at home. He says Bob had come in to get something he'd left in his dressing room. Did the guard notice anything strange? 'Well, no,' he says. 'Well, there was a hair dryer sticking out of his car. That's probably what he left in his dressing room.'

"Back home, Bob and his friend got in about five. Dorothy gets up to make breakfast and she's pretty annoyed about the whole thing. However, he's brought this standing hair dryer. She's always wanted one. She's delighted. That makes up for everything. She can't wait. As soon as she's finished making breakfast she washes her hair, and about seven-thirty in the morning she's sitting luxuriating under the hair dryer. Her hair is almost dry. She can't wait to comb it out when from under the dryer she sees Bob go to the door. He opens it and these three people come in. She's waving, thinking they're friends of his. They come over and grab the dryer off her head. They're from MGM. So they take all the pieces—falls, beards, sponges, brushes *and* her new dryer and leave. Metro was terribly upset. They wanted to prosecute. They called RKO and said, 'This is absolutely it. We've had enough trouble . . . blah, blah, blah.' RKO said, 'Fine, go ahead,' knowing MGM wouldn't do any-thing since they had two pictures coming out starring him." That's the way the story has been passed down for the last thirty-five years.

In a memo to RKO, MGM reported that rooms eight and ten in the makeup department had been burglarized of two Turbinator hair dryers ($125 each), one Eugene hair dryer ($150), plus other equipment. Fingerprints were taken and everyone was interrogated. Eventually investigators found that Mitchum's automobile had been parked by the makeup building, and they located some sound men who had seen "two very intoxicated men" loading it. The men were later identified as Mitchum and Cabeen. When Cabeen was called in he confessed. Since Mitchum was working in a series of important scenes that would last all day, he was phoned by W. P. Hendry of MGM, whereupon he admitted his participation in "the gag." A. Q. Hodgett, investigator for the MGM police department, took Cabeen with him to gather all the loot, including one eyelash curler, one Majestic clipper, one Sunbeam shaver, twenty-five small sable brushes, one bottle of spirit gum, three barber's towels, five plaster plaques, one plaster mask of Henry Hull and one bundle of hair (presumably Lucille Ball's wig?). "From the standpoint of law, both Mr. Cabeen and Mr. Mitchum could, in my opinion, be prosecuted for grand theft," the memo went on. "I do not think that these two men, regardless of the prominence of one, should go unpunished."

RKO responded that MGM should proceed, but MGM protected their investment by not doing anything. Eventually RKO sent reimbursement for $52.70 to MGM and the matter was dropped—as Mitchum probably had foreseen.

Following completion of *The Locket*, he had taken home his film wardrobe. A few days later the producer called to ask where the clothing was, and Mitchum asked what clothing the producer was referring to. It was described, and he replied that it was in his closet at home. Jack Gross, the producer, requested that it be brought back. Mitchum refused, saying he needed the clothes. The studio, according to him, was keeping him so busy he had no time to go shopping. "These fit very well and I'm keeping them," he announced. Gross said it would be impossible, and Mitchum inquired why. Wasn't it customary? Didn't they give Cary Grant his clothes? Gross disputed this, contending Grant bought them. "Yes," Mitchum agreed, "for one dollar, I checked." When Gross insisted, Mitchum informed him, "Not only does Cary Grant get his, but Bob

Cummings also does." Gross again claimed that Cummings purchased his clothing. "Well, isn't it for one dollar?" Gross gave up and sent someone around from the accounting department with a release to be executed upon payment of one dollar. Mitchum refused. "I won't pay you the dollar," he said. "I stole those clothes, and as a matter of principle I want it entered on my record that Robert Mitchum stole his wardrobe."

What to do in the face of his intransigence?

Simple. On March 14, 1946, Gross sent a memo to William Dozier, who was in charge of production.

> It was necessary that we make four changes and an overcoat (a tuxedo, a suit, two sport jackets and two pair of pants) for Bob Mitchum for *What Nancy Wanted*. This is modern wardrobe and cost the studio $580.
>
> It is my recommendation that it would be a very nice gesture on our part if we presented Mitchum with this wardrobe as a gift from the studio. Frankly, and confidentially, he needs this type of wardrobe, and as an up and coming young star it is to our advantage that he dresses in the best taste.

The same day Dozier wrote Mitchum:

> Dear Bob—
> Jack Gross has called to my attention the fact that we have purchased several suits for you as a part of your wardrobe for the picture, and has suggested that you might find these clothes useful and that you would, no doubt, propose that we sell them to you at cost when the picture is finished. This is simply to tell you, on behalf of the company, I am pleased to make you a gift of these clothes as of now, and may you wear them in the best of health.
>
> Sincerely,
> William Dozier

A clutch of new assignments, including *Pursued*, a modern psychological western; *Crossfire*, the first frank treatment of anti-semitism on the screen; *Out of the Past*, a classic example of a new genre later known as "film noir"; *Rachel and the Stranger*, *Blood on the Moon* and *The Red Pony*—all westerns—followed.

And yet, with the exception of *Rachel and the Stranger* and *The Red Pony*, work on *Desire Me* continued simultaneously as the other films were made. A preview of the film as originally written, acted and shot nearly cleared the theater before the end of the second reel. Mitchum later claimed he turned up his overcoat collar to hide his face when he left, fearing he would be stoned by angry ticket buyers.

George Cukor quit and Jack Conway took over for a few days. Marguerite Roberts attempted to rewrite the script, and Mervyn LeRoy directed the new version. Mitchum's role now consisted of a brief introduction early in the picture, as a prisoner in a wartime camp and his unexpected return near the end, revealing that his death was only the fabrication of his wife's new husband. Both Cukor and LeRoy took a look at the final cut and refused to accept the discredit of having made the film, which was a disaster.

Crossfire had only a $500,000 budget and a 22-day shooting schedule, but it was a meaty production and eventually earned five Academy Award nominations. Although Mitchum's role was considerably less important than those played by Robert Young and Robert Ryan, it provided him with high visibility in a popular picture.

The fact that he stood in third place, as it were, did not prevent Mitchum from attempting to make his mark. He and the other two Bobs realized that in a film with a lot of shouting, the low-decibel actor comes off best. So Bob Young came in under Bob Ryan, and Mitchum came in so low that he could scarcely be heard, causing director Edward Dmytryk to chide them, "Hey, fellows! We all know what we're doing, but we do have to be heard." It was at this moment that Dmytryk concluded that for all Mitchum's protests about not giving a damn, he was not as "irresponsible and vague—and—yes, wacky" as he liked to pretend. "Underneath he knows the score as few actors in Hollywood do," the director remarked. "What is more, he doesn't want anyone to realize it, but he cares deeply." His being used, as Dmytryk admitted, for "the box office value of his name," unquestionably deepened Mitchum's growing cynicism about his profession.

Perhaps not coincidentally, during the making of these films he requested permission to return to the legitimate theater for two performances in Long Beach and two in Santa Barbara. The opening was set for August 6. As it approached, Perry Lieber, head of publicity at RKO, alerted N. Peter Rathvon that, "It would mean a great deal to him [Mitchum] if you would drop him a wire," and Rathvon complied with a telegram to the Long Beach Auditorium: "BEST WISHES AND GOOD LUCK TO YOU AND THE CAST OF "THE GENTLE APPROACH."

After Long Beach, the company—plus Mitchum's wife and sons—moved on to Catalina instead of Santa Barbara. There they performed at the Avalon Theater, located in the famous big-band ballroom. Audience response was encouraging enough for the producers to bring the production to the Mayan Theater in Los Angeles. "I don't know why Bob or any of us wanted to do it," said leading lady Jacqueline DeWitt in 1983. "The premise was that he returns from the war eager to get about fulfilling his marital duties. But I, as his wife, believe that unless he gets used to the house and reacquaints himself first, it will upset him. It was the craziest idea, even for a farce. But it did prove he could play comedy. It didn't run long, but he was completely conscientious—just utterly. When people say Bob Mitchum walks through a part, that's not the same as saying somebody else walked through one. Because there is too much concentration there for him to be overlooked. He may say he doesn't take acting seriously, but he was totally professional. He resented it when others weren't. You could see he was like a quiet volcano, seething but determined not to erupt."

Having proved something to himself, Mitchum returned to films. This time Selznick exercised his prerogative by lending him to Warner Brothers for a Freudian western, *Pursued*. Since Niven Busch had written it for his wife, Teresa Wright, Mitchum was billed beneath her. As was to happen often to him, critical reception ran the gamut, from *Esquire*'s Jack Moffit, who wrote: "The picture moves Robert Mitchum into the front ranks of stardom," to Bosley Crowther, who sniped in the *New York*

Times: "[He] is a very rigid gent and gives no more animation than a Frigidaire turned to 'defrost.'"

By the time he began filming *Out of the Past*, in October 1946, his ninth film since his release from the Army, Mitchum, bolstered by a recently renegotiated contract and an increased fan following, had reason to regard himself as a lucky actor. By nature, however, he was unable to refrain from griping that he had become the studio workhorse.

In *Out of the Past* the characters inhabit a world powered by greed and corruption. Violence, death and double-crossing are the norm, rendering the film its excitement and a pervasive pessimism. Jeff Bailey (Mitchum), a former private detective with a flawed past, is sought by gambler Whit Sterling (Kirk Douglas), whom he had double-crossed by taking up with Sterling's ex-mistress (Jane Greer) instead of retrieving her and forty thousand dollars she had stolen. Bailey and the seductive, sloe-eyed Kathi had fled to San Francisco, where Bailey's ex-partner (Steve Brodie) finds them and demands part of the loot in return for his silence. Kathi responds by killing him. She and Bailey split up, and he hides out in a small town, running a garage, and there becomes involved with a local girl (Virginia Huston). When one of Sterling's henchmen (Paul Valentine) tracks him down and forces him to see Sterling about a project, Bailey is stunned to find the beautiful Kathi reunited with Sterling. The gambler is willing to forget Bailey's double-cross if he will retrieve some incriminating papers from a black-mailing lawyer who is shaking him down. When Bailey goes to the lawyer's office after hours, and discovers the man has been murdered, he knows then he's been framed. Returning to Sterling, he finds him murdered, and Kathi, gun in hand, in charge. She insists he flee with her. Trapped, he seizes an opportunity to call the police. When they run into a road block, she realizes what he's done and shoots him before she's cut down by a fusillade from the police. The film ends with Bailey's "pure" girlfriend asking his mechanic helper (Dickie Moore) whether Bailey would have gone away with Kathi, to which the mechanic nods affirmatively.

This cult film provided Mitchum with his first opportunity to carry a film, gave the delectable Jane Greer her second major role and presented newcomer Kirk Douglas with a chance to reinforce the promise he had shown in *The Strange Love of Martha Ivers*, which had been dimmed by his colorless performance in *Mourning Becomes Electra*.

In Mitchum's relationships with Greer and Douglas, he demonstrated the duality of his professional nature. Greer remembers that it was her first starring role, and she was eager to fulfill the studio's faith in her. "What I remember most is that Bob was just terrific to me and just took care of me," she says. "Even the way I looked. One costume I wore was a little too large. I think they switched at the last moment and got this dress out of wardrobe. Anyway, it wasn't right and Bob was the one who noticed it was bulging around the waist. So he stopped everything, borrowed a pin from the wardrobe lady and gathered it in and pinned me up in the back."

To create a relaxed atmosphere on the set, Mitchum gave the impression he was unprepared, which impressed his young leading lady tremendously. "I remember him saying 'What are the lyrics?' to the script person. 'I never know the lyrics,' he'd say, and she would give him the lines," Greer recalls. "I said, 'You don't learn your lines beforehand?' And he said, 'Naah.' Gosh, I learned mine a week ahead of time. I thought that might be part of why he seemed so much more spontaneous, why he was so easy and underplayed. I decided I'd do that, not be letter perfect. So I tried learning my lines under the dryer in the morning. I hoped maybe I'd look as though I was thinking. But I blew take after take, and he was letter perfect. Well, I figured out later that, of course, he knew the lines.

"But there was nothing starry about him. I think the second day that we were working we were thrown into a love scene which was a little difficult. Really difficult. As I was looking up at him under the lights, we were about to kiss. I suddenly saw this brown line around his mouth. I think, 'Is that lipstick?' It wasn't lipstick, but a sort of crumbling brown line that outlined his lips. So I said to him, 'What is that stuff around your lips? Is that makeup or something?' He fingered it a moment and said, 'No, that's my chawin' tobaccy.' So he wiped it off before the scene began." Greer emitted a roar of affectionate laughter as she recalled the moment.

The sizzling sexuality projected by the two, plus the celebrated dialogue, as when she attempts to seduce him one night and he snarls, "Get out. I have to sleep in this room," have not lost impact, even after more than three decades.

If he was protective of his leading lady, he was self-protective in his dealings with Kirk Douglas, who had been borrowed from Paramount. Cast and crew could see the two actors sizing one another up, each trying to set his own character for maximum effectiveness. This was a contest, not ensemble playing; anything went. In one of the first scenes, Mitchum opened the door of a hotel room in Mexico and there stood Douglas. The camera's eye was on the back of Mitchum's head and on Douglas's face. Mitchum made a funny face, and Douglas was completely thrown. The scene had to be repeated.

In retaliation Douglas began flipping a half dollar as George Raft had done so effectively. He was going to use it as a piece of business which would have given him the scene. By the time they were ready to go before the cameras Douglas had mastered the trick. Mitchum said nothing, but when the cameras began to roll he never looked at Douglas, but simply stared fixedly at the coin, knowing that the audience would share his response. Director Jacques Tourneur killed the coin flipping at once.

During another take Douglas nonchalantly swung a keychain. Suddenly Mitchum stuck out his finger and the chain wrapped itself around it. Chalk up another cut.

In a later take both men stood. Then Douglas sat on the arm of the sofa, whereupon Mitchum informed the director he would feel more comfortable sitting on the sofa. Had Tourneur not insisted upon returning to his original staging, both might have ended up on the floor attempting to steal the scene. Eventually Douglas realized he had to do his thing and let Mitchum do his. Mitchum had gathered enough experience to thwart any upstaging. As a result their performances complemented one another, and along with Jane Greer's brilliant portrayal of an amoral, treacherous femme fatale, transformed a complicated melodrama into what many aficionados consider "the ultimate *film noir*."

In June of 1947 RKO and Vanguard notified Mitchum of

their intention to exercise their option for his services for forty out of the next fifty-two weeks at fifteen hundred dollars a week. Already the perks attendant to his growing stature were snowballing as word of the caliber of his performance in *Out of the Past* spread. When Selznick arranged to lend him to the Charles K. Feldman Group and Lewis Milestone, Inc., for *The Red Pony* which was to be released by Republic, the deal was sweetened by a twenty-thousand-dollar bonus. Steinbeck himself wrote the screenplay, and the cast included apple-cheeked, ten-year-old Beau Bridges, Louis Calhern and Myrna Loy, who autographed a photo to Mitchum: "To Bob, with prayers, admonition and admiration, Myrna Loy." Although the finished work lacked the impact the producers had envisioned, Mitchum, as a kind of father figure, and Calhern, as the boy's elderly grandfather, registered strongly.

With Mitchum's fan letters hovering around fifteen hundred a week and other evidence that a major star was emerging, Howard Hughes, now head of RKO, and Selznick decided that competent as Paul Wilkins might be, his agency did not possess the clout to give Mitchum maximum service. Subtle machinations led to his discharging Wilkins and signing with Phil Berg–Bert Allenberg, Inc., on August 13. Two days later negotiations were concluded, abrogating the agreement signed in June of that year and substituting a new seven-year deal in which Mitchum's salary would immediately jump from fifteen hundred to three thousand a week.

Why, an outsider might ask, would his employers acquiesce to and even promote such an increase? The new contract, in a deal closed by Bert Allenberg, took effect on the day the actor began filming RKO's *Tall, Dark Stranger*, formerly titled *Rachel*. And not so coincidentally RKO was able to obtain the services of Allenberg's hot client, Loretta Young, for what was to become *Rachel and the Stranger*.

Those who were familiar with Mitchum's use of obscenity and profanity predicted trouble on the set between him and Young; as it turned out they were gazing into clouded crystal balls.

Naturally, Mitchum has a story about this. He later told columnist Roderick Mann that he paid Loretta five cents for every *damn*, ten cents for *hell*, and a quarter for *God-damn*. He claimed that when he asked, "Listen, what if I say————?" she replied, "That's free."

"Oh sure, he's said she collected half his salary in her Curse Box—which she used to fine people for swearing—but that didn't even exist in those days," says an ex-Allenberg agent who prefers to remain anonymous. "But minor details like that don't bother Bob. If he tells something and it works, the next time the story is going to be better. You know he's a little like Judy Garland that way. The story about her cruel mother got attention, and each time she told it, it increased until you would have thought the poor woman was the bitch of Buchenwald. And their relationship wasn't like that at all. Bob's stories are like that. Actually he pulled a couple of pranks that probably secretly amused Loretta, but she wouldn't show it on the set because that would have encouraged him to destroy the strict discipline she always employed while working. Between thee and me, she's a lady who knows what she's doing, and despite what he'd like you to think, he's a guy who knows what he's doing. So they got along very well. I'm not surprised. Aside from certain language hangups, she's basically an earthy lady." Mitchum's assessment: "I got a change in *Rachel and the Stranger*. Some good grade sardonic comedy plus some 'corn.'" Then he made what for him was an extraordinary admission. He said, "I enjoyed doing it."

After Mitchum joined Berg-Allenberg's roster in 1947 his professional horizons expanded to radio appearances, personal appearances and recording offers. He often had to speak with the men in charge of the various departments, especially radio. "He came in in his laconic, lackadaisical way and he listened and was listened to, and was pleasant but lacking in enthusiasm," one ex-agent recalls. "He left, and Ham Nelson, Bette Davis's ex-husband who was in the department, said, 'He's never going to do anything for us.' And I told him, 'Don't kid yourself. Wait until he sees the color of the money.' Because the guy he'd been with didn't have our client clout or our contacts to make an effort in his behalf. Bob, at that time, had no idea what kind of money was involved for somebody of his stature. So the first time something came up where he could pick up fifteen hundred or two thousand dollars he was surprised and more than willing. That original negative response had all been *facade*. Self-protection. The money really looked good to him. Because his manager had them living rather frugally. I remember running up there to the house on Oak Glen Drive with scripts, and it was a very, very unpretentious house."

In any case, the extra money to be earned in allied fields provided a few luxuries. After guest shots on *Studio One* and *The Theatre Guild of the Air* he frequently appeared on all types of radio programs from *We, the People Speak* to *Family Theater*, a religious series. He happily relinquished two weeks of his vacation to pick up ten thousand dollars headlining the stage show at the Golden Gate Theater in San Francisco. And as 1947 turned into 1948 he signed a deal with Decca Records to cut an album of six folk songs.

Just how valuable he had become is illustrated by RKO's wish to cast him in a western called *Blood on the Moon*, which was to be directed by a brilliant young newcomer, Robert Wise. Contractually it was Selznick's turn to use Mitchum (RKO had last cast him in their production of *Rachel and the Stranger*). In order to obtain him for the new western, Hughes's RKO agreed to pay Selznick's Vanguard $12,500 a week for ten weeks to secure their own $3,000-a-week contract player.

RM's first movie, *Hoppy Serves a Writ* (1943).

A pleased RM after opening night of *The Gentle Approach* at the
Avalon Theater, Catalina Island (1946).

The Mitchums at the Academy Awards (1946).

A Mitchum family portrait (1948).

Bob, Josh, Christopher, and Dorothy.

RM and Robin Ford following their arrest on suspicion of violating a state narcotics act (1948).

Dorothy vows to "stick by Bob" following his arrest.

RM and Lila Leeds receiving jail sentences in a Los Angeles courtroom (1949).

RM begins serving his sentence of sixty days.

The Mitchums ham it up at the Annual Hollywood Photographers
Costume Ball.

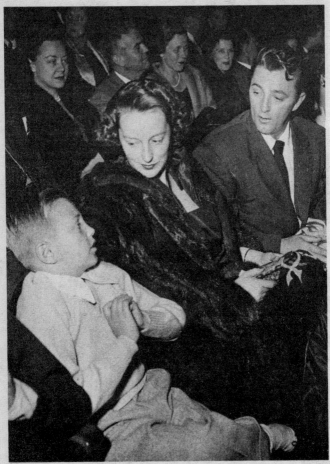

At a screening in Hollywood (1951).

RM with his good buddy "Honest Ave"—Ava Gardner—(right) and Janis Carter (left) in *My Forbidden Past* (1951).

With Jane Russell in *Macao* (1952).

A movie with a devoted following—*Angel Face*, with Jean Simmons (1952).

On loan to 20th Century–Fox for *White Witch Doctor*, with Susan Hayward (1953).

CHAPTER 6

If Mitchum's career burgeoned following his release from the Army, so did his social life. Many of his Army buddies headed for Hollywood immediately after their discharges, and the Mitchum residence became a gathering place for them. Some mornings Dorothy would find the living room carpeted with sleeping ex-GIs. Far from objecting, Dorothy, who was learning to take almost anything in stride, welcomed the visitors for it ensured that her husband would remain at home with her and the boys more often. The poker parties, songfests and bull sessions which often ran until sunup, seemed a small price to pay.

Asked by an acquaintance how she was able to put up with all the noise and confusion—to say nothing of the times when she found the refrigerator raided—Dorothy shrugged. "I married a character," she responded, as if that explained everything. In a way it did. The woman later said, "I could see she loved him and was proud of him. It's possible she also enjoyed the stream of new people who passed through their lives. She wasn't the type who would have made friends easily. She was still very self-effacing then. Very shy. This was obviously more exciting than Delaware. Life with him was unpredictable, but never dull. And I think she also found it exciting and fun to be married to an up-and-coming movie star—although I must say, he certainly didn't behave like one."

Nor did he think of himself as one. Later, when magazine writer Helen Lawrenson commented during their final meeting that she couldn't talk to movie stars, Mitchum responded, "Neither can I."

Gradually most of the GIs drifted back to where they had come from or melted into the workaday world. Still, the house continued to be crowded by people Mitchum had met in a bar or at Schwab's, plus gaffers, soundmen, grips and other crew members from his pictures.

More conventionally the Mitchums' mutual friends included some of the prewar crowd, plus rising star Jane Greer and her multimillionaire husband, Edward Lasker; Jane's stand-in, Marge Gutterman and her husband Morty, who was a talent agent with the Charles Feldman Group; Boyd Cabeen and later Cabeen's wife Dusty; and Jane Russell and Bob Waterfield, to name but a few.

At dinner one evening at the Laskers' Mitchum met William Faulkner. "Bob was at his best that night, and Faulkner was absolutely enamored with him because of Bob's way of talking," Jane Greer recalls. "I remember Howard Hughes was much talked about and Faulkner saying to Bob, 'Now this man Hughes who's taken over the studio—how does that affect you? What kind of a man is he?' And Bob, who often talks in elliptical circles, said, 'Well, he's a tall dog and I'm on a long leash, but when he throws me over that fence, the leash ain't long enough and I hang there.'" Greer recalls half of the people at the dinner party were asking what he had said, but that Faulkner understood exactly what he meant—roughly, Hughes is powerful and lenient, but when he punishes you, you're in real trouble. The two talked all evening. Soon after, Mitchum went to a bookstore where he bought all of Faulkner's works which he subsequently read with enthusiasm. They joined his well-thumbed collections of Conrad, Huxley and Thomas Wolfe on his bookshelves.

Around the same time, he encountered waspish gossip columnist Hedda Hopper at one of the famed party-giver Atwater Kent's galas. Although bobby-sox idol Van Johnson and his bride, Evie, the ex-Mrs. Keenan Wynn, were present, Mitchum was astounded that like Faulkner Hedda concentrated her attention on him all evening. Commenting on this later, he said, "Listen, it's all gravy. It's very fine gravy. But don't think I don't realize I'm just here between trains."

Boyd "Tyrone" Cabeen, who could match Mitchum drink for drink and whose imagination was as bizarre as the actor's, was not regarded as a positive influence either by Dorothy or Metro executives. Although RKO was prepared to put up with the pair's hijinx, MGM management was not. After the makeup raid, according to Cabeen, the studio attempted to ban him. He responded by indignantly taking their action before the labor board and winning a ruling: If the studio banned him, they also had to ban Mitchum for the offense. Stymied, the studio refused to allow Cabeen to stand in for the star anymore, although they were forced to accept him if he was sent for extra work by Central Casting. But on days when Mitchum was working on the lot and Cabeen received a call, he would simply throw a coat over his pajamas, drive to Metro, sign a voucher to collect his pay and go home for the day.

After the war Mitchum had also acquired a business manager, whom he came to regard as one of his closest friends. He was a florid, middle-aged man with dyed hair and a pencil mustache. He preached economy to his clients and lived extravagantly himself. Warning his actor-clients how short their years of earning huge salaries could be, he would dolefully cite former favorites who now eked out their livings as extras, salespeople, waiters, waitresses and similar low-paying jobs. Having thoroughly brainwashed the Mitchums, he persuaded Dorothy to accept ten and Bob twenty dollars a week for spending money beyond basic living expenses. The remainder of the four-figure salary Bob was earning was to be invested to provide a cushion against that day when Bob's popularity waned.

What made this economy program palatable to Mitchum was that when the two of them visited nightclubs, as they frequently did, his manager insisted upon picking up the check. Not only that, he often invited headliners to join them before or after the show. Both actor and manager were fans of hipster philosopher-comedian Lord Buckley, who performed his imaginative and inventive monologues on Sunset Strip, and he and Mitchum subsequently became fast friends. Among the other clubs Mitchum frequented, often in the company of his brother, John, was Billy Gray's Bandbox on Fairfax Avenue. Gray and Bob became such good buddies that Gray's club became another joint where the financially pressed rising star was seldom presented with a check.

Another favored spot was Slapsie Maxie's. Mitchum was first taken there by a production manager at RKO who wanted to introduce him to his young cousin, Pat Rooney, of the famed Rooney tap-dancing clan.

"He chose to be my friend," Rooney says. "You didn't choose him. He would back off and say, 'I don't like you. Fuck off!' to anyone who pushed. He was always a man's man. Very foul-mouthed. Later when I got married, my wife wouldn't go around him. He'd use any word. She objected. Or he might just decide to unzip his pants and take a piss in front of everybody. He didn't think anything of it. He regarded it as a natural thing. Some people were shocked. Yet I always felt there was a peculiarly nice kind of a—well, he was a nice guy."

At the time of their first meeting Rooney was teamed with a young fellow named Mark Rickey. They were trying to embellish their dancing act by adding impersonations of stars as well as songs and jokes. Martin and Lewis were hitting it big, and Rickey and Rooney hoped to duplicate their success. When Mitchum heard his friends were booked into the Chi Chi Club in Palm Springs, he suggested they get him a place and he'd come and see their new act. They were allotted a three-bedroom suite, so they invited him to stay with them and he accepted.

There was never any question about Dorothy and the boys accompanying him. Periodically Mitchum felt the need to get away. Sometimes he would take Dorothy; sometimes he would go off alone to read and meet new friends; and at other times he would gravitate to an action spot. Whichever it was, Dorothy wisely allowed him to wander and was waiting when he got back. Mitchum attributed his wanderlust to a nostalgia for his exploits as a teenage hobo.

In any case, he arrived in Palm Springs and caught Rickey and Rooney's show. Naturally, Pat Rooney was eager to hear his opinion. After the performance Mitchum informed his friends, "You're just great. Your act stinks." He wanted to know who wrote it. Rooney admitted he had cribbed the material from old vaudeville and burlesque routines and from joke books. Mitchum nodded and repeated that while they had talent, they needed new and imaginative material.

The next night Mitchum again attended the performance. At its close Rooney announced, "I've got a friend in the audience. Some of you will recognize him from the better westerns—his name is Robert Mitchum." Mitchum didn't acknowledge the introduction, so Errol Flynn, who had been hoisting more than a few, went over and pulled Mitchum to his feet. Surprisingly, Mitchum didn't hit him. At Rooney's urging, Mitchum even agreed to perform a song if Flynn would accompany him to the stage. He went over well, and afterward several of them went on to Don the Beachcomber's to have midnight lunch and talk about the act.

They were hardly seated when Flynn got into a confrontation with the management and threw out three waiters. Rooney was surprised that Mitchum calmly continued eating and didn't join the fray. He said so, and Mitchum explained, "It ain't my beef. I don't go looking for trouble. If Flynn wants to get drunk and out of line, let him get out of it."

With no further ado he pulled out a sheaf of hotel stationery on which he had written new material for Rickey and Rooney in longhand. The pair went through it with him and thought it was wonderful—so wonderful that Rooney promised they would put it into the show the next night so that Mitchum could see how it worked before returning to Hollywood.

"We tried it out the following evening. It was hysterical," Rooney says. "I tried to get him to come on stage and do another song, but he wouldn't budge. So I said, 'Anyway, I want you to know that Mr. Mitchum did write some of the material you've heard this evening. So your laughs are appreciated by all three of us.'"

Rooney feels that weekend cemented their friendship. When Mitchum heard the act was booked into clubs in Vancouver,

Seattle, Portland, Salem and Eugene, he said he would probably see them since he was going on location in that area about that time. By the time the Rooneys, as they were calling themselves in an attempt to capitalize on the family name, got to Portland, Mitchum was nearby shooting *Rachel and the Stranger*, and he came over to catch the show. He was aghast to find the Rooneys using the material he had given them in Palm Springs, and when the Rooneys arrived in Salem they found he had written a new act for them, with one set of jokes for the weekday crowd, another for the weekenders. For their impersonations they had been using actual dialogue from pictures featuring James Cagney, Edward G. Robinson, Jimmy Stewart and other stars. Mitchum now concocted comedy bits suited to each star's style, and wrote the words and music for an introductory song, "The Rooneys," though this had to be scuttled because Mark Rickey, who had a perfect ear when it came to capturing a star's tone of voice and inflections, proved to be tone deaf.

Rooney, who went on to become a Hollywood producer, tends to shy away from any discussion of the girls who were around during those nightclub days. This is probably out of deference to Dorothy's feelings. One aspect of a male sex symbol's life that surprised him, however, was the number of times Mitchum would be approached by some burly male who would truculently announce, "My wife thinks you're some stud!" or some such. Mitchum would try to handle it by quietly replying, "Naah, I'm just an actor trying to make a living." This would infuriate the stranger, and the exchange would sometimes escalate to violence despite Mitchum's efforts to be diplomatic. When diplomacy failed, Mitchum would deck the aggressor and then get out of the place before further trouble developed.

Friends say that Dorothy probably realized there were occasionally other women but had opted for looking the other way. Knowing intimately her husband's strengths and weaknesses, she most likely had decided that the former outweighed the latter. Friends also say that she must tend to agree with his self-evaluation as "a poor but exciting husband and good father."

If she found herself with few of the trappings of a movie star's wife, her husband's wardrobe was even more lackluster consisting as it did of the now threadbare suit, sport coats and slacks that he had worn in *The Locket*. But it was no great hardship, since Dorothy believed that their economies would ensure an affluent future.

Early in 1948 then, both, but especially Dorothy, were in for a severe jolt. His manager, whom Mitchum at this point still described as one of his "closest friends," was discovered to have embezzled almost all of the funds he was supposedly investing for them. Dorothy accidentally learned that one account which should have contained several thousand dollars had a balance of fifty-eight, and undertook an investigation which revealed that all of their savings simply had vanished.

Faced with the Mitchums' discovery, his manager refused to make an accounting. More surprisingly still, Mitchum refused to prosecute. He later indicated that he was "more hurt than angry" and that "I was eventually subpoenaed by the state as a witness for the prosecution of another matter."*

And then, according to trial records, Mitchum's secretary, Richard Ellis, received a call from the manager warning that Dorothy had better "stop making trouble" for him or he would do something violent. "He said he would do away with her," Ellis claimed.

Some time afterward Mrs. Morris and Julie implored Dorothy to persuade Bob to be treated by a psychiatrist. "Dr. Frederick Hacker, whom I visited, adjudged me rational, but suffering a state of over-amiability in which failure to please created a condition of self-reproach. He told me that I was addicted to nothing but good will of people and suggested that I risk their displeasure by learning to say 'no' and following my own judgment," Mitchum later reported.

Naturally, as time passed Mitchum applied the Sherwood Anderson touch to his psychiatric treatment, claiming that Dr. Hacker told him to tell his relatives and associates to "Go shit in a hat." He also confided that Dr. Hacker found him so perceptive about the workings of the criminal mind that he

---

*Charges were brought by a Burbank housewife who claimed she had been bilked out of $10,000 which Mitchum's manager told her he was negotiating as a loan to Ann Nichols, author of *Abie's Irish Rose*.

periodically invited him over on a social basis to discuss perplexing cases.

The circumstances that led to their losing the savings combined with Mitchum's refusal to prosecute caused a marked change in Dorothy's attitude. She began to doubt the wisdom of Mitchum's continuing as a film actor and instituted a campaign for them to move east. She confided to intimates that she felt he had "gone Hollywood," and she objected to the crowd of new friends who lived in the fast lane. Mitchum, believing she was upset and homesick, tried to pacify her by agreeing that they would spend his next layoff period in Delaware.

The latter part of April saw the family set off for what Dorothy hoped was a permanent departure from Hollywood, and what Mitchum viewed as a temporary respite for his wife—visiting her family and old friends.

By mid-June an impasse had developed. The studio was urging Mitchum's return and Dorothy was adamant about remaining on the East Coast. When he could not persuade her to leave, he went to New York hoping she would join him.

In the meantime, David Selznick, who was staying at the Hampshire House, learned Mitchum was in town and had the Selznick office summon him to the hotel to pick up a script. When Mitchum called Selznick's suite from the lobby, he was told the producer was running late with his appointments and wished him to have a drink on him in the bar. The secretary said she would call him shortly. Mitchum gulped down a couple of drinks before word arrived that Selznick soon would be free. He went to the suite where he was given another stiff drink. By now he was full of booze, but Selznick was in a talkative mood and sold him on the potential of the script which he wanted Mitchum to read at once. Mitchum agreed and got out as quickly as he could.

As he waited for the elevator, bladder bursting, he spied a sand-filled spittoon. Slipping his hands through the slits in the trench coat pockets, he unzipped his trousers, opened his coat, edged close to the spittoon, and let go—just as Selznick burst from his suite waving the forgotten script. He took one look, shoved the script under Mitchum's arm, and wordlessly fled.

In later years Mitchum improved the story, telling how he "hunkered" himself to the side of the chair he was occupying in Selznick's suite and "pissed on his white rug." Then leaving the suite, "I hadn't really finished pissing, you know, so I was waitin' for the elevator, and they had a sandbox there, so I was pissin' in the sandbox, and the door opened and Selznick's secretary stuck her head out and said, 'Your hat—you forgot your hat.'

"That was it. Hah! You can imagine David's version of the story—'This degenerate son-of-a-bitch comes in and pisses all over my wife's wig.' Oh man, I tell you." Oh man, he'll tell you anything.

Selznick specialized in prestige stars. After the incident at the Hampshire House he made an all-out effort to burnish Mitchum's public image and curb his private behavior. Both efforts were doomed. "I remember . . . they sat me behind a big desk and brought people in, like a diplomatic reception, to interview me," Mitchum later told a reporter from the *New York Times*. "The movie magazine representative, the international representative, the whole bunch of them filed in, and the publicity guy told them to sharpen their pencils and get ready to make me respectable. The trouble is I had nothing to declare, and it's just as well because sixty days later I was in the can."

CHAPTER 7

Those sixty days found him caught in a maelstrom of contradiction. Reluctantly, he realized he was going to have to leave New York and return to Hollywood without his wife and children.

Back on the West Coast he enthusiastically readied himself for costume fittings, tests and other preparations for *A Doll's House*. This would be his first opportunity to work in a Vanguard film produced under Selznick's meticulous personal supervision, despite his contention that acting was nothing more than a well-paying way to earn a living; the challenge to measure up to rigorous standards stimulated the flow of adrenaline. Later he would deliver performances far superior to the material, but at this time the amount of creative energy he expended on a role often served as a critical comment on the script.

Suddenly and without warning the prestigious production was blown from under him. A series of snags had developed and Selznick opted to abandon the project. Mitchum concluded that his future at Vanguard lay in being a Selznick chattel, to be rented to the highest bidder. Even talk of his being lent to Sir Alexander Korda to star in a motion picture based on *Out-*

cast of the Islands by his favorite novelist, Joseph Conrad, failed to cheer him.

He had cooperated with RKO in capitalizing on his he-man image by playing cowboys, cops and gangsters. This had earned him an enormous following, which in turn had allowed him to command a salary of $3,250 a week. He could tolerate such prostitution of his talent because, as his sister observed, "Acting was not central to his being." It left him little time, however, to concentrate on his poetry, writing his songs and working on his play—work that he did consider central to his being.

Disappointed about the setback in his career and depressed by the empty house at 3372 Oak Glen Drive, Mitchum began blotting out his loneliness with booze or grass, and hanging out where the laughs were. "We met a lot of extraordinary people over the years, and Bob was always laconically amused by them," says his brother, John. "For instance, we got to know Milo Anderson, a Warner Brothers costume designer. We got to be good friends with him in the early days." With time on his hands, Bob got together with Milo, John and another old friend, Elmer Jones, and the four of them took off on a nostalgic trip to Long Beach. Their goal was to look up their old pal, Dick Hunton (who in the 1980s was to become a counselor at the Indiana State Prison). "So we stopped at every third bar on the way, and by the time we get to Redondo Beach it's one o'clock in the morning. Milo was behind the wheel going no more than five miles an hour, but weaving back and forth until he touched one curb and then the other one," John remembers. "Back and forth, back and forth until finally the red light of a patrol car comes on behind us. Milo just keeps driving. I say, 'Milo, don't you think you better stop?' He did. He just sat there, and I'll never forget it because he was such a tiny, little guy. Very elegant. The cop gets out, a huge policeman—he was *big* and *rough*—and he comes over to the window and asks, 'Have you been drinkin'?' Milo looks up at him and says, 'Feeling no pain.' That was it! They took us over to the station. Brother Robert is about three-sheets, too, and he decides to take over. Now Milo is drunk, but not so drunk he doesn't realize this is a bad idea. So he tries to kick Robert without appearing to kick him—and he kicks the cop.

"Of course, in Milo goes. We stay until a friend of his sends a lawyer to get him out. The lawyer looks through the cell and sees this once-dapper peacock who now resembles a very wet sparrow peering forlornly out to sea through iron bars.

"'Want to get out?' he asks.

"'What's your impression?' is Milo's response. Well, that tickled Brother Robert to death. We had lots of fun looking up old friends for a couple of days after that."

Mitchum not only looked up old friends, he also made a lot of new ones. His use of grass earned him membership in a group that considered themselves hip and scorned nonusers as square johns and janes. Word had spread quickly that Dorothy was at least temporarily out of the picture, and Hollywood party girls descended from all directions. Vivacious Betty Rice was so eager to be friendly with a movie star that she was forever pressing free "reefers"—as they were called—on him. Others offered different sorts of favors. But the girl Mitchum responded to was a tall, red-haired, green-eyed charmer named—curiously enough—Helen Keller.

Helen shared an apartment with the ex-fiancée of George Raft, who was also a bewitching red-haired, green-eyed and baby-faced beauty. The third roommate was a vivacious blond singer and champion jitterbug dancer.

These were liberated girls who shared an elitist, contemptuous attitude toward any "square" who didn't use grass. Yet even they were taken aback by Mitchum's increasing boldness. Never before had they seen a prominent star make himself such a high-visibility risk, strutting around as he did in a straw Stetson and cowboy boots, with a reefer tucked behind each ear or carrying a package of cigarettes in which the regular ones were alternated with hand-rolled joints. Even the fearless Miss Keller warned him that he was in danger of being set up for arrest by some informer who would buy his own immunity by turning in friends to the police. Mitchum brushed aside the advice, assuring her the fuzz was too dense to recognize weed even if someone turned him in. Or, if they came around, he'd find a way of ditching it. When she insisted he be more careful, Mitchum informed her she was getting to be about as amusing as a stick in the eye. "It was as if he felt invincible," remarked

Keller's roommate. "He began hanging out with people who had reputations for being snitches."

Much as he enjoyed the company of a hip crowd, he still missed his family deeply. To entice Dorothy to return to California with his sons he decided to sell the Oak Glen house. To get a better price he set about repairing, remodeling and giving it a fresh coat of paint. His goal was to earn enough profit so that he could purchase a more pretentious home for the family in one of the canyons.

Sensible as the move was, Mitchum foolishly complicated it by involving Robin "Danny" Ford. Ford, a small, blond bartender, was attempting to become an insurance broker and real estate salesman. Mitchum good-heartedly decided to give him a boost by letting him handle the sale of his present house and find a new one. Those who knew Ford well warned that all his undertakings ended badly.

Mitchum chose not to listen. Ford began spending more and more time with him, and early in August the two of them decided to go to the beach together. There they encountered a lissome blonde who bore a marked resemblance to sex goddess Lana Turner. Her name was Lila Leeds. After a pleasant afternoon Mitchum and Ford took her to dinner. Later she confided to Ford that she liked the star, who invited her out for an evening on the town.

Then on August 31, after Mitchum and Ford had spent part of the day looking at available canyon houses, they went to Oak Glen Drive and proceeded to consume a fifth of Scotch. At some point Ford decided to check his exchange and was told there was a message to call Lila. He did so and she invited him and Mitchum to come up and see the house she and her roommate had rented. At first Mitchum refused, saying he had a script he had to read. But after several more calls Mitchum and Ford arrived at Lila's new Laurel Canyon abode, shortly after midnight. Fifteen minutes later Mitchum found himself handcuffed in a police car headed for the Los Angeles county jail. There, he and Ford were booked, mugged, fingerprinted and held for smoking marijuana. Talking freely, Mitchum told reporters, "Well, this is the bitter end of everything—my career, my home and my marriage."

He continued talking freely until an attorney arrived and silenced him. The following morning, September 1, 1948, he was released on one thousand dollars' bail and whisked to his agents' offices where the high-powered Berg-Allenberg organization marshaled its forces in an attempt to salvage his future.

There were issues to be dealt with: the positions to be taken by his employers, the industry, the press, the theater-going public, and—most importantly—his wife.

"When I approached the Berg-Allenberg building at 121 South Beverly Drive, I saw reporters and photographers hanging around the front and in the alley between our building and the stores facing Wilshire Boulevard," one of the firm's agents at the time says. "Inside the office was abuzz. The secretaries were jumping up and down, running to peek out of the windows because evidently they thought there were plainclothesmen out there. I looked, and I will say there were guys who weren't everyday pedestrians, nor were they Beverly Hills people. For some reason they had the office staked out under surveillance. Don't ask me why. Maybe they thought he was going to disappear into the wild blue yonder. He used to say he came into town on a boxcar and he would probably go out on one, too. Maybe they took him seriously.

"Anyway, what was going on in the office was that the big guns were commiserating and negotiating with Hughes and Selznick. In other words, finding out what they wanted us to do, and what we could expect their lawyers to do. Just how far were they willing to back him?

"Our office had everything going as far as power was concerned. You don't have to believe this, but it wasn't too late to do something. There were plenty of cover-ups at Metro alone. And the rumor was that at first Selznick was being cooperative and Hughes was being difficult. But in the end it didn't make any difference because Mitch just said, in effect, 'The hell with it. They caught me. They got me. I did it and I'm not going to let you get me out of it.'"

At that point his representatives concluded he needed to have some time to think and rest. In order to get him out of the office without encountering the press, it was arranged for an automobile to be driven down the alley in back of the building and up the alley between the agency building and the Wilshire stores. Mitchum and someone else from the office crawled out on one of those fire escapes which automatically descend under the weight of a grown man. He scurried down the steps and into the waiting car, leaving the press and other interested parties behind.

His destination was his mother's home at 954 North Palm in West Hollywood. H stayed there for one night before slipping back to his Oak Glen house where he went into seclusion.

Rumors spread that Selznick and Hughes were working behind the scenes—which they were—to save Mitchum's reputation and their investments. Then Selznick issued a joint memo pertaining to the matter. It was supportive, but firm about the limits of their participation. It said: "We have not engaged any attorney for Mr. Mitchum, nor do we have the slightest intention of engaging any or contributing to any alleged fund for his defense. We have never heard of such a fund.

"Neither Mr. Mitchum nor his business representatives have ever solicited us in this connection; and, on the contrary, Mr. Mitchum selected and engaged his own attorneys.

"We would, of course, not consider engaging in any so-called wire pulling nor would we be so foolish as to attempt to use any influence."

Yet the next day, Hearst's syndicated motion picture editor, Louella O. Parsons, set the tone by referring to the "shocking charge." She then quickly proceeded to the claim that Mitchum was "in a state of mental collapse" and announced that both RKO and Selznick were ready to stand by him if "he wants to be helped."

She quoted Selznick as saying he believed Mitchum should enter a sanitarium at once "to undergo treatment for his shattered nerves." Later in the story she reflected the general naiveté about marijuana at that time by writing: "None of the executives at RKO or Selznick studios is willing to believe that Mitchum is a real addict. They say he never gave any signs of being doped, and that he turned in some very fine performances."

Far from committing himself to any sanitarium, Mitchum was conferring with his lawyers, Jerry Giesler and Norman R.

Tyre, who automatically issued a statement: "There are a number of unexplained facts and peculiar circumstances surrounding the raid made yesterday in which Mitchum was involved." Giesler also expressed surprise that the police intended to turn over the case to the district attorney, and amazement when the district attorney announced that the probe probably would be expanded to investigate alleged "widespread use of narcotics in the film colony," alluding to "other top stars' reported use of marijuana cigarettes and other habit-forming narcotics." His invitation for Mitchum to testify before the grand jury was immediately rejected by Giesler.

Meanwhile, Dorothy Mitchum, Jim, Chris and Dorothy's cousin stopped at the El Rancho Vegas in Las Vegas, where Dorothy refused to grant any interviews, explaining that she wanted to confer with an RKO executive at the hotel before she did any talking. Newspaper reporters described her as "nervous and distraught," but after conferring with the RKO representative and taking seven-year-old Jim and five-year-old Chris to see the floor show, the party drove off into the night toward Los Angeles.

In anticipation of her arrival photographers and reporters gathered outside the Mitchum house at seven a.m. the following day. Finally at one p.m. Dorothy's gray Chrysler pulled up. Looking disheveled and exhausted, she shoved her sons up the steps and inserted her key into the lock. Over her shoulder she called to reporters, "Please excuse me. I'm awfully tired."

Before an RKO press representative slammed the door, reporters heard Mitchum joyfully greeting his sons and saw him embracing his wife.

The RKO press agent appeared and informed the press that Mrs. Mitchum was composing a statement, and it would be distributed to them. After an interval he emerged to read a statement, purportedly written by Dorothy:

"Everyone ought to be able to see Bob is a sick man.

"Otherwise he wouldn't be mixed up in a situation like this. Our differences were the same kind all married couples get into. We have made them up. I love my husband and am back home to stay with him.

"I am indignant that not only Bob, but our whole family should have to suffer simply because he is a motion picture star. Otherwise I do not think all this fuss would be made just because a man may have gotten mixed up with bad company.

"I am sorry I cannot answer questions today. I have driven all day and night to get to my sick husband as fast as I could and I have had no sleep at all.

"I have only one favor to ask. That is that nobody bothers our children. They are very young; they love their father and do not understand what it is all about."

Not long after the statement was read, Reva Frederick arrived. She was a dark-haired, pretty woman who wore a tailored suit and exuded a salty, no-nonsense manner which had stood her in good stead with her former employer, Earl Scheib, the auto-painting magnate. When Mitchum's male secretary departed, Reva heard about the job from the star's half-sister and had stepped in to take over.

On this particular afternoon she had stopped at a florist shop to buy some chrysanthemums to brighten up the house, and had made a second stop to choose a chic new gown for Dorothy. Having delivered her purchases, she gathered up Jim and Chris and spirited them away to their grandmother's house to shield them from the journalistic circus that was developing outside their home.

What exchange took place between the Mitchums after they were left alone only they know, and they have never revealed what demands, promises, conditions or ultimatums were made. Nevertheless, certain developments clearly indicate that Dorothy was aware of her strength and her ability to exercise power within reasonable limits.

When the press lingered, the RKO man appeared and announced Mrs. Mitchum had nothing to add to her previous statement, but it went without saying she was happy to be home, and would stand by her husband. He was also delighted to tell them that the Mitchums had reluctantly agreed to pose for reconciliation pictures for two photographers at a time.

Dorothy was wearing the ballerina dress that Reva Frederick

had delivered, and Mitchum, foregoing his western gear for a Madison Avenue image, wore gray flannels, a white shirt, and tie. For the photos they sat or stood close together talking and smiling, but the glare of the flash bulbs revealed that her eyes were red from weeping, and his face haggard. The atmosphere was so relaxed, however, that they gradually were lured into brief banter with some of the photographers.

Asked whether this was a reconciliation, Mitchum cocked one eyebrow and replied, "Reconciliation is a hard word. Reunion is better." He said he was very happy about his wife's attitude. Pressed as to whether their marriage ever had been in jeopardy, he quipped, "Every time I went to the studio in the morning."

That brought a smile to Dorothy's face as she added, "And every time he didn't shave."

When someone inquired about their immediate plans, he replied, "Lunch." Then on a more serious note, he volunteered, "I'm awfully happy that my wife feels the way she does. It's a great comfort to me."

Hollywood film studios, plagued by the incursion of television, a thirty-percent drop in box office revenues, escalating production costs and a shrinking market abroad, especially in England, were eager to avoid further inroads on their profits. So when it happened that in the Midwest heartland, moralistic attacks against the film industry following Mitchum's arrest were widespread, real concern mounted palpably.

Indiana led the offensive. The *Indianapolis Star* published an article that opened: "Now that the ugliest and most devastating of all scandals—dope—once more has smeared the motion picture industry, it will be curious in the next few weeks to see just what the overlords of Hollywood will do, if anything, to counteract a tidal wave of public criticism already sweeping in on the business." That blast was matched by the closing volley: "Right now Hollywood has the biggest problem of all on its hands. The public never did—never will—laugh off a dope scandal involving a screen favorite performer. It was a resounding narcotics sensation that first threatened the film industry with obliteration back in 1920 when the handsome

Wallace Reid, a public idol created by *The Birth of a Nation*, ran afoul of federal authorities."

Even before the *Star* article appeared, *Variety* reported "vociferous" opposition to RKO's release of *Rachel and the Stranger* from the *Bulletin,* a weekly publication of the Associated Theater Owners of Indiana. Quoting from the newsletter, *Variety* reported that the owners said: "This is not meant to heap coals on the head of Robert Mitchum. The great transgressors are those who rush in to grab off a few dollars as the result of the publicity attached to the affair. We advise every independent exhibitor who is conscious of his own local public relations to pass up the pictures, at least until the current publicity is forgotten."

In Missouri the *St. Louis Globe-Democrat* began an editorial: "'Misunderstood' Hollywood has let the lid off the garbage can again" and went on to plump its ill-informed attack with: "Now we have a young swoon actor, the idol of teenagers, caught in a marijuana party—a reefer smoking fest known to the trade as 'kicking the gong around.'"

In her syndicated column, Hedda Hopper took a milder stand: "If it is proved before a jury of his peers that Robert Mitchum violated the law, he must be made to pay the penalty just like any other citizen, rich or poor, famous or a nobody. That is the American way.

"However—and it is a BUT in capital letters—it's as deplorable as it's inevitable that because he happens to be a movie star his actions have drawn a torrent of destructive attention upon the entire industry with a free-for-all splurge in 57 varieties of scandal, malicious tongue-wagging and dirt."

For once, arch-conservative Hopper and liberal Dore Schary, Chairman of the Motion Picture Industry Council, agreed. Schary minimized the significance of Mitchum's arrest and emphasized the "good reputation of 32,000 other Hollywoodites." Hedda wrote that if Mitchum had been Joe Doakes from Center City, his story would have filled a small space on page eleven.

Across the country, Schary and Hedda, as well as other industry figures, were attacked for "pocketbook morality" put forth, it was alleged, because RKO and Republic had a well-publicized five million dollars, a sizable sum at the time, invested in motion pictures starring Mitchum.

In the face of all the controversy RKO management apparently felt it had nothing to lose by releasing *Rachel and the Stranger*. And it didn't. Box-office reports of the grosses amply demonstrated how out of touch with their readers newspaper editorial and feature writers were. Everywhere crowds lined up for *Rachel and the Stranger*. In Los Angeles sustained, lusty applause greeted Mitchum's first appearance in the movie. In Minneapolis audiences applauded the film at the end of each showing. In New York, Denver, Providence, Chicago, Omaha, Cincinnati, Kansas City—from border to border and coast to coast—*Rachel and the Stranger* was a robust hit. It was even held over in conservative Boston.

Mitchum could now rest assured that his employers were unlikely to invoke the "morals clause" to cancel his contract. The industry had adopted what he considered a galling explanation that he was a "sick man"—but he was willing to tolerate it. The press remained divided in its attitude toward him—but then it had been for most of his career. The public was rushing to his films in larger numbers than ever before. Best of all, his wife was standing solidly behind him.

Only one problem remained: how to handle his upcoming trial. One miscalculation and all the problems he had seemingly solved could be undone.

CHAPTER 8

Attorney Giesler was surprised at the DA's decision that Mitchum's was one of those rare drug cases which called for a grand jury. Most such arrests were handled at preliminary hearings before municipal judges who determined whether the evidence warranted the suspects being bound over for trial in Superior Court.

Mitchum was invited to appear as a witness before the grand jury, but since Giesler would have been unable to protect or advise him in any way, the attorney urged that he decline the invitation. The lawyers representing those arrested with Mitchum followed suit.

For his part, the DA limited his witnesses to two: police chemist Jay Allen and Detective Sergeant A. M. Barr. Allen's testimony would establish that the seized substance was marijuana. "It is not a very good grade of marijuana," he said rather superciliously. "I would call it a medium mixture." A. M. Barr identified the marijuana cigarettes—some labeled "Bob Mitchum"—as the ones taken the night of the raid, and recounted details of the stakeout. In a scant two-hour session, Mitchum, Leeds, Ford and Evans were indicted on two counts:

possession of marijuana, and conspiracy to violate the State Narcotics Act.

After one postponement, the defendants appeared on September 21 and were instructed to return on September 29 to enter their pleas. On that date Giesler attempted another delay by objecting that the indictments were not couched in English, as required by law. "It might as well be in Japanese, Chinese or hieroglyphics," he said, contending he was unable to pronounce *Cannabis sativa* which he assumed was Latin. "All I know is amo, amas, amat, which means I love, you love, he loves," he claimed, to the amusement of spectators in the court. Encouraged, he went on. "As for hemp, I thought that was used for making rope."

Judge Ambrose rapped for order and overruled the attorney's demurrers. Asked how he pleaded, Mitchum, smartly dressed in conservative charcoal-gray slacks and a blue blazer, stepped forth. "Not guilty," he said in the same distinctive baritone that had helped boost his popularity on the screen.

Leeds and Ford—Vicki Evans had jumped bail and fled to New York—echoed Mitchum. (Records do not indicate any conviction in the case of Vicki Evans.) The three were continued on thousand-dollar bonds and ordered to stand trial on November 23. Meantime, Giesler suffered three broken ribs when his car rammed into a tree, making him unable to appear, his physician said, until mid-December. Because of vacation plans of the judge and the DA, the trial was postponed until January 10, 1949.

With this long postponement assured, Howard Hughes, Sid Rogell and Jack L. Gross, producer of *Rachel and the Stranger*, began a hurried search for a Mitchum vehicle. They settled on *The Big Steal*, yet another police-gangster drama, which originally had been intended for George Raft, but had been shelved. Now the producers thought that sultry Lizabeth Scott, whom they had been trying to borrow from Hal Wallis, and Mitchum would make a hot box-office team. But Wallis, chary about having Scott appear opposite someone who might be in jail by the time the film was released, claimed she was needed for *Too Late for Tears*. Rogell then approached several other leading women, including Joan Bennett, but their agents were reluctant to risk guilt by association in the public's mind and passed.

In desperation Rogell went to Hughes with a possible solution: Jane Greer. He was well aware that Greer had had a falling out with the eccentric millionaire and he had threatened the young actress that she would never be cast in another RKO film as long as he owned the studio, even though she might continue to draw her salary. Pressed by the time factor, Hughes glumly agreed.

Rogell then called Greer and sent her the script. "Frankly, I didn't like it. I didn't really want to do any picture—even with a good script—because I'd just found out I was pregnant," she recalled in 1982. "But I loved Bob. I knew what he and his family were going through and, anyway, I really wanted to work with him again. So I said, 'Sure, I'll do it. I'd love to do it.' Little did I know! I remember when I went for the first fitting the clothes were just a disaster for me. The one outfit I wore through the whole picture, I had to dye because it had no accessories. No hat. No shoes. Nothing but this tight-fitting skirt and little bolero.

"The day we started the picture I was walking from my dressing room to the stage. Bob was coming the other way. We met just outside the stage. He looked at me and said, 'Those are the same goddamn shoes you wore in *Out of the Past*.' And he was right. He'd recognized them. 'The same damn tight shoes you're going to be crippling around in.' I knew this was bluster to cover up how moved he was that I was willing to work with him. Complaining was the only thing he could think of to do. He's a very, very sensitive man."

Rogell's scheme was to get far enough into the shooting schedule to persuade the judge to grant Mitchum parole, or at least postpone his jail term if it came to that. RKO hoped to sway opinion by pointing out that at least 150 people—actors and members of the behind-the-camera community—should not be thrown out of work. But the delay in finding a female star and other problems kept the cameras from rolling until January 4, 1949. Director Don Siegel says everyone connected with the project realized it was junk and approached it tongue in cheek. Nevertheless, they all plunged ahead as swiftly as possible to get as many of Mitchum's scenes as feasible filmed before his court date on January 10.

On that morning the Los Angeles County Courthouse was mobbed; spectators filled the courtroom and spilled into the halls as Mitchum, Leeds and Ford arrived for the opening of the trial. Frenzied fans made it impossible for Mitchum and Giesler to move until policemen cleared a path to the courtroom.

If the crowds were expecting a long, lurid courtroom circus, they were doomed to disappointment. In spite of RKO's wish that Mitchum receive probation, Giesler and Mitchum agreed that the common man would regard it as special justice for a celebrity. Giesler also urged Mitchum to plead guilty. If he stuck with his "not guilty" plea, witnesses would expose a lot of dirt which would tarnish, if not destroy, his idol status. Again Mitchum agreed. Giesler then made a motion to sever the two counts, and Judge Clement Nye granted it. Then the three lawyers representing the defendants made a joint motion proposing that the people's case consist of a reading of the 32-page grand jury transcript. The prosecutors accepted this proposal, the motion was granted, and the trial began without Mitchum having to enter a guilty plea.

Mitchum fidgeted nervously during the reading of the grand jury testimony of the DA's two witnesses, even though he knew that by dint of Giesler's clever maneuvering nothing more damaging than was already known would emerge. As he expected, after the reading he, Lila Leeds and Robin Ford were pronounced guilty of conspiracy to possess. Judge Nye set February 9 for sentencing, and the DA announced that if Mitchum drew a jail sentence on the conspiracy to possess charge, the DA's office likely would save taxpayers money by dropping the possession count since sentences usually ran concurrently on these convictions.

Giesler's next move was to keep his promise to Hughes and file an application for probation on Mitchum's behalf. Judge Nye set a hearing on that application for February.

As they left the courtroom Ford attempted to speak to Mitchum, but Giesler blocked his path. Then a swarm of reporters moved in on the lawyer, asking why he had not put up a defense for his client. "The evidence was in the transcript," Giesler answered. "And Mr. Mitchum wouldn't perjure himself. He would have had to tell the truth."

As the star emerged from the courtroom a near-riotous mob, composed mostly of females, surged toward him attempting to touch him and tear away his clothes as they screamed their loyalty and love. It was obvious that in accepting his punishment he had emerged a new kind of hero in their eyes. For his part, the cocky barroom brawler looked panicky until several lawmen formed a human wall around him and moved him into the waiting elevator.

Apprised of the fans' response to Mitchum following his conviction, Hughes and Rogell became more confident than ever that the huge box-office grosses of *Rachel and the Stranger* and *The Red Pony*, the other release, were no fluke. They were reassured that radio gossip Jimmy Fidler's weekly exhortations to audiences to boycott Mitchum films were out of sync with the public mood. Convinced that any new Mitchum picture— whatever its quality—would be a prime moneymaker, they urged Siegel to rush *The Big Steal* to completion before the star's sentencing.

Immediately after Mitchum's arrest Hughes had ordered a man named Kemp Niver to keep a discreet eye on him. Now, as shooting on *The Big Steal* resumed, Hughes was more interested in protecting a valuable property than having Niver remain unobtrusive. Coworkers on the film noticed that Niver arrived with Mitchum each morning, stayed with him on the set during the day and left with him after shooting was completed.

Some mistakenly concluded that Niver, a six-foot, 200-pound-plus behemoth of a man, was Mitchum's bodyguard. "Not so," Niver said in 1982. "I was Hughes's undercover security, and after Mitchum got arrested I was assigned to him.

"To go back, I graduated from the Police Academy in the same class as Tom Bradley, Los Angeles's first black mayor. My first partner in a patrol car was Ed Davis. He became chief of police here and then a state senator. I became a detective attached to the district attorney's office until World War II.

Afterward, I set myself up as a private detective—'Discreet About Others' Indiscretions.' It was at a time when the House Un-American Activities Committee was coming to Hollywood. Howard Hughes hired me to gather dossiers on every RKO employee earning over $750 a week. He wanted to find out how many card-carrying Communists he had working for him. He didn't really care. He just wanted to know. So in about a year I had twelve people working under me compiling that information.

"Then Howard took me off that and assigned me to Mitchum. Not as a bodyguard; he could take care of himself. My job was to keep the undesirables away from him, and that wasn't easy. Because Mitchum is an actor, and that, of course, covers a lot of things. Actors are not like you and me. They are products of arrested development. That doesn't mean they aren't more intelligent by far than the average walking-around-on-the-street guy, but they are actors. And they're a special breed who need constant attention—which can bring on a lot of trouble," Niver explained.

"So Hughes and Mendel Silverberg of the studio said they wanted a witness to everything he did. They said then if he is ever in a situation where the shit hits the fan, you can get him out so at least it doesn't land on him." Niver smiled, then said, "Of course, I was with him two years and my duties expanded."

Meanwhile, Siegel pushed the company to turn out as many pages as possible each day. In the script Mitchum played Army Lieutenant Duke Halliday, who is on the trail of a $300,000 payroll which was heisted from him, he believes, by Jim Fiske (Patrick Knowles). When he catches up with Fiske in Mexico, Halliday is surprised to discover his superior officer, Captain Blake (William Bendix), is also in on the robbery. Blake kills Fiske, and Joan Graham (Jane Greer) distracts Blake long enough for Halliday to overpower him and retrieve the money. That accomplished, Halliday and Joan set out for the United States to return the money and remove the smirch from Halliday's character. It was Siegel's plan to film all of Mitchum's big scenes before his sentencing date, and to finish the film using a double in the long shots. Try as he might, however, he was not able to pull it off.

On February 9, Mitchum and Leeds again appeared before Superior Court Judge Nye. The probation department reported Mitchum had told them that although he earned $3,250 a week, he was "constantly obsessed with the phantom of failure" and had become the target of "parasitic-type individuals" as a soft touch. The department's conclusion was that he was "psychologically ill-equipped for his sudden rise to fame."

Before sentencing him Nye sternly lectured him. "I realize you are idolized by hundreds of thousands of people. By dint of hard work and native ability you have gained national prominence that up to now has meant nothing but glory to you. However, you have overlooked the responsibilities that go with such prominence. You have failed to set an example of good citizenship.

"I am sorry for both of these defendants," Nye told spectators, "but respect for law and order must be taken into consideration. This case has attracted attention not only locally, but throughout the world, and I am treating it the same as I would any case of a similar nature. This sentence must serve as an example for hundreds of thousand of fans."

Nye then proceeded to sentence Mitchum and Leeds to a year in the county jail. Suspending those sentences, he placed both on probation for two years, the first sixty days of which were to be spent in Los Angeles County Jail.

Pandemonium ensued. Photographers jostled one another as Mitchum and Leeds posed patiently. When a reporter asked Mitchum whether he had brought supplies in anticipation of his incarceration, he smiled. "Not even a toothbrush. I travel light, but I guess this is too light." With that a deputy sheriff handcuffed him and led him to the ninth floor where they took an elevator to the twelfth, the one on which the cells are located.

There, Mitchum became prisoner number 91234, and was assigned to a barren cell containing a steel bunk with a thin mattress ("I've slept on worse"), a wash basin and a toilet. His clothing, except for his own expensive dark brown cordovans, was replaced by jailhouse denims.

Lights were out at ten p.m., but Mitchum's insomnia allowed him little sleep between then and the predawn wake-up call. At six-thirty he marched with the other prisoners to the messhall where he had a breakfast of oatmeal, sweet roll, applesauce and coffee. Back in his cell he followed jailhouse routine, sweeping and mopping the floor inside and in front of his cell, washing down the bars, scrubbing the basin and toilet and making up his bed. As he worked, his spirits rose noticeably and his ability to adjust easily to any situation stood him in good stead. The previous day he had said, "This is the last time anything like this will ever happen to me. It has been a sad lesson. I hope it will save other people from a similar fate." Now, experiencing jailhouse camaraderie, he announced, "I'm beginning to like it here. There's lots of activity. Whatever work assignment I get will be all right with me."

That was fortunate, because Giesler was unsuccessful in obtaining a stay of sentence until *The Big Steal* was completed. Judge Nye countered Giesler's contention that innocent people were being thrown out of work. "If we tried to take all the innocent people into consideration in every case, we would have to take down all the jails and penitentiaries."

At his press conference Mitchum was cooperative with both reporters and photographers; his only condition was that there be no behind-the-bars photos that would embarrass his children. "I know I have to pay the penalty," he said, eating humble pie, "but I want everything as upbeat as possible for the kids' sake." So he posed mopping floors, eating lunch, cleaning his cup and spoon, and purchasing milk and cigarettes.

Later, on several occasions, he was called upon to pose for photos with the warden and visiting personages. On one unforgettable day he was startled to have the guards place him in shackles to take him across the quad. He protested that he was no violent criminal, nor was he planning an escape. There must, he said, be some terrible mistake. Nothing he said deterred the guards. The group began the trip with Mitchum struggling and swearing. As they emerged from the building he spotted an unfamiliar photographer lurking near the door and a number of those he recognized at a distance. The realization that he was being set up threw him into a rage. The thought that news pictures of him in shackles would give children an opportunity to torment his sons apparently filled him with panic. In spite of the shackles, he tried to take a swing at the photographer who was preparing to make a shot, and fell. Immediately the photographer snapped a picture of him writhing on the ground. At the sight of the flash Mitchum began crying, then screaming with rage. His emotional torment was so undisguised that a couple of friendly photographers who had been hanging back rushed the opportunistic cameraman and tore the film out of his camera, according to a friend of his.

Otherwise Mitchum adjusted easily to the county jail. Hearing that he was to be transferred to the Sheriff's Wayside Honor Farm at Castaic threw him into a funk. Interviewed as he awaited his physical, part of his certification for the move, he told reporters, "I've been pretty happy in the tank here. And I'm really proud that the men in the tank recommended me to the jailers to be the trusty. That's considered quite an honor. The men and I got along well, and I was to take over my new job as a trusty on Saturday. No, I'm not happy about leaving." What he did not tell the reporters was that one reason for his unhappiness was that it would end his wife's daily visits with news of his family. He was inclined to request that he be allowed to remain in the county jail, but reluctantly bowed to pressure applied by Hughes and Rogell. They argued that in addition to benefiting from the sunshine and fresh air he would automatically receive a ten-day reduction in his sentence. Those ten days, they contended, were crucial in finishing *The Big Steal*.

Upon their arrival at the Honor Farm, Mitchum and the other new trusties had to submit to another thorough physical, after which they traded their jeans for overalls and endured a lecture on rules. They would arise at dawn—no problem for a film actor—have breakfast at six-thirty; report for work at eight—in Mitchum's case, the cement plant; eat lunch at eleven-thirty; return to work at twelve-thirty p.m.—where Mitchum would juggle ten-pound cement blocks—until four-thirty; and shower and clean up for dinner at five-thirty p.m. Following the evening meal each prisoner would be free to attend class at the prison farm school, go to the library, watch a movie, wrestle, box, or whatever until retiring at ten p.m.

Reluctant as Mitchum had been to leave the county jail for Castaic, he once again found himself reacting positively to his new surroundings. Naturally news photographers appeared during his first day at the farm, and he was very cooperative. If the photo of him handling cement blocks without work gloves earned guffaws among laborers, he demonstrated he had not forgotten the skills he had mastered on his grandmother's farm in Delaware. Slapping a heifer named Daisy Mae on the rump, he ordered, "Git over there!" Then, seating himself on a stool, he demonstrated his milking expertise so successfully he drew applause from the press. For an encore he directed a teat at a cameraman and squirted a stream of warm milk toward him.

Next day, work gloves in place, Mitchum settled into the routine at the cement plant. The heavy labor agreed with him. He began to lose the slight roll of flab at his waistline. A confirmed insomniac who had not had more than four hours of sleep (and irregular sleep at that) since his breakdown during the Second World War, he now happily told anyone who would listen that he was off the Hollywood merry-go-round and was sleeping like a baby. "I haven't had so much sleep in years," he said contentedly. His chief regret was that he was unable to see his sons, and that Kemp Niver brought Dorothy to visit only on Sundays. When a reporter inquired how he felt about Judge Nye's refusal to grant him parole, Mitchum vigorously denied harboring any resentment. "I don't think it was a bum beef at all," he said. "If I had gotten probation, it would have gone against public opinion."

Not that prison life was free of problems. At the minimum security facility, some control was maintained by rewarding prisoners for reporting infractions of the rules. This led eager beavers to plant evidence on fellow prisoners and earn points by snitching on the supposed offenders. In Mitchum's case, obviously the plot was to secrete marijuana in his room. When it was found, he would be penalized and the fink rewarded.

Tipped off to the danger, Mitchum always searched the premises the moment he returned. If marijuana had been hidden and he found it, he took it to the guard. After a couple of such incidents he began making his bed in an unorthodox way; when he returned, it was easy for him to check whether his bedding had been tampered with. If it had, he would search out the contraband and flush it down the toilet. Invariably guards would arrive for a search shortly thereafter. And invariably the first place they would look was the spot where the finks had told them the stash was planted.

Mitchum quickly solved this problem by requesting a locked cell.

A few days after Mitchum's arrival at Castaic, Perry Lieber remarked on the telephone to Kemp Niver that Howard Hughes was one of the craziest men he had ever worked for. Not that this was news to Niver. A few months before he had been called by Hughes in the middle of the night and sent to a New York address to await instructions. He had waited fifteen days and nights without further communication. Finally he called the studio and was grilled about where he had been for the past two weeks. He explained and was told Hughes had intended that he keep a certain actress under surveillance. Now her visit to Manhattan had been canceled, and he was to report back to the studio at once.

Lieber informed Niver that Hughes had called him, saying that he wanted to visit Mitchum at the Honor Farm, but under no circumstances was his identity to be known. Not an easy assignment.

Niver called the sheriff, and swearing him to secrecy, explained the situation. In 1982 Niver still shook his head in disbelief as he imagined the call that took place between that sheriff and the captain at Castaic, with the sheriff saying that a man, to whom complete privacy and every courtesy was to be extended, would be arriving soon. When the captain inquired who the visitor was, the sheriff said only that Niver would vouch for him.

Niver eventually arranged for the captain to smuggle Hughes onto the Honor Farm and hide him in the captain's own office. There the secret meeting between Hughes and Mitchum took place.

Hughes, who, a number of acquaintances claim, would have liked to have been as bold and carefree as Mitchum, told the actor he admired his pragmatic decision that it was in his own best interest to serve time in jail. He believed Mitchum had reached the correct conclusion and had earned the public's admiration.

"I want you to know directly from me that we're going to

keep your contract," Niver overheard Hughes assure the actor. Then Hughes added that if there was anything Mitchum wanted, the studio would get it for him.

Mitchum allowed there was something. "Fifty thousand dollars to get a suitable home for my family."

Hughes instantly said arrangements would be made.

"Howard had been two hours late for the appointment, which was normal for him," Niver says, "but there was a problem. He wanted to talk and this collided with the jail's schedule. Still, the meeting went right on through the dinner hour, and the prisoners were kept locked up unfed until he finished his visit and left."

On the way home Hughes told Niver that Mitchum was to have whatever he needed, but he also specified that Niver make sure that a quantity of vitamins and chocolate bars were sent to the prisoner.

"Now in those days the competition among columnists was fierce. Louella Parsons, Hedda Hopper, Jimmy Fidler, and the others all employed legmen. What one of them wouldn't have given for the story of how Howard Hughes had made the prison stand still and was sending his locked-up star vitamins and chocolate bars," Niver says. "Why, Louella would have given her legman a five-hundred-dollar bonus for that information."

Hughes okayed the loan Mitchum had requested—almost, but not before Mitchum was released. On July 15, 1949, RKO loaned not Bob, but Dorothy Mitchum, $49,500 at five percent per annum to buy a new house. According to the agreement, beginning on October 13, $250 was to be withheld from Mitchum's paycheck every Thursday up to and including August 17, 1950, when he went on layoff. Upon his return to work on October 12, 1950, $500 was to be deducted every Thursday while he was on salary until the principal and interest had been paid in full. But in the fall of 1951 the Mitchums requested and received permission to refinance the loan through the First National Bank in Beverly Hills and to pay off RKO. Nevertheless, from the moment the loan was made through Hughes, Dorothy Mitchum was dealing from a position of strength.

* * *

Those developments lay in the future. As time neared for Mitchum's release, visits from coworkers on *The Big Steal* disrupted the regimen at the Honor Farm. Officials decided to transfer him again, and on March 24 he arrived back at the Los Angeles County Jail. He now supported a deep tan, a mustache and a trim waistline, having taken off between five and ten pounds. Asked how he regarded his stay at Castaic, Mitchum replied: "It was a relief to get away for a while. It's the first vacation I've had in seven years. I worked hard, slept well, and believe it or not, batted eight hundred on The Rancho softball team. We won the last eight games. That farm's just like a weekend in Palm Springs—a great place to get in shape." Then he added, mischievously, "Only you meet a better class of people."

A week later on March 30 he and Lila Leeds were released, although terms of their probation prohibited them from associating with each other.

Quizzed about his plans, Mitchum said he was returning to RKO to go back to work because he was broke and in debt, but added, "I've been happy in jail because I've had privacy. Nobody envied me. Nobody wanted anything from me." This led him into a discussion of ideas that had struck him during his incarceration. In his opinion, crime detection was highly efficient, but the penal system left a lot to be desired. "You get a new chimpanzee and put him in Griffith Park Zoo and everybody rushes to look him over. And if the keepers don't feed him well and take the best care of him, the public raises hell," he said. "But you put a man in a cage and nobody seems to care how he gets along."

Did he have a solution? He suggested that each new prisoner receive a psychiatric classification in order that he might serve his sentence under conditions—including psychiatric treatment—designed to insure rehabilitation.*

By special arrangement Mitchum was released from custody

---

*Later he donated a variety of gum, candy and other vending machines to the Wayside Honor Farm to make the prisoners' lives more pleasant. A couple of years after he made this gesture, his pal, Steve Brodie, visited an acquaintance incarcerated there and took the authorities to task because Mitchum had received no credit for his contribution. After doing some checking, the administration put up a plaque which read: DONATED BY ROBERT MITCHUM.

in the first hour of March 30. As soon as he was processed a waiting deputy drove him to his home where his patient wife and jubilant children, plus other members of the family and a few close friends, were awaiting his arrival.

The following Monday he reported to the studio for resumption of production on *The Big Steal*. Complications of all kinds arose. Mitchum was tanner, leaner and healthier looking than he had been in the scenes shot before he was jailed. Jane Greer was now noticeably pregnant. Before they could leave for location shooting in Mexico, Mitchum's probation officer had to notify the Mexican Consulate General that permission for the actor to enter Mexico had been granted "subject to the observance of the regulations and laws of the state of Mexico."

Mitchum, accompanied by Niver, joined the company there to do shots for which his stand-in had not been able to double. And as soon as child-care arrangements were made, Dorothy arrived to lend "a calming influence." Using all their ingenuity in devising a series of long shots and closeups, the director and cameraman produced enough footage eventually to earn surprisingly amiable reviews, including one from the usually hypercritical Bosley Crowther in the *New York Times*.

Meanwhile, Hughes, pleased with Mitchum's work, acquired Selznick's share of the actor's contract for $400,000 and assigned him to *Holiday Affair* opposite Janet Leigh. A frothy, sentimental Christmas love story that might have been better suited to Cary Grant and Irene Dunne, it pleased few critics. However, the audience reaction was good. Patrons attending the first showing at the Hill Street Theater in Los Angeles applauded and shouted their approval as Mitchum closed a speech by toasting his rival, Wendell Corey, and telling Leigh, "But I still think you should marry me."

Upon completion of the film RKO renegotiated Mitchum's contract, giving him $3,750 a week for forty out of fifty-two weeks. Uncharacteristically, Mitchum dashed off a thank-you note to Sid Rogell after signing the new document.

Wasting no time in putting him to work, the studio teamed him with Faith Domergue in *Where Danger Lives*, and with glamorous Ava Gardner in what was first called *Carriage Entrance*, but was retitled *My Forbidden Past*. Mitchum, as

he so often did to the despair of theater owners and the irritation
of RKO, disparaged the latter film to syndicated columnist
Hedda Hopper while it was being made. "In *Carriage Entrance*,
the picture I'm doing with Ava Gardner, I was first pencilled
in as a real square john. We didn't have much of a script to
start with, so I suggested the first scene be about like the
climactic one in *Ecstasy*. I figured if we were going to give
the public a shock, we might as well do it up brown."

When Hughes called him on the carpet for these remarks,
Mitchum sloughed off the reprimand and asked Hughes, who
allegedly had had an affair with Gardner, whether he ought to
go to bed with her. Hughes attempted to needle him. "If you
don't, everybody will think you're a pansy," to which the sharp-
witted Mitchum shot back, "If you want to discuss your problems, I'll discuss mine." At that Hughes gave up and, according
to Mitchum, said bemusedly, "You're like a pay toilet. You
don't give a shit for nothing, do you?"

When the picture was finished RKO sent Mitchum and
Gardner on personal appearances to ascertain whether there
was any residual hostility toward Mitchum over his arrest. To
the contrary, his skirmish with the law seemed to have acted
as an aphrodisiac. Mobs of screaming, swooning women blocked
the stage doors wherever he played. Kemp Niver and Dorothy
were kept very busy preventing his admirers from slipping
backstage or waylaying him at the hotel. Heads, as marijuana
users were then called, jammed theaters and were forever trying
to give him grass by palming it off during a handshake, wrap-
ping it with a gift, leaving it in his mailbox at the hotel or
rapping on his door—only to be greeted by Dorothy or Niver
who scared them off.

Even representatives of the establishment were excited by
him. The manager of the Chicago Theater called Ned Depinet
at RKO to tell him that Mitchum and Ava Gardner were at-
tracting the greatest business the theater had done in many
years. In Depinet's memo to Hughes he reported that "While
Ava Gardner is receiving a wonderful reception, all bedlam
breaks loose when Mitchum appears on stage. He had to take
five encores at the first show."

Depinet was especially pleased to learn that the conservative

Chicago Tribune had given the two stars a cocktail party attended by Mrs. Bazy McCormick Miller, publisher of the *Washington Times-Herald* and president of the *Tribune*, as well as other members of the McCormick family, and leading *Tribune* editors and writers. His reception was not universally warm, however; he *was* snubbed and slighted in various quarters.

The most painful humiliation occurred a couple of years later. His son Jim, who was enrolled in an exclusive private school, wanted his father to attend the Christmas program and party as other parents did. Dorothy and Bob Mitchum went together, but Mitchum's reception by the principal was frostier than a visit to the real North Pole. During the holiday vacation the Mitchums received word from the school that it had been decided that little Jim would be happier elsewhere. An inquiry revealed that while the child was innocent of wrongdoing, neither the principal nor the board felt it suitable for "Joan Fontaine's little one," "Betty Hutton's girls" or other children to be exposed to a man with Mitchum's record.

Mitchum was deeply wounded personally, but even more concerned about his son's reaction. Several liberal parents of other pupils—the Dore Scharys, the Dean Jaggers, Jane Greer and her then husband, Edward Lasker—were outraged when they learned of the incident. "Eddie and I talked it over with the others and considered the possibilities. We could have taken our children out of the school, but we really wanted Jim reinstated because we felt it was so unfair to have a child punished for something the father had done," Jane Greer says. "So my husband called the head of the school and really let her have it. Then Dore Schary called Eddie and said, 'Edward, you lost your temper. You have to use tact with these people. I have made arrangements to attend a meeting with them and I will settle it.'

"So Dore met with them at their monthly meeting. He explained beforehand that he had to attend a sneak preview of a film at eight-thirty. And since the meeting started at seven, he'd appreciate it if he could go on early. The meeting began. They talked about what color the benches should be painted, whether to serve tomato or orange juice, and so on. Well, finally it was seven-thirty, then eight o'clock. Dore is motioning to the woman and the head of the school board, but they refuse to recognize him. At eight-fifteen they'll hear from Mr. Schary. 'Mr. Schary is very important,' the head of the school announced, 'and he has something he'd like to say to us, but we wanted him to know other things are important, too. Mr. Schary.'

"Dore was very angry at the high-handedness. He picked up the table and slammed it down. Then he yelled at everybody and stomped out without waiting for the discussion. He was so angry he didn't even go to the preview. He phoned my husband and said, 'I just blew it, too.'

"The upshot was that the school didn't take Jim back, and all of us—the Scharys and I think the Dean Jaggers—withdrew our children. Which was just as well because it was a very snobbish school.

"It's ludicrous now, but it was very tough for Dorothy and Bob during that period. Because he didn't realize the magnitude of his 'crime' in some people's eyes. Incidents such as that hurt him deeply.

"I have great admiration for how they—especially Dorothy—handled things. She took responsibility, and I must say handled matters superbly—to have the children turn out well."

CHAPTER 9

The period of Mitchum's probationary term might be expected to stand as one of the most difficult in his life. For a man who rebelled against any supervision, delivering an oral or written weekly report on his activities was humiliating. Even more demeaning in his eyes was having to account to Kemp Niver for his whereabouts twenty-four hours a day.

Only at home was he free of his obligations to RKO and Niver; consequently, he spent more and more time there. But the modest house on Oak Glen was crowded and poorly situated. Now that the boys were older, they roamed the neighborhood, and Chris had already received minor injuries when he raced off the sidewalk into the path of an automobile. Taking everything into consideration, Dorothy and Bob decided to look for a roomier and more secluded place—and one removed from the area where he was likely to run into the crowd with whom he had been involved prior to his arrest.

Tony Caruso suggested they join him and his wife, Tonia, on "their side of the mountain." A quick check with realtors turned up a house at 1639 Mandeville Canyon Road, just around the corner from the Carusos. The Mitchums took one look and set in motion the machinery to purchase it.

In midsummer of 1949 they took possession. By comparison to the Oak Glen place, this was a spacious structure—more suitable in every way for the residence of a rising film star. "We've got a swimming pool, but no furniture," Mitchum informed columnist Hedda Hopper, who interpreted the remark as another of his put-ons. In point of fact, other than a few beds, dressers, chairs and lamps, the entire contents—two large, braided rugs and other New England-style furnishings—of their former home were swallowed up by the enormous family room that overlooked the garden.

Since payments on the loan from Hughes, previous legal fees and other obligations left them with little ready cash, the Mitchums postponed decorating plans beyond the family room, the bedrooms and the kitchen. Gradually Mitchum, who told Sidney Skolsky he felt himself to be "an accomplished interior decorator," put together the furnishings for the living room. While Dorothy neither praised nor criticized his work, as soon as they became financially stable she contacted a professional set decorator while her husband was out of town and gave the pro a free hand on the room. "The result was very modern-modern—grays and blacks, as I remember," says a friend. "Very formal for these informal people who were happiest in the New England family room where they could put their feet up, or outside by the pool. The living room was beautiful. It just didn't have anything to do with them. But I guess they liked it."

Immediately after their move, Mitchum's lifestyle began undergoing a noticeable change. Since the studio discouraged stars—in fact, prohibited them—from night prowls with stand-ins, grips, gaffers and casual bar buddies encountered along the way, the Mitchums frequently entertained at home. With the exception of Tarzan, a close friend he had made at the Honor Farm in Castaic who was often a guest at the house, most of the people with whom Bob and Dorothy socialized were industry people who lived nearby.

At first they and their neighbors simply drifted together late on free afternoons. Exactly who began referring to this loose association as the Mandeville Canyon Gang is long forgotten, yet forty years later just who did and who didn't belong is not open to question. Mention of someone who was not a part of the group will bring a response, "No, no. He lived in the Canyon, but he wasn't a part of the gang."

Unquestionably the catalyst—founder is too formal a word— who brought such diverse personalities together was Ollie Carey, widow of Harry, and herself a fixture in John Ford films. A forthright, funny, earthy woman, Ollie Carey became den mother to the group. More than one middle-aged, former resident nostalgically recalls some hot December evening when Ollie and her group, bundled in mufflers and stocking caps, appeared at the door to do their Christmas caroling.

If Ollie was mistress of entertainment, Mitchum was the storyteller. So persuasive was he in recounting stories of his youth that some of the gang regulars remember them vividly today. Many of the stories centered around the exploits of his brother, John, Tony Caruso and himself. In John's absence, he always would pull Tony down beside him before launching into a story. Periodically, as he embellished an incident with exciting, humorous details, he would poke Caruso in the ribs and demand, "Isn't that right, Ole Tone?" Caruso, so caught up in the magic Mitchum was weaving, would vigorously nod his head. "Yeah. Yeah. And then what did we do?"

The other Mandeville Canyon Gang regulars were the Carusos, Richard and Jean Widmark, Gregory Peck and his first wife, Greta, Dean Jagger and his wife, and Jerry Devine and his first wife. Devine, a former child actor, was a successful radio writer who later went on to be a successful producer. A walking computer of New York theatrical lore, he enlivened the get-togethers with little-known anecdotes about famous theatrical personages and productions.

All the regulars naturally brought their kids to these neighborhood get-togethers. There might be a ballgame for the kids and men while the women gossiped. Anybody who wanted to went in the pool. "These were very low-key and unpretentious affairs. But a lot of laughs," Tonia Caruso recalls. "Basically all the men got along together and so did the women. That was the basis of it."

The most frequently recalled incident did not happen at one

of the Gang get-togethers, however, but at a Fourth of July celebration which included a number of the Mitchums' other friends. Upon hearing a loud crash, from the area between 1639 and the corner of Sunset Boulevard, Mitchum sprinted toward the roadway with his guests in pursuit. An automobile and a motorcycle had collided and the motorcyclist lay cradled in his female companion's arms, bleeding profusely. "Oh, my darling, my poor baby," she was sobbing. "I'm here with you, darling. Speak to me, please." As she threw her head back to get her hair out of her face, she caught a glimpse of Mitchum. "Oh, my God! It's Bob Mitchum! Look, honey, look!" she shouted to the gravely wounded man, dropping his head on the pavement in her excitement. Luckily, an ambulance arrived before she could request Mitchum's autograph.

The close-knit social life was but one pleasant facet in the Canyon. All of the Mitchums adapted well to their new home. The boys had plenty of space in which to play; Caruso frequently dropped by to give Mitchum a lift to work and home again at night; and Dorothy, whose extreme shyness had made her a shadowy figure during her first years in Hollywood, grew more at ease among the Canyonites who gradually helped her become more comfortable with the entertainment industry's social scene.

But it was on March 3, 1952, that the bigger house became even better suited to their needs and an even happier place with the arrival of the Mitchums' only daughter at the Good Samaritan Hospital. She weighed seven pounds, ten ounces. In a sentimental gesture they named her Petrina for her father's grandmother.

Only one major annoyance disturbed those early days, according to Kemp Niver. Himself. "My job was still to keep an eye out to stop anybody from getting Bob into trouble," Niver says. "He always had to let me know where he or they were going and what they were going to do. And that created a little bit of hostility on his part. I was—you could say—establishment, a square, the kind of guy that anyway bothered him. We locked horns a few times because we looked at things differently. I was a necessary evil from his point of view. But both he and his wife knew that if the police found him within twenty feet of marijuana, he was going back to the joint. So I made a deal with him. I said, 'Under no circumstances, take any chances. And I will stay near the phone as long as you're out of the house. You can always get me, and I'll come where you are.'

"To show you how careful he had to be, one night he and Mrs. Mitchum went to their dentist's office to get their teeth cleaned and a little other work done. They came out and started to get in their car, and right on top of the ashtray was a great big lovely marijuana cigarette," Niver recalls. "They locked the doors and put in a call to me. I got there, and as soon as I could I got them into my car and took off in theirs.

"All the while he was on probation I went on the road with him and Dorothy, because people were always showing up at his suite. There'd be a knock at the door. They'd say, real quiet, 'We got one for you,' then they'd leave and he'd call me to take care of whatever it was they'd left behind for him. He could never let down for a minute."

With this constant focus on the legal dangers his use of marijuana had brought, Mitchum took to kidding friends and coworkers about how loose things were. Invited to the birthday party of Henny Backus, the Mitchums showed up with a pretty little bauble for her. "It was the first time I'd seen him since his release, and that night he was in great form," she recalls. "As I opened the box, he whispered in my ear, 'Underneath that trinket is hidden lots of marvelous grass. It was planted out back and fertilized with real elephant shit.'"

Later in the evening, Henny asked him, "Was it awful in the can?" According to her recollection, he replied, "No, I was at an Honor Farm." She inquired what he did there. "Had a little plot, grew myself a little grass," he replied gravely. "Every night made myself a little roach. Slept like I hadn't since I was a baby."

She also asked about his stay in Mexico finishing *The Big Steal* and wondered whether he by any chance had met the president of Mexico, who was looked upon by many as a glamorous figure. Mitchum nodded affirmatively and went on developing his theme. "The president came right over to me with a pocketful of roaches," he told her. "Came up smoking a roach. Handed me one, too."

Henny said later that she felt elated that his arrest had not made him bitter. "He hadn't lost his sense of humor," she says. "Of course, the stories weren't true. What is true with him?"

Nor was Mitchum any less high spirited in his behavior at RKO. Perhaps he had sufficient confidence in Howard Hughes's investment in and regard for him to take risks. Several employees who worked there at that time have expressed the opinion that Hughes increasingly envied Mitchum's free-spirited way of living on the brink. For years after the actor left RKO's employment, Hughes delegated one underling to update Mitchum's telephone number periodically should he ever want to call him. Earlier, he *had* called one night and whisked the star off on a personally conducted tour of the Spruce Goose, an encounter that was mildly disappointing to the millionaire. He had heard that Mitchum once worked at Lockheed Aircraft and assumed the two of them could engage in a stimulating technical conversation about planes. Unfortunately, Mitchum knew nothing and cared less about the subject of aviation.

"Howard was an attractive man. He was a rich man. He wielded a lot of power, but I think he secretly would have liked to have been Bob Mitchum," says Jim Backus. "Because of who he was, Howard's conquests were unquestionably staggering. But Bob Mitchum could have gone right on being a bum, and beautiful women would still have fallen all over him. And I think Howard was canny enough to realize that."

Another RKO employee claims that Hughes once offered to allow Mitchum to run the studio, only to have him point to actor Dick Powell, who was sitting nearby, and say, "He's the one you ought to be offering the job to."

Mitchum's method of dealing with Hughes generally contained a certain cheekiness. He customarily spoke of his employer as "The Phantom," except when he was feeling angry and wanted to put him down, at which time he called him, "Mr. Howard T. Hughes." (Addressing anyone formally is always a signal of displeasure on Mitchum's part.)

Certainly Mitchum felt confident enough to indulge in outrageous behavior on the RKO lot. Rumor had it that Hughes had certain dressing rooms bugged. Mitchum assumed that if anyone were a candidate for electronic spying, it was he. Proceeding on this theory, he would enter his bungalow and walk around the dressing room, saying something to the effect, *Hey, Phantom. I know you got it bugged. Where is it? And where's my stash? If you don't tell me, I'm going to have to report it. Answer, Phantom. I know I'm bugged.*

"Once after going through that routine," says Backus, who worked in a couple of Mitchum films, "he demanded an answer, and when he didn't get one, he picked up the phone and got the policeman on the front gate. 'Officer, I'm reporting a robbery,' he said. 'My stash has been stolen.' Now that takes chutzpah. Of course, I think he did it chiefly for shock value."

Consensus is that the assignments he drew in such films as *Where Danger Lives*, *His Kind of Woman*, *My Forbidden Past*, *Macao*, *The Racket* and such later ones as *Second Chance, One Minute to Zero* and *She Couldn't Say No* provided him with little challenge. So he distracted himself in various ways—like tweaking management's nose.

Another was to manipulate the press as a means of embarrassing the studio. "They come up with the same plot, essentially the same dialogue, even the same suits—all they change is the leading lady," was a complaint he repeatedly raised over a period of years. He claimed to have first-hand knowledge that some of these scripts had been foisted on RKO and, subsequently, on workhorses like him by powerful agents who controlled sought-after stars and insisted the desirable star and undesirable script be contracted for as part of the same deal. Assuming this to be the case, he said he was unable to regard acting as a serious profession. After all, how much pride could a man take in belonging to an industry whose greatest star up to that time had been Rin Tin Tin?

Columnist Sheilah Graham happened to be visiting the set when a drunken extra was being ejected. Ever alert for a possible scoop, Sheilah asked Mitchum the man's identity. He replied very seriously that it was a sad, sad story. That man was the producer of the picture, he said, clucking his tongue in mock sympathy. Only by chance at the last minute did the RKO publicity department learn what he had told her, present the true facts and kill the story.

A favorite anecdote among long-time Mitchum watchers is unverifiable. This perhaps apocryphal tale centers on his interview in connection with *One Minute to Zero* by (a) an inexperienced fan magazine writer, (b) an unworldly secretary subbing for her boss who was ill, (c) a college journalism student. In any case, Mitchum allegedly became bored by the inane line of questioning and decided to have some fun. Asked by the interviewer whether he had a favorite sport, he assured her he had. What was it? Hunting. Hunting what? Poontang, he replied. She was unfamiliar with that. Where did one find it? she asked. Just about anywhere, he said. He'd found some right in his dressing room. He'd seen it at Hollywood and Vine. There was good hunting atop the Empire State Building. Could he describe it, she wanted to know. Well, it was soft, covered with hair and reacted to excitement. It had to be shot. Couldn't be trapped. And there was a difference of opinion whether it was good eating.

Although no one can produce a copy of the story, numerous individuals swear the piece found its way into print intact and caused a mild sensation.

If so, it might help explain Mitchum's citation by the Hollywood Women's Press Club as "the most uncooperative actor" of 1950. Not that this disturbed him. He wired the club assuring them: "Your most gracious award became a treasured addition to a collection of inverse citations. These include prominent mention in several ten worst dressed American lists and [inclusion on] a society columnist's [list of] ten-most desirable male guests, which happily was published on the date I was made welcome at the county jail."

He later appeared at a luncheon at the Beverly Wilshire Hotel, with forty-eight members of the Women's Press Club, telling them that if they anticipated his bringing a flock of doves of peace, they were in for a disappointment. "I won't do it," he said, grinning at them. "I'm afraid the hotel would arrest me, and I'm still on probation. I have to be careful." Then he treated club members to champagne, which he eschewed and downed several martinis instead.

The censure was not limited to the press. Ned Depinet,

corporate president of RKO, wrote Sid Rogell about "muffling" Mitchum's deprecating remarks about the industry, then, in the same letter, loosed a second blast at a columnist: "Which reminds me that someone should try to muzzle Jimmy Fidler, particularly as regards to Bob Mitchum. No matter what Jimmy talks about that is critical of actors, he always seems to find some excuse to drag in poor Bob, and he unloaded on him again last night. How about having Perry Lieber talk to Jimmy and see if he can prevail upon him to let Mitchum have a breather and give him a chance to redeem himself. Unless Fidler is completely hypocritical he should not condemn a fellow eternally for one mistake."

The outcome was that Rogell spoke to Bert Allenberg, who extracted a promise from Mitchum to be more tactful in the future. Whether or not Lieber spoke to Fidler is unrecorded, but the attacks eventually abated somewhat.

Surely Mitchum's chief problem in keeping out of mischief at RKO was surfeit of time on his hands. Blessed with a photographic memory, he spent far less time mastering his lines and characterizations than most other actors. Two directors he would work with later gave vivid testimony of this. On *His Kind of Woman*, John Farrow walked onto an unfinished set the first day of shooting. Rather than waste time, he assembled Mitchum, Jane Russell, Vincent Price, Jim Backus, Raymond Burr, Charles McGraw, Tony Caruso, Leon Ames and other principals around a table and suggested they read the 110-page script aloud. Mitchum underplayed it all the way.

After finding the set was still incomplete, Farrow gave the cast a five-minute break. When they returned, they read through the screenplay again, and several of the group realized that Mitchum did not open his script once. When one of them expressed surprise, Mitchum shrugged. "Next time I'll do the camera directions."

On loan to 20th Century-Fox for *White Witch Doctor*, Mitchum enraged director Henry Hathaway, an amiable man off the set, but one who has a reputation as something of a tyrant on the set, by asking, "What are the lyrics?"

"Haven't you studied your scene?" Hathaway demanded.

"Not yet," Hathaway recalls Mitchum responding.

Hathaway says he was at first furious, then astounded. "By God, I've worked with actors who were stopped by a half page of dialogue after they'd really studied it. Mitchum looked over the scene, got up and did those six pages in one take. Six pages. And part of his dialogue was in Swahili."

Afterward, Hathaway telephoned Howard Hughes to report that Mitchum had just performed one of the most phenomenal feats of memory he had ever witnessed. When Mitchum heard about the call, he asked, "What did he expect at these prices? A bum?"

In the early 1950s, Mitchum went through a series of chameleonlike changes. Unlike many earlier coworkers, Hathaway, Lizabeth Scott, with whom he made *The Racket*, and others perceived him as a loner. Scott felt there was a strong resemblance between him and Humphrey Bogart, with whom she had made a picture. "Bogart said to me while we were working together, 'You know, this profession for me is truly embarrassing,' and I sensed Bob to some degree felt the same way.

"As soon as a scene was over he'd go into his dressing room. He had a guitar there. He'd strum away, writing songs and singing. There was something passionate and very compelling and emotional about the whole thing."

Around this time Mitchum was flirting with the notion of becoming a recording artist. Earlier he had issued an album of folk songs on the Decca label, but nothing much had come of it. In the latter part of 1950, Eleanor Corrigan, who was the publicity agent for *Your Hit Parade* on CBS radio, heard him sing with Mark Warnow's orchestra at a tribute to Hollywood composers. Struck by his voice, she sought him out to tell him he ought to record. He brushed off the suggestion.

A few weeks later at a christening party at Dean Jagger's house, Corrigan heard Mitchum sing again. "He sounded like a young Bing Crosby to me," she says. "None of us were feeling any pain, so I informed Dorothy and him that I was going to try to get him a recording contract. Later at the bar, I ran into a CBS v.p. and told him Bob ought to have his own radio show. He looked at me and said, 'You must be working for the wrong network. Don't you realize he has a marijuana arrest over his head?'

"That didn't stop me," Corrigan recalls. "I got on the phone with Paul Weston, who was head of Columbia Records. He became interested in having Mitchum do some songs with Jo Stafford, their top girl singer."

Weston offered Mitchum the opportunity to record "No, John, No" with Stafford, plus "Roving Gambler" and "Streets of Laredo" as a single. Howard Hughes immediately rejected Columbia's proposal, but Mitchum announced he was proceeding. This brought the following memo from the RKO legal department: "We are informed that notwithstanding refusal of permission you have announced that you will make the records. This will be a breach of our employment contract with you dated August 18, 1947, and would cause irreparable damage. We intend to take legal action enjoining recording, distribution or sales or broadcasting of any commercial records by you."

Mitchum never bothered to reply, but six months later the RKO legal department informed Hughes that no recordings had been cut.

With such creative endeavors prohibited, a bored Mitchum indulged his youthful fondness for practical jokes. Early on, when his friend Steve Brodie was working in a swords-and-wigs picture on a sound stage adjoining Mitchum's, Brodie suddenly felt an excruciating pain in his left leg during a dueling scene. He went to his dressing room, pulled down his leather pants and saw a bruise the size of an orange on his calf. Nobody could figure out what had caused it. The studio nurse gave him a pill for pain and he resumed work. That evening before he went home, the script girl said to him, "Mr. Brodie, you have a lot of good friends at RKO." Brodie replied that he certainly hoped so, and she responded, "But you have one especially good friend who's always getting into devilment." Brodie immediately concluded she was speaking of Mitchum; an inquiry revealed he very likely had been shot by an air gun.

At seven p.m. that night Brodie purchased a small box of itching powder at a Hollywood Boulevard magic shop. Returning to the studio he told the janitor he had been having a drink with Mitchum and had left his wallet in his friend's dressing room. The janitor threw him a pass key. Brodie went to Mitchum's quarters and proceeded to dust the powder under the band of his hat, in the armpits of his shirt, in the crotch and behind the knees of his trousers. Then he joined the janitor for a couple of friendly drinks and left.

Next morning, under the lights, Mitchum began to act as if he were suffering from St. Vitus's dance. He attempted to scratch every place at once, saying he thought he was going crazy. At this point, his helpful friend Brodie happened along and suggested a cold shower. "That's the worst possible anti-dote," he said in recalling the incident. "Once you get cold water on itching powder you can't get it off." As a result Mitchum was unable to work for three days at the cost of ten thousand dollars a day.*

Time passed. Mitchum terrorized the set with a water pistol, firing it at three paces. He also retold how, as a neophyte, he innocently ate a slice of raw onion and roquefort dressing before playing a love scene with Greer Garson. Now he deliberately partook of garlic before doing an intimate scene with feisty Susan Hayward. She said nothing, but before their next embrace, *she* ate garlic. One again a truce was temporarily called.

In spite of such behavior, and his claim that his gate bore a sign reading "No Peddlers, Actors or Agents Allowed," undoubtedly, aside from the $3,750 a week he was collecting, what made his working days bearable were the friendships he was developing among actors. Despite his insistence that he preferred the company of plain workers who were not connected with the motion-picture industry, he was accumulating more and more ties with creative people.

Occasionally, as in *My Forbidden Past*, the expected screen conflagration failed to ignite. As Lynn Bowers wrote in the *Los Angeles Examiner*: "It seems to us that Robert Mitchum wasn't as enthusiastic about his love scenes with the lushly lovely Ava as some fellows might have been, given the op-

---

*Two years later, Mitchum approached Brodie in a bar, tapped him on the shoulder and knocked him off the stool, saying, "I just heard about the itching powder, you dirty son-of-a-bitch!" Brodie responded that he still had the bruise, but to this day Mitchum denies giving it to him.

portunity." Nevertheless, the two performers became good buddies with Mitchum calling her "Honest Ave—because she doesn't have to pad her bust."

Mitchum and director John Farrow met quite by accident and embarked on a marathon drinking match. At one point Farrow said he would like to do a picture with Mitchum, and the actor responded that he would enjoy working with the director. During the next four hours they dreamed up a story, decided on Susan Hayward as the ideal leading woman, and assembled an entire package in their heads. Congratulating themselves on their accomplishment, they staggered to their cars. Next morning a hung-over Farrow called to inquire whether Mitchum was serious about proceeding with their plans. Mitchum hedged. Eventually, each man revealed that he remembered nothing about the story they had spent the evening fantasizing. Nevertheless, Mitchum eventually spoke to The Phantom and RKO took on *Where Danger Lives*, produced and directed by Farrow, with Mitchum, and Hughes's latest protégée, Faith Domergue, in the leads.

Farrow also directed him in *His Kind of Woman* ("What kind of woman would that be?" Mitchum inquired), which was completed May 23, 1950, but sat on the shelf unreleased and waiting to be doctored until September 1951. It was one of the twenty-three shelved films that Jerry Wald and Norman Krasna proposed to rescue as part of their five-year contract at RKO. Originally intended to launch Jane Russell and Mitchum as a smoldering love team, the film was notable mostly for Vincent Price's comic, flamboyant performance as a hammy matinee idol.

His Kind of Woman may not have been considered a very good picture at the time it was made, but it was what Hollywood called a happy set. In a small part, at least, this was attributable to Mitchum's generosity. Each lunchtime he would lead between twenty and twenty-five of his coworkers, including Jane, Farrow, Price, Raymond Burr, Anthony Caruso, Jim Backus, Marjorie Reynolds, his stand-in Tim Wallace and others to his bungalow. "All the pals would fall into place and he'd yell to his secretary—Reva Frederick—'Hey, ole Reev, break out the ice.' After everybody had a snort, he'd yell, 'Hey, ole Reev, get your hard ass in here. Let's have Chinese food for every-body!' Well, even from the Coral Isles across the way, it had to cost fifty or sixty bucks even in those days. She'd sign for it because he was the only one of us—except Jane when she was there—who was a quote movie star unquote who could afford to pick up the check," says Jim Backus. "He never thought of it that way, but he was."

If Mitchum did recognize his star power, he was careful not to flaunt it before his coworkers. On several occasions when he realized his stand-in had had a rough night, he stood-in for the stand-in. Also, in the early 1950s it was the producer's option whether or not there would be free coffee and rolls on the set for the actors and crew. During *His Kind of Woman*, Tony Caruso volunteered to drop by and drive Mitchum to the studio each morning since they lived so close together. After a couple of days he began asking Caruso to let him off at the coffee shop across from RKO. He said he wanted Caruso to be on time, but that he was going to be a little late. If anyone asked, he was getting his coffee. For several mornings, Mitchum, who had a reputation for punctuality, arrived from thirty to forty-five minutes late. "I finally asked him why he didn't tell them he wanted coffee. He said no, they would catch on pretty quick," Caruso says. "What he was doing was getting it for everybody. If he had complained, they'd only have given it to him. He didn't want that. He just backed off and let them figure out what he was after. When the coffee cakes appeared, he was on time again. That's the way he operated."

A problem with the picture arose when Hughes became beguiled by Price's outrageous portrayal, and added a long comedic sequence. This scene weighted the picture toward comedy. "I think Bob was disappointed at the direction the script took, because if he had known about the comic tilt, he would have played his character in a lighter vein," Price says. "But he's such a dear man it would never cross his mind to be upset. He's heaven to work with. And he's just really one of those diamond in the rough types, in whose character you can't find any sort of holes because he's so open and honest. He's a dear man.

"He writes his poetry and his songs and tells his stories—

some true, some not. It doesn't matter, because they're all funny," Price continues. "But he is a complete anachronism. He claims he doesn't care about acting, but he's an extraordinary actor. He's one of that group of people in Hollywood who are such extraordinary personalities that people forget they're marvelous actors."

Price is just as enthusiastic about Jane Russell. "He and Jane and I all became friends," he says. "Jane I still see and talk to a lot, and I think she really adored Bob, loved him deeply, but without any hankypanky. Because she's a very straight girl. And he loved her. It was just a marvelous combination."

One story about Russell that Mitchum tells occurred during the promotional tour for *His Kind of Woman*. Sometimes he says that Russell, Price and he were in Des Moines, Iowa, at other times, Chicago. Wherever they were, Russell was being interviewed by an uptight reporter much to Price's and Mitchum's amusement. "He asked Jane all about the church she built in the Valley for her family, and she said, yes it was true, she had hammered on the shingles herself. Then the reporter asked her, 'What about this big ad for the movie where you're leaning over?'—and she was leaning waaaay over, I can tell you. The reporter asks, 'How does this go along with your church activities?'" Mitchum recalls. "Well, Vincent and I were sitting on the window sill about thirty stories up, and if he hadn't caught me, I'd have gone right over backward and messed up the Loop, because Jane just looked straight at the guy and said, 'Christians have big tits, too.'"

Initially Hughes had envisioned teaming Russell and Mitchum in a series of films loosely patterned after those made by Bogart and Bacall. But aside from *His Kind of Woman* only *Macao* ever was made. Begun in 1950, but not finished until 1952, it was nominally directed by Josef von Sternberg, although Nicholas Ray reworked portions of it and later estimated that he was responsible for approximately fifty percent of it. Like so many other RKO films, this was an unambitious formula melodrama. It is therefore surprising that Hughes and his associates were able to introduce so much confusion into what should have been basically simple action. In a day when ambiguity was a dirty word, *Macao*'s murky development brought some harsh judgments from critics and audiences alike. Commenting on the problems in his autobiography, von Sternberg wrote: "This was made under the supervision of six different men. . . . And instead of fingers in the pie, a half dozen clowns immersed various parts of their anatomy in it."

Mitchum, Bill Bendix and some of the other actors in the cast blamed von Sternberg's autocratic Prussian methods for bringing on the trouble. The whole company went on location, sleeping outdoors in big tents mounted on cement foundations. By day, von Sternberg harassed the actors with his perfectionist demands. Night after night the actors retaliated by visiting calamities upon him. Once they collapsed his tent as he was in the midst of getting into his pajamas. Another night they placed a pebble in the hubcap of his car. On still another they rubbed limburger cheese on his engine. Asked why they did it, Mitchum said von Sternberg took himself and the picture too seriously. "It was just another crummy melodrama," he explained. "We weren't out to win the Pulitzer Prize or anything."

Macao marked the last film Mitchum began while under probation. And on January 12, 1951, his County Deputy Probation Officer, David Byrne, announced that Mitchum's term would end that day. He assured the public that no favoritism had been shown. Mitchum had reported weekly and obtained permission whenever it was necessary for him to leave the country as part of his work routine.

Then on January 31, Judge Nye officially wiped away the felony conviction, ended probation and expunged the record of the case to remove any legal disabilities Mitchum might otherwise have suffered.

CHAPTER 10

In 1951 Mitchum was earning $4,500 a week and had managed to extricate himself from the financial quagmire in which his legal problems had flung him. He was also free from the restraints that probation had placed upon him.

Late in September he set out with the *One Minute to Zero* company for Colorado. RKO had obtained the cooperation of the Defense Department in shooting a Korean war story utilizing official Army equipment. The location was six thousand feet above sea level, twelve miles southwest of Colorado Springs. A couple of weeks into filming, premature winter weather hit, creating grueling working conditions for the actors even though they wore winter underwear beneath their summer uniforms. To warm themselves after a particularly bitter day's filming on November 8, Mitchum, Charles McGraw, Richard Egan and two or three other cast members stopped for a hot-buttered rum at the crowded Red Fox Bar on the ground floor of the Alamo Hotel where the company was staying.

McGraw and a six-foot, 180-pound private got into a heated exchange which escalated into a shoving match. When it looked as if McGraw were going to get roughed up, Mitchum moved in, seized the private by the lapels, shook him and attempted to prevent him from throwing any more punches. The soldier skillfully extricated himself from the clinch and loosed a wild uppercut at Mitchum. In the jammed area, each man was handicapped in landing punches, but as the crowd pushed back, the two fighters sent glasses crashing and knocked over tables and a piano. Sending his opponent to the floor with a punch, Mitchum dived after him, and the two of them mixed it up until onlookers separated them.

Mitchum rose, only slightly the worse for wear, but the soldier lay unconscious until removed by stretcher to an ambulance which took him to the Camp Carson Hospital.

During the investigation that followed, an off-duty MP claimed that Mitchum had kicked the private in the face. McGraw, Egan and several soldiers contradicted this assertion and no charges were brought. Mitchum insisted he had been "aggressive like a policeman" in an attempt to break up the fight.

Next morning on November 9, newspaper headlines screamed:

ROBERT MITCHUM IN BAR BRAWL
SOLDIER WINDS UP IN HOSPITAL

The incident might have rated only a paragraph had Mitchum's adversary not turned out to be a Camp Carson football player, a former light heavyweight professional boxer with a record of twenty-six wins—nineteen of them knockouts—and two losses between 1946 and 1947. In one bout, he had rated a spot in the semiwindup match on the first Joe Louis–Jersey Joe Walcott heavyweight title match. Naturally, the clash between the ex-fighter and the screen's bad boy rated coverage.

"Mitchum was blamed for something he didn't start," says Egan. "The military authorities were going to withdraw permission for us to continue filming until Howard Hughes stepped in and pulled some strings to get the cameras rolling again. But there was no question of Bob kicking anyone. Rightfully, he could have pressed charges against the private for assault with a deadly weapon. That's what the hands of a boxer are classified outside the ring. But Bob refused to say anything to defend himself, which is typical of him."

One group of acquaintances cannot be shaken from the belief that he is basically what he seems on the screen: a hard-drinking, rough-talking swinger who is destined for endless trouble. At the other extreme are those who perceive him as the most sensitive, caring, creative and lonely man in Hollywood.

Jerry Devine holds a middle-of-the-road position. "I can understand what both groups feel," he says. "Because I think I saw him before he really had his act put together. There were a lot of Bobs floating around in the early days. He hadn't consolidated them into the image he would wear so successfully later.

"Having written radio crime shows, I think I have a pretty good reading on con men," Devine says. "And Bob—I say this in a complimentary sense—is a master con man. One of his charms in those days—and possibly still is—was that he could become anything you wanted him to be. If he was with roughnecks, he'd mix it up. And he could fight. If he was with a group of hookers, he'd use all the hooker language. He automatically fell into that chameleonlike thing that good con men can do. When he was with a gathering of priests—which would be unlikely—he would talk about his days as an altar boy."

Unlikely? While filming *One Minute to Zero*, Mitchum found he had a great deal in common with the rising young leading man Richard Egan. Egan was later to say, "Working with him I learned a lesson of generosity that I have seldom encountered in this business. To him the better the actors, the better the picture. That may not seem like much, but it is not as common as you would think. Many a career has been inhibited because a star didn't want strong competition. Mitchum not only didn't object, he welcomed you."

Back in Southern California and eager to share the acquaintance of this remarkable fellow, Egan called Mitchum the next time his brother came down from San Francisco and asked to bring him to the Mitchums' home. Father Willis Egan and Mitchum hit it off beautifully and began a friendship that included endless hours of their exchanging religious and philosophical speculation.

* * *

One Minute to Zero, an insignificant movie from any vantage point, was shoved out of the Criterion Theater in Manhattan on October 24 to make way for Mitchum's *The Lusty Men* which proved an important stepping stone in his career. Among the forty-odd films in which he had appeared up to then he selected it along with *The Story of G.I. Joe* and *Rachel and the Stranger* as one of this three favorites.

Over the years, it has remained special enough to him to stimulate the Sherwood Anderson syndrome. In 1982 he told an interviewer that there had been no script—only an idea of *his*. In his recall, he'd suggested the subject to producer Jerry Wald and then he and director Nicholas Ray had contacted Tom Lea, who had written a story about rodeos for *Life* magazine. Lea's response to their query about cowboys had turned out to be so colorful that Ray had said, "Great! We'll shoot his letter!"

Wald and Hughes had insisted, Mitchum continued, on assigning Horace McCoy to do a script. It turned out to be totally unusable, so Mitchum and Ray improvised a story which they pitched to Susan Hayward. When she asked whether it was written, Ray grabbed up a handful of scratch paper, waved it under her nose and assured her it was. According to Mitchum, he and Ray wrote most of the scenes although eventually Wald took a hand with the "finale," which turned out to be so bad that Mitchum's secretary finagled a key to the film vault, searched out the final reel with Wald's scene on it and tossed it into the incinerator, which necessitated reshooting the ending. "It turned out to be a pretty good picture—even though it had a lousy title," commented its star.

David Dortort, who was later to become the producer-writer of the long-running *Bonanza* television series, has a less fanciful version of *The Lusty Men*'s genesis. "The way it came about was that Jerry Wald and Norman Krasna had recently brought their unit over to produce and release through RKO. I had worked for Jerry at Warner Brothers, and I came up with this original idea which I called *Cowpoke*. Until that time the only contemporary western figures in pictures were Gene Autry and Roy Rogers, singing cowboys. But those films had nothing to do with real working people on ranches. I said, 'Let's do an in-depth, realistic kind of story of the transient, the day laborer who has to break broncs and do everything, and then when he is forty-five, too old to get in the saddle, is fired with no pension. We'll show how in order to compensate for that these men go to rodeos to pick up some day money. The day money is literally what keeps a lot of them going, especially the ones courageous enough to take on marriage.'"

Dortort says Wald was sufficiently fascinated with his pitch to send him on the Rodeo Cowboy Association circuit for four or five weeks to pick up color and general research on rodeo cowboys. By the time he returned, Wald had read an article in *Life* magazine by Claude Stanush about a rodeo cowboy named Bob Crosby. A national champion for three consecutive years, Crosby had had nearly every bone in his body broken at least once. Wald proposed buying the article so Dortort would be free to incorporate whatever he felt was necessary to add dimension to his script. Dortort agreed.

He wrote a screenplay which Wald showed to a director who liked it. Somehow Henry Fonda also obtained the script and upon encountering Dortort told him, "*Cowpoke* is one of the most creative, original, thrilling scripts, I've read." The neophyte Dortort responded, "Why don't you play the part?" only to be told by Fonda, "I would love to be able to play it, but Jerry wants to go with Mitchum." In point of fact, Wald wanted Mitchum badly enough to agree to pay RKO fifteen thousand dollars weekly for ten weeks and to give Mitchum costar billing opposite Susan Hayward in order to obtain his services.

About Mitchum's response, Dortort says, "He just flipped over the script because he said he'd been a rodeo bum himself briefly." As Jerry Devine pointed out, when you're with hookers talk hooker talk, etc.

Dortort says the original director withdrew at this point and Nicholas Ray read the script with an eye toward taking over. "He felt it needed a little implementation of the love story—the so-called triangle," Dortort remembers. "I had been concentrating on the plight of the rodeo man, the reasons he went into the rodeo—sort of doing a *Grapes of Wrath* around the rodeo economy. Jerry said he'd like to bring in Horace McCoy, a fine writer with a lot more experience than I in writing about women. So Horace and I collaborated on the rewrite.

"Horace was quite a drinker, and I used to drink with him. Over drinks at Lucy's Restaurant on Melrose, we decided how the credits should go. He felt it should be Screenplay by David Dortort and Horace McCoy, and I, in a mood brought on by a vast alcoholic haze, insisted it be the other way around. I said, 'You're older than I am.' And that's the way the Writer's Guild approved it.

"Mitchum may have added a line, ad-libbed on the set as actors sometimes do, but nothing more," Dortort says. Also contrary to the impression Mitchum likes to convey about not taking his craft seriously is Dortort's vivid recollection of the explosive fights between the actor and the director over interpretation of scenes. "Each one would appeal to Jerry Wald, who was, deep down, a devout coward. He would duck both of them so that sometimes decisions were made right on the set. Sometimes Mitchum would win and sometimes Ray would. But Nick felt he could always get the final word in the cutting room. Now *that* caused some tremendous fights between him and Jerry, because Jerry wanted the film a little more commercial.

"Finally we went to the sneak preview out in Pasadena. We looked at the picture and it was gorgeous. Mitchum, Susan Hayward, Arthur Kennedy and Arthur Hunnicutt—everyone in it was so right. The audience response was enthusiastic and we were all very pleased with it. It was a grand night."

What viewers responded to in 1952 and still respond to in 1984 is the gritty, demythologizing of the legend of American cowboys as romantic figures. And perhaps never before had Mitchum delivered as affecting, authentic and powerful a performance. In this instance, even the *Saturday Review*'s Arthur Knight, who often was unimpressed with Mitchum's understated style, wrote that he was "outstanding in a generally superior cast."

Mitchum had seriously applied himself because he considered the material worth his time and attention. Whenever he had contempt for a script, he turned up without bothering to prepare for his role. This applied to the two films in which Howard Hughes assigned him to appear opposite Jean Simmons.

The first script, known as *Beautiful but Dangerous, She*

Had to Say Yes and *Enough for Happiness* before it became *She Couldn't Say No*, pleased Mitchum under none of those titles. Rather than appear in it, he went on suspension on April 29. Though his only daughter had been born less than two months before, he literally dropped out of sight. No one—not his wife, his agents or his secretary—knew how to reach him to warn of the studio's notification that his default might deprive RKO of Jean Simmons and that they would hold him responsible for any loss.

Finally on the evening of May 8, he telephoned his secretary, Reva, to say he was in Mississippi, headed for New Orleans, and would "probably" return to Los Angeles sometime the following week. Early on the ninth, Reva phoned the William Morris Agency and delivered his message. She said that Mitchum had refused, as he had done since being called for *Beautiful but Dangerous*, to speak to anyone at the agency or the studio. Later in the day, she called an executive at RKO and notified him that her boss was headed for Dallas to visit his brother, John, and she might possibly get in touch with him when he arrived. Through her, RKO made contact with the recalcitrant actor and persuaded him to fly to Los Angeles on the twelfth of May. Next day, he appeared to take his medical examination for cast insurance, passing easily. Reluctantly, he undertook the lead in RKO's feckless attempt to resuscitate the screwball comedy genre. The result was pathetic. Mitchum, who played a Cary Grant–type doctor, sourly suggested RKO take him out of acting and make him a script doctor instead.

Viewing the second Simmons film, *Angel Face*—loosely inspired by yacht murderer Beulah Louise Overell, who blew up her parents—it is not at once apparent why Mitchum resisted making this film so strenuously. That is, not until one hears Otto Preminger's story.

In his autobiography, Preminger tells of being given the script of *Murder Story*—the original title—by his employer, Darryl Zanuck. In repayment for past favors from Hughes, Zanuck proposed to lend Preminger to Hughes to direct the film. Preminger found the screenplay unshootable, but reluctantly agreed to talk over the assignment after Hughes arranged a middle-of-the-night meeting on the streets of Hollywood. It seemed that he wanted to get one more film from Jean Simmons before her contract expired, but he had only eighteen working days to do it in. To complicate matters, he and the actress had had an acrimonious personal quarrel; to spite him she had cut off her hair at the roots. She was confident she had thwarted him and he was determined to outsmart her. Zanuck, he confided, had assured him that Preminger could accomplish the feat in the allotted time. In return, Hughes promised the director the right to hire as many writers as necessary to put the script in shape. He further promised that Preminger would work free of interference. "All I want to see is a test of the lady wearing a wig of long beautiful black hair," Preminger quotes Hughes as saying.

Preminger had the script rewritten and retitled *Angel Face*. As eventually shot, Jean Simmons plays a psychopathic beauty who attempts to murder her stepmother, fails, vamps the ambulance driver who has revived her stepmother, persuades him to come to work as their chauffeur, engages in a torrid affair with him, tampers with the transmission of her stepmother's auto and sends the hated stepmother and, unintentionally, her father hurtling over the cliff to their deaths. On trial for murder, she and the chauffeur marry in hopes the jury will acquit them. Freed, the chauffeur prepares to leave her, and she kills both of them by sending *her* Jaguar backward over the cliff.

Filming began on June 18 and was fraught with dissension. Simmons was miserable. Mitchum was unhappy. On the first day of filming, according to one cast member, Preminger was delayed in arriving by a last-minute change. When at last he walked onto the set, it "looked like a Gypsy caravan or an orgy scene from the Bible. People were smoking, drinking, dancing to portable victrolas."

Shotgun Britton, the 1928 All-American football player turned makeup artist, was the first to draw Preminger's ire. "Mr. Makeup Man! The actor here needs attention. Why is he not ready? Hurry!"

"Okay, Hitler," Shot responded. "Keep your goddamned boots on. I'm comin'. It's shady and downhill, you know."

Preminger fired him on the spot.

At that Mitchum intervened. "I wouldn't do that if I were you. I wouldn't fire anybody, Dutchman, because The Phantom is going to put him right back on." With that he walked out.

Next morning, all of them returned, including Shot. Both men had sent messages of complaint to Hughes.

Undeterred, Preminger browbeat one person after another to keep to schedule. The climactic courtroom scene fell on a Friday. The defendants, Jean Simmons and Mitchum, had finished their big scenes. They had only to react. The defense lawyer, played by Leon Ames, delivered his summation and, after a tongue-lashing by Preminger, repeated it. The time was getting on toward five p.m. when Preminger called for Jim Backus, whom he had cast as the district attorney. Suddenly Backus realized that if he lapsed in his lines so much as once during his four-page summation all the extras would have to be called back for a half-hour's work the following Monday. "That I realized and it was enough that I realized it," Backus says. "But Preminger said, 'Now, Mr. Backus, you're going to play this scene and I am going to do it in one shot. Not going to break it up with the camera. And if you make mistake, let me remind you that people will be in terrible trouble.'

"So I started with the handicap of that warning. I looked over at a big, fake-silver water pitcher that you find in all courtroom scenes. Bob and Jean filled their glasses. I began my speech. In the parlance of the one-camera take with a crane, I went to each member of the jury pleading continuously. It wasn't cut one by one. I kept having to cross the courtroom to an engine that had been removed from the car. I knew nothing about automobiles. And I had to use so many technical terms. 'The transmission apperscope, as you can see—do you happen to be a mechanic, sir?' Gibberish. But I pleaded to each member of the jury and crossed to the automobile several times. As I came to the end of my plea, I had a piece of business where I crossed, poured a glass of water, looked at Bob and Jean and said, 'The State rests.'

"This I knew, and I decided to milk it. So I took all the time in the world. Very dramatically, like I'd seen Lionel Barrymore do, I looked at Bob with those half-lidded eyes of his. I deliberately reached over and grabbed the pitcher. I filled the glass, lifted it and swallowed. It was straight vodka! Well, when your stomach is expecting water and gets vodka—well, I sputtered and thought, *Oh, my God, I gotta do this thing over again and we'll have to wait until Monday to do it*. I waited for that fateful moment. Finally Preminger spoke. 'It's a print! I like what Mr. Backus do with the coughing. It's very dramatic. I like that—him choking almost to death. Very good. Yes.'"

Angel Face, coolly received by the critics, has attracted a devoted following. In his program notes for a showing of it at the Los Angeles County Art Museum, Tim Hunter wrote admiringly of the film's abstract quality and noted that rarely has an American melodrama proceeded with such cryptic, implacable logic toward its somber ending.

Hunter concludes: "The Mitchum character, of course, believes he's in total control of the situation right to the point when he's driven backward off the cliff to his death. In his prime at RKO, Mitchum was the great *loser* hero of the American screen. Always quick to figure all the angles, he was nonetheless not smart enough to keep himself from getting killed. In *Angel Face* he virtually sleepwalks to his doom. It is certainly Mitchum's most somnolent performance and one of his most oddly impressive. He and Simmons surely smolder up a storm in this dark, brooding, jewel of a *film noir*."

Gossip had it that the smoldering on screen was carried off screen as well. Mitchum, on occasion, has half-facetiously gone on record as believing that he should always have affairs with his leading ladies, but that his wife would object.

Despite the friction engendered between Mitchum and the studio because of his resistance to the assignments being handed to him, RKO exercised their option at five thousand dollars a week on September 21, 1952. From Mitchum's point of view it must have seemed that the studio had lost interest in building his career and was willing to sell his services to anyone willing to pay the price. Although 20th Century–Fox and Wayne–Fellows would be successful in obtaining his presence, an examination of RKO's records indicates numerous offers were turned down. Lester Cowan, who had given Mitchum his big break, was refused when he tried to borrow him for an all-star production he was working on. Republic attempted and failed to persuade anyone at RKO even to read a script in which they proposed to costar him with Joan Crawford. Universal–International was turned down when they attempted to secure his services for the leading role in *Lone Hand* and again when they submitted the screenplay for *Saskatchewan*. In his report on the latter, the chief story analyst spelled out the businesslike view the studio took in regard to Mitchum's career. Of the script, he wrote: "Adequate romance can do Mitchum no harm *if* one wanted, but chances are U–I will do this on an economy basis and consequently it will have no production values. Kind of role normally filled by Jeff Chandler, Steve McNally, Randy Scott. After *Lusty Men*, we should be wary of using Mitchum in ordinary westerns like this. Picture has no stature and is not 'big' in any sense. *Unless* we are no longer interested in furthering Mitchum's career and increasing his stature, my vote would be no." That vote prevailed.

Between November 10, 1952, and January 23, 1953, however, RKO loaned him to 20th Century–Fox for *White Witch Doctor* to fulfill part of the reciprocal agreement under which they had obtained Susan Hayward's services. This tale of a nurse and cynical trader's adventures in the Congo circa 1907 might have interested him had producer Otto Lang and director Henry Hathaway persuaded the studio to send the production company there. As it was, a second unit was dispatched to capture local color while the soap-opera plot was acted out on the backlot. Aware that Hayward was a perfectionist who had no time for levity, Mitchum refused to accept any stand-in except Tim Wallace, for he was determined to have some amusing company. When there was a complaint about Wallace's $175-a-week salary, Mitchum straight-facedly informed 20th's representatives that the rough-speaking Wallace was also his drama coach. Truth be told, he was his confidant, gofer, drinking buddy and pal.

Later, director Hathaway commented that although his relationship with Mitchum was civil, he always felt a lack of contact. "He's such a bright guy, but he started very few conversations with me. If I started one, he was never mean or insulting, but he just looked at me with those droopy eyes and I got the feeling he was thinking, *This is my life. Why don't you leave me alone?*"

Dissatisfied as Mitchum was with *Witch Doctor*, he was even less contented with the one in store for him at RKO. Once again, as he had prior to his period of probation, his professional frustration started him bar hopping and hanging out until all hours, ignoring his family. And once again Dorothy began to make *her* dissatisfactions known. Now as the mother of three it was inconvenient to pack up and return to her family in Delaware. This time when she laid down her ultimatum, he was the one who packed his clothes and moved into an apartment for a trial separation. It lasted two weeks. On March 16, he and Dorothy dined together to celebrate their thirteenth wedding anniversary and a week later he was back home with his family. If all of their differences had not been settled, it had become apparent to both that the positive elements of their relationship far outweighed the negative ones.

"She is East Coast—down-east crafty," said a former employee in analyzing the relationship. "It's not that I want to say she is a calming influence on him, but I really feel he enjoys her company. Like every man in pictures, he'll get sidetracked. So lots of times in the early days Mama had to sit home alone, but the kids were little so it didn't disturb her too much as long as she knew he wasn't in any trouble. At least, that's what she said to me once. There were a lot of people at that time asking her why she didn't divorce that knothead. Her attitude was, 'Well, why should I? I'm the mother of his children. And anyway where would I find anybody like him?' Deep down I think she weighed the life she was living against what it would have been if she'd married some yahoo who went to an office or owned a little business. Anyway for all his tomcatting around, Mitch has always been a family man."

Shortly after their reconciliation, Mitchum prepared to go to Mexico where RKO would be shooting a Technicolor, 3-D, action-adventure film, *Second Chance*, costarring Howard Hughes's girl-of-the-moment Linda Darnell. Arrangements were made for the Mitchum children to be cared for and Dorothy accompanied him—enjoying one of those benefits the former employee had alluded to.

Both Mitchums enjoyed their time in Taxco and Cuernavaca. They agreed that the Mexicans had developed a way of doing their jobs yet reserving time to enjoy their lives. The pace attracted both of them. Then Mitchum discovered a two-family fishing village on the mainland side of the Gulf of California at the mouth of a river. He was eager to acquire a large parcel of land at once before others discovered it. Dorothy was reluctant about bringing three children to an isolated spot where there were no doctors, hospitals or other modern necessities. The acquisition was postponed and although Mitchum talked about retiring there for a time, the subject gradually faded from his conversation.

As for the picture, the leading characters in the familiar triangle were a rubber-legged prizefighter (Mitchum), a professional killer (Jack Palance) and a fugitive gangmoll (Linda Darnell). When columnist Hedda Hopper visited the location and asked what Mitchum thought of the movie, he once again annoyed RKO by proving a tougher critic than the man on *Newsweek* and than reviewers on several metropolitan newspapers. Nevertheless, he refused to pretend he had enjoyed making it.

Then, in mid-July, after a hassle over who was to receive top billing, Mitchum's representatives triumphed over the Marilyn Monroe forces and RKO instructed him to report to 20th Century–Fox for *River of No Return*. "He got the best billing. She dominated the choice scenes," Ruth Waterbury said at the time. "Zanuck and Preminger—he's the director—are certainly going to protect the studio's hottest property no matter what the billing. But it won't do Bob any harm to be seen opposite her. If Joe DiMaggio weren't around, I have a feeling they'd be a very hot item."

As it turned out, Mitchum fared surprisingly well as the secretive frontiersman, who, after his release from jail, turns up in a tent city during the 1870s to be reunited with his ten-year-old son (Tommy Rettig). The boy has been looked after by a sexy saloon singer (Marilyn Monroe). Mitchum and Rettig settle on a wilderness farm which is adjacent to the River of No Return. One morning, Mitchum sees a couple on a raft in distress. He rescues them and they turn out to be the saloon singer and her gambler husband (Rory Calhoun). He learns they are on their way to register a gold claim which Calhoun has won in a poker game. When Mitchum tries to persuade them not to return to the treacherous river, hot-headed Calhoun steals his horse and gun and vanishes. Monroe remains to nurse Mitchum and look after Rettig. An Indian attack forces the three to flee on the raft. Pressures from the attacking Indians combined with the dangers of the river cause Monroe and Mitchum to quarrel and in a fit of temper she tells him she knows he has been in prison for murder. The boy overhears this and rejects his father's attempted explanation of the crime. Back in the city, Monroe seeks out Calhoun and urges him to clear himself with Mitchum. He flourishes a gun and when she tries to take it away from him, Rettig, who is looking at a rifle in the country store, sees Monroe is in danger and shoots Calhoun. Mitchum tongue-lashes her for bringing about more trouble and she angrily returns to the saloon to resume her career. Mitchum obtains a wagon for his and Rettig's return to the farm. Then at the last moment he stomps into the barroom, tosses Monroe over his shoulder and the three of them set out to make a new way of life.

All but a few of the scenes were shot on location to allow Preminger and the cinematographer the opportunity to show off the new Cinemascope wide-screen process of capturing scenic wonders and hair-raising action. A special train was hired to carry the cast and crew plus Marilyn Monroe's coach Natasha Lytess, Monroe's husband, Joe DiMaggio, and his pal, ticket broker Georgie Solotaire to Banff in the Canadian Rockies.

Mitchum and Monroe, acquaintances from his Lockheed and her *hausfrau* days, were delighted to be working together. But problems arose on the set as soon as shooting began because Preminger was exasperated by Miss Lytess's insistence that Monroe drop "the soft, slurred voice," which Preminger liked, in favor of what he later described as "such grave ar-tic-yew-lay-shun that her violent lip movements made it impossible to photograph her." According to him, Mitchum saved the scenes by ignoring Monroe's stilted delivery and facial contortions until Preminger was ready for the cameras to roll. Then Mitchum would swat her on her derriere and say, "Now stop that nonsense, madam! Let's play it like human beings. Come on!" Startled, she would allow her natural talent to eradicate the mannerisms that had been smeared over her naturally ingratiating personality.

Finally, however, Preminger lost patience and barred Miss Lytess from the set. Until Monroe succeeded in getting Darryl Zanuck to countermand the director's edict, Mitchum and she enjoyed a light, kidding relationship. "Marilyn was always filled with sly humor," he says. "She'd jokingly say, 'What a set! A girl doesn't get much action around here!' Once when she'd said something of the kind, my stand-in piped up, 'What about a round robin?' Marilyn didn't know what that was. 'You and me and Mitch,' he said. 'OOOOOH, that would kill me!' Marilyn replied. 'Nobody's died from it yet,' he told her. 'I bet they have,' she said. 'But in the papers it says the girl died from natural causes.'"

During a scene in the barn, as Mitchum took Monroe in his arms, she began to move slightly as she tilted back her head and opened her lips tremulously. Suddenly, he looked at Preminger and inquired in a loud voice, "How the hell can I take aim when she's undulating like that?" Nobody laughed more heartily than Monroe.

What both Monroe and Mitchum shared was respect for each other's courage. He earned hers early. In one of the few scenes shot at the studio, he stood on an oak raft in front of a process shot of the raging river while special effects experts shot steel-headed arrows all around him and between his feet. The force of the projectors drove the arrows so deeply into the oak that heavy tongs were required to pull them out. This action was repeated five or six times before Preminger was satisfied he had obtained what he wanted.

After returning from Canada, Mitchum granted an interview in which he expressed his admiration for Monroe: "This new medium Cinemascope is great, but it's going to turn a lot of actors gray over night. . . . The amazing thing is how well Marilyn and Tommy Rettig, who plays my son in the movie, have adapted to it."

Later, he revealed that Monroe had tried to save his life. She, Rettig and he were on a raft on the river when he realized they were headed for a huge rock beyond which was a waterfall. He cautioned her and the boy to lie flat on their bellies on the raft, telling them not to panic but warning that this could be a matter of life and death because the raft could be torn to pieces. "Pretty soon I saw a little rescue boat," he said. "There was only room in it for Marilyn and the boy. And it already had a big hole in the bottom. But Marilyn refused to get aboard unless they squeezed me in. She said, 'He's sick and besides he wouldn't be here if it weren't for me having to do the scene over.' So I pushed into the leaky boat and held my elbow in the hole to keep the water out. Any girl with that much guts, I think, is a really great dame." At another time, he remarked, "Marilyn and I are a lot alike. There's not one single day when we can do one single thing completely gracefully. We're always in the soup."

After the picture was completed, the Mitchums invited Monroe and DiMaggio to attend get-togethers with the Mandeville Canyon Gang, Marge and Morty Gutterman, Jim and Henny Backus, Jane Greer and Eddie Lasker and Vic Mature as well as various other friends. Looking back, Jerry Devine says of those years, "The Mitchums' move to Mandeville represented a very, very concerted move toward respectability because before that they'd been schlocking around Hollywood and Dorothy wanted to get things pulled together. So they wound up with what were essentially neighborhood people. It was man-wife parties. There were no drugs. Just booze. No wife-swapping or anything exotic. Very circumspect lives, we led there. I mean if a man was going to do anything he did it without any of the group knowing. So the parties were frequent, but it was the kind of thing where the men wound up in the kitchen and the women were off somewhere else talking domestic as hell.

"When people find out I used to live near Mitchum—non-professional people who like to look on the lurid side of our world—they expect to hear about wild parties. So I tell them there was one night when there were these two unescorted ladies at the Mitchums. They perk up. You can see what they expect to hear. I tell them everyone else was man and wife—and the two unescorted ladies were Marilyn Monroe and Jane Russell. They were unescorted because Joe DiMaggio was in New York and Jane's husband, Bob Waterfield, was off playing football someplace. Pretty tame stuff if you're looking for scandal notes."

Still Mitchum's life continued to have its ups and downs. On August 28, while the *River of No Return* company was still in Canada, RKO exercised its seventh and final option for forty out of fifty-two weeks. Mitchum began to balk immediately when he learned that they next proposed to cast him in *Susan Slept Here* opposite Debbie Reynolds. Not that he lacked admiration for the young star. His beef was that he didn't want to attempt a full-fledged singing and dancing part. By November 12, the situation between him and the studio had deteriorated to the point where they were telegraphing him in care of the William Morris office:

YOU ARE INSTRUCTED TO REPORT AT THE OFFICE OF ROSS HASTINGS IN THE RKO GOWER STREET STUDIO, 10 A.M., NOVEMBER 13, 1953 TO ENTER YOUR SERVICES IN "SUSAN SLEPT HERE."

C.J. TEVLIN
RKO PICTURES

The next day, Mitchum replied by wire that he found *Susan Slept Here* "interesting but impossible."

On November 17, he was suspended without pay. When word spread that he was sacrificing five thousand dollars a week because he felt inadequately prepared, one well-meaning friend advised him to do the film. How much could it hurt him? In other words, collect the money and play it safe. Mitchum fixed him with a reptilian gaze and responded, "That's not for living—that's for the cemetery."

He certainly was not playing it safe around midnight on December 3 when Motorcycle Officer J. N. Ryan clocked his black Jaguar traveling at seventy mph through the Wilshire and San Vincente intersection. After a chase, Ryan pulled the vehicle over and ordered Mitchum out of the car. As he emerged, he flipped his keys to Ryan, informing him the driver's license was probably in the trunk and inquiring what he had done.

"Seventy-four in a 35-mile-per-hour zone," Ryan informed him.

"You got any witnesses?" Mitchum reportedly asked.

The officer admitted he did not.

"Well, neither have I. See you in court," Mitchum said, as he produced a second set of keys, scrambled into his Jag and took off, leaving Ryan writing up a ticket for a disappearing car.

Unable to catch the actor, Ryan went to the West Los Angeles station house where he found Officer David Sellers taking a complaint over the phone from Mitchum that someone had stolen his driver's license. Ryan took over the call and demanded to know why Mitchum had run out on him.

"I didn't know you were a cop, Dad," Mitchum said. "I thought you were a bandit or something. So I went home."

A warrant was issued for his arrest, charging him with (a) escape from lawful custody, (b) resisting, obstructing and delaying a public officer in the performance of his duty, and (c) doing seventy miles per hour in a thirty-five mph zone.

He was not at home when the police showed up at the door at three a.m. An obviously distraught Dorothy said that he was out with a friend.

His lawyer quietly posted his $250 bail. Then on December 5, Municipal Judge Freund granted him a continuance until December 8. On that morning the judge dismissed the charge of escaping from lawful custody, telling Mitchum, "It was a rather silly thing to do."

"I agree, Your Honor," the actor replied.

"It was a stupid thing," Judge Freund added, pausing to give Mitchum a chance to agree. When Mitchum remained silent, Judge Freund continued, "However, it was not too serious." He then fined Mitchum $50 for speeding and $150 for resisting, delaying and obstructing Officer Frank and dismissed the escape charges. These fines drew a protest for being excessive from Mitchum's attorney and the judge allowed the $5,000-a-week actor three days to raise the money.

Explaining his behavior later, in view of the fact that he had not been drinking, Mitchum speculated that when faced with a stressful situation, his impulse was to hide his panic by "cracking wise."

Chastened by this latest brush with the law, Mitchum notified RKO on December 21 that he was ready, willing and able to return to work. The studio, however, advised him that his suspension would not be lifted until a decision had been reached on whether to take advantage of the six-weeks time allotted to prepare for use of his services or the time when Dick Powell, his replacement in *Susan Slept Here*, checked off the lot. Since the six-week period would end February 1 and Powell was scheduled to complete his stint on January 20, RKO finally chose the former as a means of letting Mitchum know that all was not forgotten and forgiven.

Questioned about his mounting problems, Dorothy attributed them to his inability to submit to authority of any kind. "Bob has the rugged independence of an Army mule," was her succinct explanation for his trouble-littered past and present.

April 1954 found Bob and Dorothy in Cannes mingling with six hundred other stars, starlets, directors, reporters, photographers, producers, promoters, publicists, party girls, relatives and assorted wheeler dealers at the International Film Festival.

Attending a picnic in connection with the festivities on nearby Lirins Island, the Mitchums were standing on a cliff overlooking the sea when a crowd of sixty photographers approached and began snapping photos. In the ensuing furor, Dorothy got shoved aside in favor of a 26-year-old, Egyptian-born, British actress, who was clad in a pink bikini with a transparent, veiled top over her 37-inch bust. Several photographers urged the starlet to remove the top. After almost no hesitation, she whipped it off. In the resultant scramble for a better angle, three photographers were pushed or fell into the sea, one broke his elbow and another fractured an ankle. Mitchum was joining in the spirit of the occasion with relish until he saw Dorothy glaring at him. To appease her, he threw his arms around the would-be actress to shelter her and covered her naked breasts with his hands, giving the paparazzi photos that would surface in the sleaze press around the world.

A short sharp reproof from his wife was enough to cause him to disengage himself and get through the mob to her. As they fled, he was heard protesting, "What else could I do? I had my back to the sea. Jump into the water?"

Next day, as the Mitchums were checking out, the still irate Dorothy slapped down a shot of the previous day's scene and demanded of newsmen how they would like such a photo of their spouses spread throughout the world. Mitchum was more philosophical about the situation, saying that if the girl wanted to have her picture taken like that it was none of his affair.

Two days later, a publication in Hamburg, Germany, was seized by the police for carrying the photo. And with each new development, Dorothy's response became more intense. Now she threatened that if women continued to come on too strong, she might just begin "to bust them in the chops."

Apparently she said much more to her husband in private because when they arrived at the Los Angeles Airport at approximately the same time as the topless actress on the night of April 19, Mitchum rebuffed suggestions that he pose with the notorious starlet. Unable to resist a quip, however, he informed the press that he had already seen more than enough of her.

With his contract entering its final months, Mitchum's relations with the studio grew increasingly tense. How much of his trouble arose from RKO's determination to punish him and how much from Howard Hughes's sloppy business tactics is difficult to assess. Certainly studio executives found themselves suffering from as many costly and embarrassing snafus as Mitchum did.

Ten days after returning from Cannes, Mitchum received a letter from Lew Schreiber at 20th Century–Fox threatening that 20th would instigate legal proceedings against him if he did not report to the studio to appear opposite Susan Hayward in *Untamed*. Mitchum's agents replied that he was "ready, willing and able to render his personal services for RKO Pictures, Inc. (and by extension to 20th) by contract in accordance with the terms of his said employment up to and including August 15, 1954." As of August 16, however, he was committed to another company. "Since you have threatened to institute legal proceedings against Mr. Mitchum," the agency went on, "this letter is sent to notify you formally of Mr. Mitchum's position and to make entirely certain that Mr. Mitchum's reliance on the rights and protections granted him by the Labor Code, Section 2855 will not submit him to any criticism or subject him to any claim that he has directly or indirectly caused you damage."

The Morris office then wrote RKO denying Mitchum had been notified of any commitment to 20th Century–Fox. On May 11, Mitchum, Schreiber and the Morris agents were startled to learn that RKO had loaned the actor's services to Wayne/Fellows Productions, Inc., for William Wellman's *Track of the Cat* beginning May 17 and running through July 10.

The news brought an angry protest to RKO from 20th pointing out that their second unit had already completed three hundred scenes for *Untamed* which had been shot in South Africa, using doubles for Mitchum and Susan Hayward at a cost of $260,000.

This had been done on assurance to Darryl Zanuck by Hughes and attorney Greg Bautzer that Mitchum had read the scenario and would perform, providing the picture was finished before his contract expired.

Nevertheless, on May 17, Mitchum began shooting *Track of the Cat*, the story of a psychologically warped mountain family terrorized by a killer panther. Director William Wellman's self-indulgent and pretentious production was laden with symbolism, but he made little use of a cast headed by Mitchum, Beulah Bondi, Teresa Wright, Tab Hunter, Diana Lynn, William Hopper, Philip Tonge and Carl "Alfalfa" Switzer. Trumpeted as a possible multiple Academy Award winner before its release and heralded as the fulfillment of a long-deferred dream of Wellman's, it disappointed everyone including the director. He said of it later, "It was a flop artistically, financially and Wellmanly." He bemoaned the audiences' indifference to the sparing use of color—everything except Mitchum's red jacket and Diana Lynn's yellow scarf was in black and white—and their failure to connect the marauding panther which did in both Bill Hopper and Mitchum with the evil inherent in Mitchum's character.*

To further confuse matters for the accountants, RKO had sent Wayne/Fellows a $50,000 bill for Mitchum's services. John Wayne immediately objected that the previous January, Hughes had agreed to lend Mitchum to one of Wayne's companies for $100,000. Contracts previously prepared for Wayne/Fellows were returned to RKO along with a $100,000 check. RKO then drew up new contracts in the name of Wayne's Batjac company.

RKO, meantime, had fallen behind schedule in shooting *The Conqueror* which starred Susan Hayward. Since she would not finish until July 24, *Untamed* could not begin until July 26 which therefore made it impossible for 20th to complete Mitchum's scenes by August 15.**

Mitchum refused to budge. RKO retaliated by sending a

---

*In 1982, when asked to name his least favorite picture, Mitchum promptly chose *Track of the Cat*, explaining that the location at Mount Shasta in thirty feet of snow during the summertime had been torturous.

**Untamed* was eventually filmed with Susan Hayward, Tyrone Power and Richard Egan.

wire in care of the William Morris office ordering him to report for loanout to Filmcrest Productions, Inc.'s *Cattle Queen of Montana*.

These instructions brought a stinging reply to Ross Hastings from the Morris agents. It read in part:

> In behalf of and as agent of Robert Mitchum . . . [we point out that] it would have been physically impossible for him to be contacted in sufficient time to report at that time and on the date indicated in [your] telegram. . . .
>
> . . . A reading of the script of *Cattle Queen of Montana*, the motion picture referred to in your letter indicates without any doubt that the role of "Colorados"* is a secondary role; that assigning Mr. Mitchum to this role—that of portraying an Indian—is done to embarrass and harass him . . . and is done to hold him up to ridicule not only in the entertainment industry, but to the public at large. You are not acting in good faith under said contract.

Publicly Mitchum shrugged off the disagreement. "I glanced through the script, but I'd rather go fishing and that's what I'm going to do."

He never worked for RKO again.

---

*It was eventually played by Lance Fuller in his screen debut.

CHAPTER 11

Upon leaving RKO, Mitchum set up offices at 9200 Sunset Boulevard, almost exactly where the showbizzy Sunset Strip ends and quietly opulent Beverly Hills takes over. In this move, like the one from Oak Glen Drive to Mandeville Canyon, he took another step away from the nomadic young rebel who announced that he had arrived in a boxcar and expected to leave in one. Now as a would-be producer and in-demand, free-lance actor, he had adjusted sufficiently to stardom to feel comfortable maintaining a suite of elegant but sparsely furnished offices.

On hand to look after his interests were Gloria Westmore, recently recruited from RKO's publicity department, and the faithful Reva Frederick. Reva, who had come to work for him as a part-time secretary, had over the years worn many hats. In addition to secretarial duties, she had served as a baby sitter, gofer, confidante, shopper, waitress, manager, press agent, accountant, bartender, business manager, apologist and friend— to name only a few of her duties. Some saw her as a fiercely loyal sister; others, despite her physical attractiveness, were reminded of one of those salty, show-biz mother figures, "the jungle mother" as Gypsy Rose Lee felicitously named them.

Still others likened the relationship to a marriage with the sexual component eliminated. "Bob was always saying *yes* when he meant *no* and it was up to Reva to get him off the hook," one of their long-time acquaintances said. Whatever the basis for the relationship, they seemed to understand and trust one another completely.

On the surface this extended beyond Mitchum to his entire family. But as Reva became more and more entrenched as his alter ego, Dorothy confided her reservations about paying out money for such services to friends and often espoused her belief that she could easily and efficiently assume Reva's duties herself. In the end, only reminders that such a full-time undertaking would interfere with her duties as a mother and would prevent her from traveling with her husband when he went on location dissuaded her from attempting to take over.

The office provided a retreat where Mitchum could escape from family and indulge in those private pursuits that he kept separated from the *mucho macho* image he projected on the screen, an image which press agents, intent on building stardom for him, trumpeted across the nation. It was in the office early in 1955 that he completed several new pieces of special material for his sister Julie, who had been engaged to headline the show at the Bar of Music in Los Angeles shortly.

It was at the office, too, where he worked intermittently on an original story for a film which he hoped to produce, star in and write. He claimed that his most highly guarded activity, however, was composing the poetry which expressed his most deeply felt sentiments, secrets that, he confided to his family, nothing on earth could persuade him to share.

Mitchum's first five films following his departure from RKO neatly illustrate both the pitfalls and opportunities that lay in store for the free-lance actor. Of those five, all of which were released through United Artists, *Man With the Gun* (1955) represented the kind of no-risk, run-of-the-mill western that might very well have been made under his RKO contract. He played the kind of hero he often had enacted before and, if he had wished, could have made an unchallenging career out of portraying until television came along, took over and wore out the formula.

The chief lures of *Foreign Intrigue* (1956) and *Bandido!* (1956) were the high compensation and the opportunity to travel at company expense. For *Foreign Intrigue* Mitchum was paid $150,000 plus a promised seventy-five percent of the profits, a prospect he found so tempting that he signed the contract before reading the script.

On June 12, 1955, he and Dorothy sailed for Europe on the tramp steamer *Fern River* to escape the spotlight. On a stopover at Casablanca, Mitchum proposed visiting the native quarter, which suggestion was greeted by the ship's crew with apprehension. He was warned about frequent uprisings, but he was not to be dissuaded. He, Dorothy and three friends wandered about making purchases before settling at a table in a small square for some drinks. Gradually a mob gathered—approximately three hundred by Mitchum's estimate—to see the movie star. Aware that revolutionaries often used crowds such as these to incite riots, he casually alerted his companions and signaled for their car to pull up from a side street. As it approached, he smiled at the crowd which was roaring his name. Waving genially at them, he simultaneously shoved Dorothy and their three companions under his arm and into the automobile. The others' expressions of relief at their escape were interrupted by Mitchum's announcement of his intention to return to the quarter for dinner that evening.

Once the Mitchums were settled in Paris, he began work and Dorothy spent her free time attending the showings of such couturiers as Jacques Fath, Pierre Balmain and Christian Dior. As soon as school recessed for the summer, they sent for Jim, fourteen, and Chris, eleven, to join them. Petrina, who was only three, remained in California in the care of a nurse. After spending weeks traveling from Paris to Stockholm, Marseilles, Nice and Monaco with the movie company, Dorothy took the boys to Rome for sightseeing. The junket was only a partial success; the boys compared everything unfavorably to the California beaches and dismissed the Colosseum as "a junk pile."

Realizing Jim and Chris were too young to enjoy exploring other cultures, Dorothy conferred with their father and they devised a system that pleased all concerned. Each evening they provided the boys with such American fare as hamburgers, hot dogs and Coke. Afterward, they left them in a theater showing

American films. While Chris and Jim were thus occupied, the Mitchums and producer-writer-director Sheldon Reynolds were taken to a different out-of-the-way French restaurant by Reynolds's associate producer, a French woman named Nicole Milinarre. Dorothy and Reynolds found the experience an epicurean delight, but Mitchum was less taken with it. When Dorothy urged him to show a little enthusiasm, he shrugged. "I just don't care that much about food. It embarrasses me to see people putting stuff into the holes in their faces."

Creating a scene embarrassed him not at all. Outraged when the captain in the bar at the Eden Roc refused to relax a rule and serve sandwiches to his party late in the afternoon, Mitchum took childish delight in obliging requests for his autograph from two waiters. For the first he wrote: "Your headwaiter is an idiot. Bob Mitchum." For the second, he scrawled: "I will never come here again. Bob Mitchum." Then he stood up and led his party out of the establishment.

Nevertheless, he enjoyed working with Reynolds and later sang the producer-director-writer's praises to anyone who would listen. "Shelly finished *Foreign Intrigue* in ten weeks. And the total cost was around $625,000," he said with the appreciation of a man who has a piece of the action. "In Hollywood, the same thing would have been a $3,000,000 production."

Speaking of this miracle to columnist Dick Kleiner, he explained its accomplishment in terms of organization and planning. "Shelly doesn't waste any time or money. He had forty-seven minutes of film finished and in the can before the deadline for him to start shooting," Mitchum marveled. "He used the same camera and some of the same locations he'd used for the TV series."*

One thing that impressed him, he told Kleiner, was Reynolds's adeptness in manipulating European officials. Reynolds could obtain police permits for filming on a moment's notice—as opposed to delays that sometimes stretched into days or even a week with Hollywood-oriented producers.

That the picture eventually received lethal reviews and he himself personal attacks seemed not to bother the actor in the slightest. Let Bosley Crowther of the *New York Times* fume:

*The television series *Foreign Intrigue* ran from 1951 to 1955.

"Mr. Mitchum, whose mental processes have never appeared overly alert, is favored at least in this instance, by not being overly taxed." Mitchum well knew that the audience to which the film would appeal probably never read *any* reviews—to say nothing of those in the *Times*. Let the critics rant, he could be confident that the money would roll in.

At one point during a lull in filming, Mitchum squeezed in a visit to his maternal aunts, uncles and cousins in Oslo, Norway, and he and Reynolds managed a quick scouting trip to North Africa. Upon his return to the United States, he was confronted with widespread rumors that he was launching a soft-drink business on the Dark Continent. Was it true? Mitchum said it was not. "Shelly and I noticed the Arabs use hashish," he explained. "So as a gag we said we were going to introduce a drink called 'Hashi-Cola' in Africa. Trouble is, people took us seriously."

If *Foreign Intrigue* was chosen to replenish his bank account, *Not As a Stranger* (1955) was selected to move him into prestige productions. Among his fellow actors were two Academy Award winners, Olivia de Havilland and Gloria Grahame, as well as Frank Sinatra, Broderick Crawford, Lee Marvin, Charles Bickford, Myron McCormick and Harry Morgan. Unfortunately, a turgid, melodramatic, best-selling book had been turned into a turgid, melodramatic script, and, despite the presence of good actors and a documentary feel to the medical scenes, first-time director Stanley Kramer was unable to invest the picture with an emotional depth that went beyond the surface, soap-opera variety. Nevertheless, from Mitchum's point of view *Not As a Stranger*, the largest-grossing film in which he appeared, brought him to the attention of people who ordinarily would never have attended any of his RKO movies.

Perhaps the most joyous part of making *Not As a Stranger* was that Mitchum found several kindred spirits among the cast who could use a break from Kramer's heavy-handed seriousness. Even Olivia de Havilland, who tended to take her work seriously, developed a light, bantering relationship with him. Dancing with her at a party, he found her body encased in a tight girdle from her armpits to her knees. As they moved about the floor, his leg encountered the rubber barricade and bounced back. He facetiously advised her she ought to boil the garment.

Thereafter, whenever she became uptight he suggested, "Go boil your girdle." At the picture's wrap party, she presented him with a beautifully done-up package containing a boiled girdle.

Also to Mitchum's liking was the number of hard drinkers in the cast. On one occasion the group—which included Brod Crawford, Lee Marvin, Myron McCormick and Sinatra—staged a barroom brawl in the dressing rooms, partially demolishing furniture, uprooting telephones, smashing windows and sending all 240 pounds of Crawford hurtling off a second-floor balcony in the name of good fun.

Just as Mitchum had nicknamed Marilyn Monroe *Madam*, he dubbed Sinatra *Snodgrass*, and Sinatra called him *Mother*. Sinatra had arrived on the set one morning "completely beat." Mitchum, who understood his plight, guided him to one of the operating tables on the set, applied cloths soaked in witch hazel to his eyes and proceeded to administer an alcohol rub which put the sufferer to sleep. When he finally awoke, he felt so well that he smiled gratefully at Mitchum and murmured, "Mother!" And "Mother" to him Mitchum remained—so much so that for several years thereafter, Mitchum received horrendously sentimental Mother's Day cards from Ole Blue Eyes.

Sinatra later spoke to writer Helen Lawrenson of the interest he and Mitchum shared in music. "For anyone who's not a professional musician, he knows more about music from Bach to Brubeck than any man I've ever known." When Lawrenson reported this compliment to Mitchum, the professional cynic raised an eyebrow and said, "That shows how much Sinatra knows about music!" Thinking it over, Lawrenson concluded the response typified Mitchum's "defensive self-mockery that is at once an attitude toward life and an armor against it."

In a May 1982 issue of the Los Angeles *Reader*, David Ehrenstein chose to highlight a revival of *The Night of the Hunter* (1955) as a Critic's Choice selection:

> From its opening moment, with the face of Lillian Gish magically materializing out of a star-filled sky, to its last shot of a snow-covered farm house as comfortably banal as a calendar illustration, *The Night of the Hunter* is one

of the more unclassifiable films ever made. . . . As directed by Charles Laughton, this 1955 production is a film of looming expressionist shadows, homespun back-fence chatter, psychopathic sexual craving, and victorious maternal wisdom. It is also along with Lang's *Moonfleet* and Erice's *Spirit of the Beehive*, one of the finest, truest portraits of the childhood experience.

In January 1983 *The New Yorker* had this to say in its capsulized review of a revival at the Little Theater of the Public Theater:

Despite its peculiar overtones of humor, this is one of the most frightening movies ever made (and truly frightening movies become classics of a kind). Robert Mitchum is the murderous, sex-obsessed, hymn-singing soul-saver with hypnotic powers, and his terrified new wife (Shelley Winters), who has a boy and a little girl from an earlier marriage, becomes his fervent disciple. He is something of a Pied Piper in reverse, adults trust him, children try to escape. The two kids' flight from the madman is a mysterious, dreamlike episode—a deliberately "artistic" suspense fantasy, broken by the appearance of a Christian variety fairy godmother (Lillian Gish). The adaptation of Davis Grubb's novel was James Agee's last film work, and this shadowy horror fable was the first and only movie directed by Charles Laughton; it was a total financial disaster, and he never got a chance to direct again.

The same month, Carrie Rickey was asking in the *Village Voice*:

. . . Is there an image more terrifying than the sight of Robert Mitchum, playing an unregenerate parson, soulfully singing "Leaning on the Everlasting Arm" on horseback as he soullessly stalks two young children who are in possession of their father's cache of bills? . . . Fortunately for us, Laughton's right hand knew what the left was doing, and his film is a distinctively American Gothic interpretation of German Expressionism, with tilt pans, Stanley Cortez's moody cinematography, and a startling appearance of Lillian Gish as the incarnation of Good combating Mitchum's unreconstructed Evil. A movie about the American nightmare of greed, about the precipitous experience of two innocents, about the triumph of spirit over will, *The Night of the Hunter* embodies the evil of the Pox Americana and its transcendence.

The curious history of *The Night of the Hunter* began with Paul Gregory's reading the novel and drawing it to the attention of Charles Laughton. Gregory, whose previous experience was limited to the stage, was from the beginning determined to have as director, Laughton, his coproducer and director of Gregory Productions' theatrical triumphs. The quest for financing was made most difficult by their combined lack of experience behind the camera. "From the moment I read the book I knew there was only one man to play the preacher," Gregory says. "Bob Mitchum. There's a quicksilver turn about him. You never know what to expect. Speak to him and you never can predict whether he's going to be friendly or attack you. He's a fascinating fellow—a little scary. Perfect for that part, because he was and is one of the most wondrously unique human beings who has ever been in films. An absolutely unique man. He looks unique. He acts unique. He walks unique. But all I hoped then was that we could get him.

"Charles and I gave him the book. Charles told him that it would call for him playing a diabolical crud. Mitch said, 'Present.' That amused Charles and he said he wasn't supposed to know about such things. Being English and doing the classics made him a professional noncrud. And Mitch told him, 'Charles, I'll take care of that department if I like the book.'"

Gregory and Laughton were apprehensive about his response, but they need not have worried. The story's baroque, sinister, decadent quality excited Mitchum.

"Luckily," says Gregory. "Because in all candor, the production rested on him. I couldn't have financed it without his name. As it was, that made it possible for me to get the money through United Artists. From old man Heller in Chicago. Six hundred and ninety-five thousand dollars is what it cost. Charles's reputation as a stage and screen actor didn't mean a thing because they knew he was nervous as a cat about undertaking this. He'd never directed a film before."

Gregory engaged James Agee to write the script. "The credits say Jim Agee wrote it, but he was rolling around on the floor drunk most of the time," Gregory continues. "He turned in a screenplay four times thicker than the book. Eventually Charles took on Dennis and Terry Saunders, whose only experience was an Academy Award—winning short they'd done as students at UCLA, to bounce ideas off."

"The script was pretty much Charles," Dennis Saunders agrees. "Charles tried to tell Jim Agee what to do, but Jim didn't understand what was wanted. Charles ended up doing most of it."

Laughton also had a hunch that he wanted Lillian Gish for the spinster who has turned her farm into an orphanage.

"The first I heard of it some people called me from the Museum of Modern Art here in New York and asked if I knew why Mr. Laughton was running all my old films," Gish remembers. "I said I didn't. And then the phone rang and he wanted me to have tea with him, Mr. Gregory, Mr. Agee and the cameraman and two or three others. He said he was making a picture with Mr. Mitchum and he wanted me to be in it. I asked, 'Why?' And he said, 'When I first went to the movies they sat in their seats straight and leaned forward. Now they slump down, with their heads back or eat candy and popcorn. I want to sit them up straight again.' Of course, I was eager to work with Mr. Laughton. And I came to like Mr. Mitchum very much."

After securing the services of Lillian Gish, Gregory and Laughton settled on Shelley Winters to play the doomed young widow and mother. The old pros predicted the neophyte film makers were asking for trouble putting Winters and Mitchum in the same cast. "Not at all," says Gregory. "She wanted to do it so badly she was on her best behavior. I can tell you quite honestly she was darling." (Asked about her years later by *Today*'s Gene Shalit, Mitchum responded, "Well, Shelley defeats herself a lot. She's so self-conscious and so insecure that she visits it on other people which is unfortunate for her.")

As for Mitchum and Laughton, they formed a mutual admiration society from the beginning. After viewing some of the dailies and assessing Mitchum's work as the murderous itinerant preacher with L O V E tattooed on one hand and H A T E on the other, Laughton delivered the opinion that "Bob is one of the best actors in the world."

Unable to accept such extravagant praise any more gracefully than he had accepted birthday or Christmas presents as a child, Mitchum said he was only doing the same thing he had been doing ever since he started working in pictures. "I haven't changed anything but my underwear."

Undeterred, Laughton persisted in telling anyone who would listen that Mitchum would make the best Macbeth of any living actor. To which Mitchum countered he didn't know anything about that kind of acting. He said he subscribed to the Spencer Tracy school: "Learn your lines and don't bump into the furniture or other actors."

Almost thirty years later, Lillian Gish maintained she had to go back as far as D. W. Griffith to find a set so infused with purpose and harmony. "I didn't work with Miss Winters, but in all the scenes I had with the children and Mitchum, there was not ever even a moment's doubt as to what we were doing or how we were doing it," she recalls. "To please Charles Laughton was our aim. We believed in and respected him. Totally.

"One thing that bothered me at first—as you know, the story is a conflict between good and evil. Black and white. The battle between the two. Early in the filming, Mr. Laughton said to me, 'For Mitchum to play this all evil might be bad for his future. He has the power to convince audiences he *is* what he plays. I'm going to handle his characterization so that a few amusing things will break the evil occasionally. I'm not going to ruin that young man's career.' And I thought, 'Oh dear, what will that do to our story.' But I agreed with him because I saw he was more concerned with Mr. Mitchum's future than the film. Which was the mark of the man. And happily his method didn't hurt—it may even have helped the film."

Pleased as Laughton was with Mitchum's performance, he was so distressed by the actor's calculated verbal shock tactics that at one point he admonished him to remember that everyone has skeletons in his closet. "Most people walk past such a closet, note the door is closed and tiptoe politely on," he said. "You, however, not only open the closet door, you reach in and seize the skeleton and shake it. You must stop brandishing skeletons, Robert, you really must."

Recounting the warning later, Mitchum said, "I knew what he was talking about. I'm blunt and I make people feel guilty. And I suppose my own style is so elliptical and aphoristic that people think I'm saying one thing when I'm really talking about something else. I could be describing my mother and some dude will think I'm talking about a beer garden in Munich."

Despite all the mutual admiration, the production was not trouble-free. "The major culprit was that horror named Bert Allenberg," says Paul Gregory. "He put Mitch into *Not As a Stranger* knowing full well that Stanley Kramer was going to start shooting before we finished. And it was such an awful thing to do to us. We had to shoot on Sundays and such things to get rid of Mitch's scenes. That put him and Charles and everybody else under pressure. But Mitchum came through. He even came to the set one Sunday after we'd closed down to pick up one final shot Charles needed."

For his trouble Mitchum eventually received unprecedented personal reviews even though the picture initially didn't fare well. In lauding the actor, William K. Zinsser of the *New York Herald-Tribune* made the inaccurate observation that Mitchum, whose "acting perhaps has never been praised before, gives a performance that will surprise everybody." In the *New York Times*, Bosley Crowther wrote: "The atmosphere of the sticks is intense, and Robert Mitchum plays the murderous minister with an icy unctuousness that gives you the chills. There is more than malevolence and menace in his character. There is a strong trace of Freudian aberration, fanaticism and iniquity."

In 1982 on the *Tonight* show, Mitchum told Joan Rivers that Preacher Harry Powell in *The Night of the Hunter* was probably his favorite role; that Laughton was the best director with whom he had ever worked; and that Shelley Winters got what she deserved lying there dead at the bottom of the river.

The juxtaposition of such personalities as Mitchum and Laughton was too tempting for the scurrilous but widely read journalistic rag, *Confidential*, to pass up. In the May 1955 issue, the editors ran a story titled "Robert Mitchum . . . The Nude Who Came to Dinner."

In the brouhaha that followed they admitted this was a "pretty crazy story" even though it was about the "world's number one fun lover these days." Then they went on to describe "an elegant binge" for some twenty guests cohosted by Laughton and Gregory at the latter's Santa Monica beach house. *Confidential* described things as being on the dull side until Mitchum and "a pretty dish" arrived. According to the magazine writer, he had been delayed by a bottle of Scotch and immediately proceeded to seize a second which he "nursed on." The writer complimented his "girl friend" on a fine job of "piloting him to the dining room when the dinner bell rang." But the anonymous beauty purportedly choked on her appetizer when she glanced up to see Mitchum "removing every bit of his clothing."

All of the other formally dressed dinner guests were hypnotized as the naked actor "returned to the table to seize a bottle of catsup." As *Confidential* told it, he spattered his body with red goo as he inquired, "This *is* a masquerade party, isn't it? Well, I'm a hamburger."

One guest took his performance good-naturedly, the writer reported, but Laughton angrily ordered Mitchum to get into his clothes and leave. Mitchum, *Confidential* claimed, responded by dancing around, spattering the room with catsup until his "babe corralled and persuaded him to put on his duds." After she led him away, the magazine fantasized, the guests returned to eating because, "in Hollywood they're used to guys fried— not French fried, just plain fried."

Since there was not a word of truth to the story, on May 9, 1955, Mitchum sued the magazine, publisher Robert Harrison, editor Gordon Rushmore, managing editor A. Govoni, associate editor Ray Breen and purported author Charles Gordon for one million dollars. The suit prepared by attorney Jerry Giesler claimed the piece had damaged Mitchum's professional reputation and exposed him and his family to "public scandal, embarrassment, disgrace, contempt and ridicule."

In filing the suit, Mitchum was aware he would bring the story to the attention of hundreds of thousands of people who otherwise would not have heard of it. Some members of the film colony felt it would have been wiser to have ignored the piece; others applauded his action. At the time, Mitchum said simply, "It was something that had to be done. It's a matter of principle with me rather than concern with financial returns. It could very definitely affect my career as an actor. It deeply concerned my wife and my two sons and my baby daughter, Petrina. . . . That left me with no alternative but to take legal action against them."

A month later publisher Harrison filed a motion in Santa Monica Superior Court to quash the suit on grounds that his company did not—and never had—done business in California nor had it ever owned or rented property in the state.

Several continuances were granted on Harrison's motion. Meanwhile, a "Miss Smith," who identified herself as secretary to "Mr. D," called Paul Gregory to arrange an appointment. When she was unsuccessful, a "Miss D" called to say he could avoid "injurious scandal" for his business associates by meeting her at Frascatti's located at Crescent Heights and Sunset Boulevard. Gregory found her sitting with a man and another woman. He and "Miss D" went to an empty booth where she proposed he "buy off a writer's commitment" for a scandalous article about Mitchum, Laughton and Laughton's wife, Elsa Lanchester. The price was eight hundred dollars. Gregory refused, knowing the story was false.

Mitchum's case against *Confidential* and *Confidential*'s motion for dismissal dragged along until March 8, 1956, when the motion by *Confidential* was granted, apparently on technical, jurisdictional grounds. Nevertheless, Mitchum's stand encouraged others to pursue court action against the scandal-mongering magazine. Suits by Maureen O'Hara, Dorothy Dandridge, Liberace and others resulted in the magazine changing both policy and management before it finally collapsed.

Looking back, Mitchum reflected, "It's not been cheap to fight. But someone has to put a stop to it."

RM and Marilyn Monroe were old friends delighted to be working together in *River of No Return* (1954).

A prestige production for Mitchum—*Not As a Stranger,* with Olivia de Havilland (1955).

Perhaps RM's favorite role—the preacher in *The Night of the Hunter* (1955).

A performance endowed with gentleness—*Heaven Knows, Mr. Allison*, with Deborah Kerr (1957).

On the set of *Thunder Road* with his son, Jim, whom Mitchum
cast as his brother (1958).

His performance in *Home from the Hill* (here with George Hamilton) earned RM the National Board of Review's nod for best performance by an actor (1960).

With Deborah Kerr again in *The Sundowners*, considered by many to be one of Mitchum's great performances (1960).

With Shirley MacLaine in *Two for the Seesaw* (1962).

With Carroll Baker in *Mister Moses,* the first full-length feature to be filmed in Kenya (1965).

Ryan's Daughter, with Sarah Miles (1970).

With Dorothy (1970).

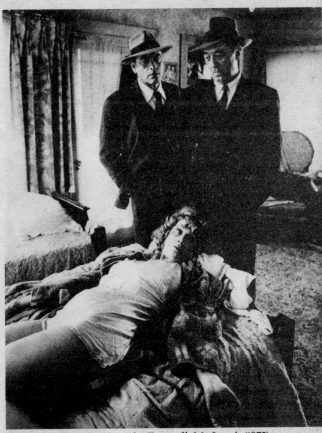
RM plays Philip Marlowe in *Farewell, My Lovely* (1975).

In a supporting role in *The Last Tycoon* (1976).

The star-studded cast of *That Championship Season,* from left to right, (top row) Bruce Dern and Paul Sorvino, (bottom row) Stacy Keach, RM, and Martin Sheen (1982).

Robert and Dorothy at the premiere in New York (1982).

On location for *Maria's Lovers* (1983).

CHAPTER 12

Early in Mitchum's career his unique outlook and method of dealing with the industry fascinated the Hollywood press. When costume designer Orry-Kelly tried to do him a favor by saying to Louella Parsons for the fourth or fifth time, "Louella, you know Bob Mitchum, don't you?", Mitchum piped up, "Screw it, Kelly. She's never going to print my name anyway." Far from being offended, Parsons interpreted his remark as an indication of the high regard in which he held her syndicated column and was charmed. Later she frequently ran friendly items about him.

During the time he was under contract to RKO, Hedda Hopper dropped by his dressing room one afternoon and began asking questions he considered inane. After answering several, he abruptly stood up and said to the powerful columnist, "Never mind the small talk, Hedda. Wanta fuck?" She shrieked, dropped her pad and pencil and fled. "Instead of getting mad, she loved Bob for it," says Mitchum's former stand-in, Boyd "Tyrone" Cabeen. "The columnists and reporters all just loved him. Because he'd say anything. That's what made him such a good interview."

Cabeen would seem to have a point, judging from some of

the anecdotes that have found their way into print. What other star would tell reporters such stories—true or not—as these? When an interviewer mentioned Eleanor Roosevelt, Mitchum volunteered he had once been "a guest at Eleanor Roosevelt's place. I saw this pink nightgown and just for a gag put it on over my clothes. Noel Coward walks in at this point and says, 'My dear. You look simply divine!' and kisses my hand. Next time I see Eleanor at a party she says loudly so everyone hears, 'Why Bob, last time we met you were in a pink nightgown being kissed by Noel Coward.' What could I do but admit it?"

He regaled the same gullible reporter with an improbable but funny story of meeting Gina Lollobrigida at the entrance of the Beverly Hills Hotel. "She was going on the Johnny Carson talk show, live that night. She says to me, 'How on earth do you keep that figure? Is it some special diet?' I tell her, 'No, lady, by isometric farting!' She went on the show that night, and sure enough the talk got around to diet. She's got no sense of humor, that dame, and she says, 'I saw Robert Mitchum today, and he keeps his figure by isometric farting!' Carson nearly fell off his chair." The fact that Carson's television show has been taped ever since moving to California seems not to bother Mitchum, who never lets a fact ruin a good story.

Actress Janet Gaynor, who is married to producer Paul Gregory, feels that the press and general public were intrigued because on- and off-screen Mitchum's attraction was rooted in his lack of inhibition. "All of the rest of us were so intimidated by what the studio said the public would or wouldn't stand for. But not him. That was his charm—that not caring."

After World War II new rebels appeared on the screen and Mitchum no longer automatically commanded top-of-the-column position. Speaking about this to a *Los Angeles Times* writer shortly before he left for the Caribbean to make *Fire Down Below* in 1956, Mitchum gave the impression that he had at last decided to monitor his behavior. More importantly, he observed that other colorful mavericks were taking some of the play away from him. "This guy Brando. How I welcomed him on the scene. I knew he'd get a lot of the heat," he said. Later in the interview, he denied he was abandoning Hollywood.

Now that his sons were tired of spending school vacations in Flathead Lake, Montana, he explained that he and Dorothy were looking for a working farm on the East Coast so that the children would realize everyone didn't grow up lying around a backyard swimming pool. "But this will always be home," he insisted.

A few days later he boarded a plane with director Robert Parrish, costars Rita Hayworth and Jack Lemmon, and the rest of the *Fire Down Below* company. The story they were setting out to shoot was essentially a romantic triangle, and was to serve as a comeback film for Hayworth who had voluntarily retired for several years of real adventure. Lemmon would also break away from his demonstrated mastery of light comedy to execute a tour de force as a sailor trapped on a burning ship. In the story, Mitchum and Lemmon, who are joint owners of a boat, agree to help a fleeing adventuress escape deportation by taking her to an island where passports are unimportant. On the way, the innocent Lemmon falls in love with her, but she rejects him with the memorable good-but-awful line, "I'm no good for you. No good for anyone. Armies have marched over me." Eventually she falls for the decadent Mitchum and receives an equally potent bit of good-awful dialogue from him. Displeased by her lack of response to his kiss, he shoves her away, announcing, "I'm proud. I don't make love to the dead."

As they set off for the Caribbean, Mitchum found Hayworth, Lemmon and Parrish congenial companions. Relaxed, he spun one colorful tale after another while consuming a full bottle of rum, and was in an exhilarated mood as he debarked from the plane, carrying a piece of hand luggage. In answer to a question from someone in the assembled crowd as to whether he had anything to declare, he held up the bag and replied, "Only two kilos of marijuana and a quart of Jewish blood I've taken by transfusion so I can stay even with those guys."

He had barely checked into his hotel before his "joke" had reverberated to Irving Allen and Albert R. Broccoli's Warwick Films in England, coproducer Harry Cohn's Columbia Studios in Hollywood and the State Department in Washington, D.C. For a brief time, there was a distinct possibility that the company would be expelled from the islands. Mitchum professed to be dumbfounded. "Don't these people have any sense of humor?" he repeatedly asked members of the company.

Recalling another occasion when Mitchum encountered a similar problem, Jim Backus says, "Bob has never learned to distinguish what is innocent fun and joy on a soundstage from what appears to be an insulting remark on the street. It's not uncommon for people who know and love one another to call each other by ethnic names. But it's done with affection. It becomes dangerous when outsiders are present. Now Mitchum used to call me the Militant Wasp. He had a thing going with John Farrow, a Catholic. He called him the Count of Malta or the Knight of Malta or the Militant Catholic. Someone else could have been the Militant Jew. Or he might say, 'Get your slimy Irish ass over on the set.' Done with love, that's common show business exchange. But taken out of context, out of an atmosphere where everyone understands the situation, it can seem dangerous and not very nice."

Whatever it seemed to outsiders, Mitchum was blithely unconcerned. The second night in Trinidad, instead of keeping a low profile, he and other members of the company visited various spots featuring steel bands and calypso singers.

"We listened to these guys who had been making their livings for decades going from table to table improvising calypso lyrics," Jack Lemmon says. "All at once this son-of-a-bitch Mitchum got up and began making up lyrics along with the professionals. He must have gone for twenty minutes, moving from table to table, just as the pros had been doing, making up lyrics that were absolutely brilliant. I was just totally thrown. He was as good as they were. It just totally knocked me out."*

Next day, the company found itself stymied by the rain. There was no shooting, and rehearsals were soon taken care of. Everyone connected with the film was staying at a big old colonial hotel and most of them spent the day wandering aimlessly about the premises.

Around eleven p.m., Lemmon realized Mitchum had not put in an appearance all day. No one else recalled having seen him either. "I started to track him down," Lemmon says. "I

*When Mitchum returned to the U.S., he signed a contract and recorded a calypso album for Capitol Records in March of 1957.

found him in his room. He'd been there for thirteen hours. He told me he had sent some runners up into the mountains to get some bark from the Hawaiian Umm Umm tree.* It was supposed to be a powerful aphrodisiac. It took the runner four hours to go up and down a mountain to get it, but he came back with a pound and a half of this bark. Mitchum now had a pot of boiling water, hoses, tubes, everything to extract the juice from this bark and make a potent tea-soup. He also had a young native couple sitting there all day into the night. He kept feeding them this stuff to see what would happen to them. They just looked at each other and at him. Puzzled. They didn't feel a thing. Not a goddamned thing. But it figured he'd do this because Mitchum always has been inquisitive."

Eventually the weather cleared and the movie company moved from Trinidad to the smaller island of Tobago in the southernmost part of the Caribbean. Before that happened, though, Dorothy and the Mitchum's five-year-old daughter, Petrina, arrived to provide a stabilizing influence. One evening the Mitchums were enjoying a quiet dinner at the hotel—Petrina was already in bed—when three inebriated American sailors spotted the macho movie star and decided they would find out for themselves just how tough he really was.

One staggered up and asked whether he could take a punch at the star. Mitchum obligingly stepped away from his table and told the gob to be his guest. The sailor tapped him on the chin. Mitchum was not fazed. The sailor unleashed a killer punch, but Mitchum counter-punched, knocking his assailant out. With that, the second sailor grabbed a chair and threw it at the star. When it missed, the third sailor picked up another chair and charged. Mitchum knocked it out of his hands and flattened him. Retreating to the railing of the dining deck, he turned just in time to seize sailor number two, hoist him over the railing and toss him into the pool forty feet below.

Moments later, he was fighting with sailor number three again when he felt a sharp object banging his skull. Dispatching the third sailor with a haymaker, he whirled to confront the new aggressor who turned out to be Dorothy. She was banging

*In *Lemmon* by Don Widener, Mitchum identifies the bark as *bois bundy*. "I don't know the exact translation, but whatever it is I think it means *hard*—hardwood."

him over the head with her sandal, shouting, "Stop it now! You're beginning to enjoy this." Eventually the waitress evicted the sailors and the Mitchums resumed dining.

When it has suited his purpose, Mitchum has set the incident on Sunset Boulevard and his aggressors have been members of a wedding party. He has also connected it with *Heaven Knows, Mr. Allison* rather than *Fire Down Below*. Those who know him well are inclined to shrug off the variations. "Oh sure," Julie Mitchum Sater says, "both John and Bob appropriate one another's experiences in the interest of entertainment." And Boyd Cabeen claims that after someone told Mitchum and him some colorful experience, the star often would change names and details and recount it as, say, one of Cabeen's experiences. Later with more extensive revisions, he might tell it with himself as the central character. Still later, with many more improvements, he would tell it again. "Sometimes it got so unrecognizable, I'd have to inquire when we were alone whether that wasn't the story so and so told us," Cabeen recalls.

Probably no story has given Mitchum more mileage than his shark yarn. Where and when the tale was born is unknown. But during his early days in Mandeville Canyon, he informed a Bel-Air hostess that his brother had once humped a shark. At approximately the same time, he told a neighbor that he and several acquaintances had had a gang bang with a shark. While making *Where Danger Lives* with Faith Domergue, he said an actor on the lot had done it. She was repelled at the thought of anyone "having relations with a dead old thing," but Mitchum reassured her, "Oh, our friend is a sport, not a necrophile. That shark was throbbingly alive!" He added that there had been rumors the shark was a male, but said he didn't believe it made any difference with sharks. "Anyway, it wasn't a serious affair," he reassured her. "I mean he didn't kiss it or anything."

Walking along the beach in Tobago with Lemmon, he once again told his shark story. Lemmon regarded it as one of his friend's fanciful tales invented to banish boredom on a cloudy afternoon when shooting was held up. But months later, on the set of another movie, he was sought out by an agitated stranger who introduced himself and then inquired whether Mitchum had told Lemmon, "I hump sharks."

Taken aback, Lemmon laughed and admitted having heard the story but assured the man that he regarded it as merely a joke and advised him to forget about it.

"Forget it! How can I?" the man demanded. "How would you like it if someone went around telling that story about you. I tell you it's not fair. You hump *one* little shark . . ."

Lemmon cracked up, but later marveled at the trouble Mitchum had gone to in order to provide yet another amusing twist to the tale of the shark.

When the company departed the Caribbean to complete shooting in London, Lemmon and Mitchum were quartered in apartments across from one another at 22 Grosvenor Square. Lemmon was about to be divorced from his wife. "Without mentioning any names—because I refuse to—it just so happened that I ended up with a cocktail and dinner engagement with a rather prominent young lady. I told that son-of-a-bitch across the hall that she was being brought to my flat for a predinner cocktail. Well, about ten minutes after the lady and her entourage arrived, in comes a large plant with a note. I don't know what the hell the note said because I never read it. I knew immediately who sent it. The plant was festooned with tiny balloons. All blown up condoms. I was mortified. And he was sitting across the hall in hysterics. I didn't know what to do. I said, 'Oh, English balloons. All white.' A typical Mitchum trick.

"But listen, if you're not a prude or a nut, it's awfully hard not to like and respect Bob. He can at times, I will admit, he can throw you for a minute. In front of people, there can be embarrassment. But his outrageousness is not a turn-off because he doesn't do it to get attention. Lord knows, he's a public figure, and with his career, he doesn't need to do anything to attract attention. So you learn to accept that for the unusual moments—with a really unusual guy. And boy, it is worth it to be a friend. Not a close one because he lives in Montecito and I live here. But if Bob lived here, I'd sure see a hell of a lot more of him. There is no question the man is unique and always will be. Because he ain't gonna change."

* * *

Back to Tobago.

Not for retakes of *Fire Down Below*, however, but for a new project called *Heaven Knows, Mr. Allison*. The plot involves a nun, Sister Angela (played by Deborah Kerr), and a Marine, Corporal Allison, stranded on a South Pacific Island during World War II. Censorship problems had blocked previous attempts to bring it to the screen, but screenwriter John Lee Mahin and director John Huston were confident they could convey the bittersweet relationship without running into problems with moral policemen. As they treated the story, Sister Angela has not yet taken her final vows, and she registers disapproval of the corporal's forwardness when he observes that he never realized there were pretty nuns. He quickly retracts by adding, "Well, I got the corps like you got the Church." Meanwhile, in the course of events, the script has Sister wracked with fever which requires the corporal to strip and wrap her in blankets. For the rest, the story concentrates on their struggle to find food, survive the elements and avoid capture by the returning Japanese before a hundred real-life U.S. Marines storm and retake the island.

Perhaps what eventually endows Mitchum's performance with an unusual gentleness is Huston's direction, but it may be attributable to the actor's friendliness with Deborah Kerr. At their first meeting, she was somewhat apprehensive, greeting him with, "Good morning, Mr. Mitchum. How are you?"

"Beaten to death by gorillas," the hung-over actor replied.

In recalling that exchange, Kerr said she was immediately prepared to like him. As they talked, she found him intelligent, sensitive and surprisingly gentle—the opposite of what she had been led to expect by his screen presence and the press.

A camaraderie developed between them which lasted throughout this film and two more.

"Within hours, we were sitting on the soft pink sand and I was listening to an extremely sensitive, a poetic, extraordinarily interesting man. Not just a vain actor concerned only with his role and his looks, but a perceptive, amusing person with a great gift for telling a story, and possessed of a completely unexpected vast fund of knowledge," she wrote of him in the introduction to Alvin Marill's *Robert Mitchum on the Screen*. "Throughout the shooting of the movie, which was a trying, particularly rugged one, Bob was at all times patient, concerned, and completely professional, always in good humor, and always ready to make a joke when things became trying. . . . Here on this remote island in the Caribbean, I came to know and admire his facile acting. We discovered we could work together like a good doubles pair at tennis. His timing is always perfect and he makes the very difficult task of 'acting' seem as easy as falling off a log. . . .

"*Heaven Knows, Mr. Allison* was a charming, touching, unusual story that could have verged on the tasteless in less sensitive hands. . . . But Bob's wonderfully innocent bewilderment at his own predicament made the relationship between two human beings a most moving and gently humorous happening."

Mitchum's response to her was and is, "The best, my favorite." He told the late Thomas Thompson, "She sure ain't the cool, unapproachable dame she makes out to be. They [Huston, Mahin and 20th Century–Fox] were trying to figure out a way to work in a love scene with me. So they wrote this dreadful dream sequence, and she had a wig shipped over from England to wear. It arrived late, sort of green, and she put it on and modeled it for me. She asked how I liked it, and I said, 'Well, it all depends. Are you a natural greenie?' She hit me and shouted, 'You never even bothered to find out!' Later on, out of acute boredom, we decided to make a musical version of the picture, and she and I wrote great songs. One of them was to be sung by Deborah in her nun's drag, and it went, 'Since I met Father Dunne, it's a ball to be a nun, he's getting to be a habit with me.' Ah yes, life would be kind if I could live it with Deborah around."

The relationship that developed between Mitchum and John Huston was also one of mutual admiration. Huston saw Mitchum "in the Bogart mold," and Mitchum regarded Huston as rivaling Charles Laughton as the best director with whom he had worked. Huston put him through a lot of tough action, Mitchum recalls. For instance, in one scene he lassoed a 300-pound turtle in an attempt to obtain food for Sister Angela and

himself. The turtle took off and Mitchum had to swim under-
water. He kept bumping into things and only narrowly missed
being bashed into a coral reef. Afterward, he asked the natives
about those things he hit. "They said, 'Oh, that *bikyam*,'" he
reported. Alligators! Afterward, Houston said, 'How was that,
kid? How was that?' I said, 'John, look, I just got off this
bloody island from another picture. You know it's no novelty
to me. If you like it, print it. If you don't, tell me what to do
and I'll do it again.' The whole British crew, in the presence
of the mighty John Huston, froze. But John said, 'Swell, kid,
swell.' I saw that twinkle in his eye and I appreciated it.

"The only thing he ever said during the whole filming was
when I looked across to him after he said, 'Cut!' and he said
to me, 'Even more, kid, even more.' I said, 'Really?' He said,
'Even more, even more.' I said, 'Okay.' I recognized this was
a man who has a great visual sense and very often he's done
with that scene and he's on to the next vision before this one
is shot.

"But John made making that movie fun and he continues
to make moviemaking fun. He's one of the few people who
sees the real basic fun in the genre of motion picture communication and I admire him for it."

Huston often has cited Mitchum's willingness to give his
all physically as well as artistically—working with a twisted
ankle, a cut foot, and almost skinning his chest, arms, and
knees sliding down a coconut palm. Repeatedly, the actor
crawled through hip-high weeds before Huston secured a take
that satisfied him. When Mitchum stood up, blood oozed from
his chest where the stinging nettles had punctured his skin.
Spotting what had happened, Huston apologized and inquired
why Mitchum had not complained. Mitchum shrugged. It was,
he said, Huston's job to get the shot, and, for the salary he
was being paid as an actor, it was his obligation to provide
what the director was after. "You work for John Huston, you
suffer," he kidded. "What else can you expect?"

Both Deborah Kerr and Huston became fervent Mitchum
boosters. She announced that as an actor her costar was a
hundred times better than either he or most other people thought.
And whereas Laughton had seen Mitchum as the best potential

Macbeth of his generation, Huston was convinced he would make a memorable King Lear. "He is a rarity among actors, hard-working, noncomplaining, amazingly perceptive, one of the most underrated stars in the business," Huston concluded.

When asked why he had never performed in the classics, Mitchum admitted he once had considered committing himself to a season at Stratford. But apparently he had lacked the courage to go through with the plan, opting instead for a series of adventure films. "Those pictures I could do and walk away from," he explained. "Once they're finished I'm not involved. Furthermore, I don't let anyone down. I don't want that responsibility. I don't want that deep involvement."

This attitude was reinforced by a condescending thread that ran through the reviews. For example, *Time*'s man sniped away even as he praised Mitchum's portrayal of the Marine, writing: "Actor Mitchum, even though as usual he does nothing but slob around the screen, has succeeded for once in carrying off his slobbing with significance." This patronization was reflected in numerous other reviews and at award-giving time, although Kerr was nominated for an Academy Award and was named best actress of the year by the New York Film Critics. Mitchum's expectations came to nothing.

Publicly, Mitchum assumed the attitude that he couldn't care less. Friends say that privately he was deeply disappointed. His method of dealing with the situation was to produce and star in a series of unambitious adventure pictures which hopefully would make him a large amount of money and free him from participation in the cultural-critical sweepstakes.

The action pictures that followed immediately—*The Enemy Below* (1957), *Thunder Road* (1958), *The Hunters* (1958)—were the kind of films which he had in mind. Ironically, *The Enemy Below*, counted on for its commercial appeal, failed at the box office but was tapped as one of the ten best films of the year by the National Board of Review, and *Films in Review*'s critic cited Mitchum as "surprisingly effective . . . an able actor . . . no longer [to] be dismissed as merely a dimpled chin."

The Hunters, *The Angry Hills* and *The Wonderful Country* performed about as—or below what was—expected of them, but *Thunder Road* turned out to be a surprise to everyone connected with it. United Artists looked at the finished print and concluded it would be savaged by metropolitan critics. A first-run showing in Manhattan was bypassed, as were most other urban markets. The targets were drive-ins and grind houses in rural areas, especially in the South.

The genesis of the picture lay with Mitchum himself. Even before he finished his contract at RKO he had begun making notes and developing the bare bones of a plot for a film. Periodically he put it aside, only to take it up again. Eventually he completed a treatment that satisfied him. Since he knew nothing of the mechanics of script writing, he decided to hire Walter Wise and James Atlee Phillips to put the story in script form. When their screenplay exceeded his expectations, Mitchum undertook producing it—with a firm assist from Reva Frederick, who was always at his side—through his DRM Company. Not only did he cast himself in the lead and his older son, Jim, as his brother, but he also wrote the music to Don Raye's lyrics for "Whippoorwill" and "The Ballad of Thunder Road."*

Probably Mitchum's shrewdest decision was to hire Arthur Ripley to direct. Ripley was an eccentric talent who found it difficult to function within the restrictions of the studio system. Since 1954 he had headed the motion picture division of the theater arts department at UCLA, but his roots stretched deep into the beginnings of filmmaking. His first job had been cleaning negatives for Kalem Films in New York in 1908. From there he moved to Vitagraph as chief cutter, a position he also held with Universal, Fox and Metro. In 1916 he was to make his debut as a director but clashed with Rex Ingram, who had brought him to Southern California to do *Alias Jimmy Valentine*. A lifelong foe of heavy plotting, Ripley had tried to simplify the script. Ingram fired him. Thereafter, he wrote gags for Mack Sennett, served as editorial supervisor for Irving Thalberg at MGM, and collaborated on scripts before taking up directing. His first work was in short subjects featuring W. C. Fields, Robert Benchley and Harry Langdon, among others.

*One of his few slipups was failing to record the title song under the credits. However, he did record it for Capitol Records and in October 1958 it hit the Hot 100 Chart in 62nd place. Capitol reissued it in 1962 and it again hit the chart in 65th place.

An adversary of the star system, he once wagered he could shoot a successful picture in five days. Spending nine weeks writing the script and three days rehearsing the cast, he then shot *Prisoner of Japan* in five days at a cost of $19,000. The film eventually grossed $350,000.

Among his productions prior to *Thunder Road* were *Voice in the Wind* with Francis Lederer, *The Chase* with notable performances by Robert Cummings, Peter Lorre and Steve Cochrane in dramatic roles, and *Atlantis* with Jean Pierre Aumont and Maria Montez, as well as several comic trifles.

Claiming "the story is all," Ripley disagreed with the film establishment over their reliance on top stars and proven box-office formulas. *Thunder Road* with its small budget, location shooting in Transylvania County near Asheville, North Carolina, and its relatively unknown cast was a project that appealed to him.

The story spotlights a family of moonshiners—a father who manufactures the booze, the older son (Mitchum) who drives it to market, and his younger brother (James Mitchum) who aspires to emulate his brother, but for whom the family has higher aspirations. The clashes between the hill people, the representatives of the syndicate who are trying to muscle in, and the federal revenue agents who are trying to shut down the operation keep the action lively.

Envisioning something beyond a B movie, Ripley directed it to appeal both to the redneck good-ole-boy crowd and to the intellectuals such as Richard Thompson, who in 1970 would publish a scholarly appraisal of it. Thompson points out that the moonshiners represent rural individualism; the gangsters, urban industry; and the revenue agents, state control. He argues that "these stages have a one-to-one relationship with the thematic past, present and future of the film. The entrepreneurial figure linking the three states of economic life, Dolin/Mitchum— the one man possessing the social skills to deal with all the forces in the drama—is also an existential pluperfect-subjective tense linking the antagonistic conjugations of the film."

Ironically this cult film is still frequently shown on television and in theaters throughout the South. Perhaps it is just as well. Thompson in his analysis commented, "It is a work whose charm is open only to those who have first-hand knowledge of the world it depicts. Audiences must be primed with this experience in order to recognize and respond to Mitchum's vision, a truly *maudit* vision because by its very form and structure it is damned. A work like this frustrates critics straining to infuse popular art with culture, because it brings them face to face with an audience for whom criticism is irrelevant and 'art' is a cool word. For this group, *Thunder Road* is a private myth irradiating the secret corners of a lost existence with the savor of true existentialism."

CHAPTER 13

More and more, because he could no longer take refuge in relative anonymity, Mitchum found himself suffering from what he later described to writer Helen Lawrenson as the intrusion into his life of "the mealymouth bores." Of life in the movie colony he said, "It's a dull, aching euphoria. You have no friends," and then consciously or unconsciously quoting his mother he added, "You have disciples.

"This whole place has no relation to real life, real people," he complained. "Oh there are real people here, but they're in the oil refineries and the factories, not in movieland. This is Atlantis."

Why, Lawrenson inquired, did he stay if he were truly unhappy? In reply he launched into a story about President Calvin Coolidge. "He used to have to go to a lot of formal dinners and he hated them. So one time Alice Longworth asked him, 'Why do you do it?' and old Cal said, 'Well, I have to eat somewhere.' . . . That's why I make movies, I guess, I have to eat, and I'm too lazy to work." Eventually, he predicted, he would retreat to an island he knew where "There's no hotel, no phones, nothing—I'll just lie there in the sun and lick my wounds."

When he was not spinning fantasies about retreats to isolated islands, he focused on the Carolinas as a likely place where he could go back to his roots, back to where his relatives lived. In Asheville, during the shooting of *Thunder Road*, the manager of the motel where he was staying came to his room and said, "Mr. Mitchum, I'd like a word with you." Mitchum asked what was on his mind. The manager said, "Well, there are some people down in the lobby who want to see you. They say that they're your cousins." Mitchum asked, "Are they real mean-looking? Indian-looking? Blackfoots?" The manager assured him he had described them exactly. "They look like they'd take your scalp off in a minute." Whereupon Mitchum said, "They're my cousins all right. Send them up." It was with them he looked forward to settling.

But it wasn't to the Carolinas that he and his family moved. Dorothy by chance discovered one of the prettiest tidewater estates on the East Coast, approximately twelve miles from Trappe, Maryland.

Belmont Farms and its three hundred acres were reached by a long lane. The alternate approach was by boat since the farm had two miles of verdant coastline on Chesapeake Bay. The water and the long lane provided Mitchum with exactly the kind of solitude he sincerely believed he yearned for.

The Mitchums' announcement that they were selling their Mandeville Canyon home to move east naturally aroused a great deal of curiosity among personal friends and the press. Mitchum repeatedly assured everyone that he had no intention of abandoning his career. "I'm only a plane ride away," he insisted.

What to the objective viewer quite clearly appears to be the midlife crisis of a 45-year-old seems never to have occurred to him. At first he claimed that he and Dorothy were motivated by a desire to protect the children from acquiring Beverly Hills values. They wanted their kids to be free to choose their own lifestyles. That explanation seemed lame, however, since Jim would remain in Hollywood to pursue an acting career and Chris was almost ready to enter college. At other times, Mitchum said the farm appealed to Dorothy and him because of its isolation. He likened it to moving to a foreign country without the inconvenience of a language barrier. He advanced a third reason—perhaps the one that came closest to the truth—saying that he wanted to get to know himself before it was too late.

Belmont Farms seemed an ideal place to do just that. The big old house, built in 1850 during a period when most of the Eastern Shore, as the area is known, belonged to plantation owners, was surrounded by a working farm. Professional farmers leased the land to plant oats, barley, wheat and corn. Mitchum had nothing to do with it; the farmers took care of everything from the breaking of the land through the harvesting of the crop.

Mitchum himself initially owned two quarter horses—a stallion and a mare—and some white-face Hereford cows. Once, when Helen Lawrenson visited, he took her out to see a favorite stallion and a black mare, volunteering that he personally had taken the mare to Yukon, Oklahoma. Mystified by this information, Lawrenson asked why the mare had had to go there. "To get laid," Mitchum informed the writer and then launched into a story about how on the return trip she had broken out and got on the highway, requiring Mitchum and six other wranglers to capture her. "We put on a regular rodeo out there on the highway," he said, adding, "I think she had it in her head to go back to Oklahoma."

Once the Mitchums were settled in, Dorothy responded rather differently to their new surroundings than her husband did. She definitely missed their Southern California neighbors and found life at Belmont Farms lonely. Asked whether he missed Hollywood, Mitchum professed amazement that anyone would pose such a question. "Do I miss Hollywood life? What Hollywood life? I never traveled with the mob." Then indulging in his penchant for exaggeration, he said, "I've only been in one movie star's home, Kirk Douglas's—and that was for all of ten minutes. Certainly you can't say I've given up society for Maryland because I've never taken it up. I'm not bound to anything or anybody."

What he undoubtedly envisioned at that point was the life of a gentleman farmer. In addition to the horses and cattle, he amused himself by zipping around the bay in a little power cruiser and, although he was against hunting on the principle that it was immoral to kill animals for sport, he enjoyed fishing.

When the weather was bad, he said he had his books and his music to occupy him. He also continued writing verse. He was happy as a clam with his new life, bragging that he had burned another bridge behind him, implying that here was proof positive that he had never been caught up in the movie-star syndrome, that he remained the good ole' boy he'd been when he took up residence in Long Beach in the early 1930s. "My unsocial nature is well known," he said. "In Maryland, I can be as unsocial as I like and nobody gives a damn." He claimed that his fellow Marylanders protected him from bothersome fans by issuing complicated misdirections to Belmont Farms.

During the first year he made every effort to sell Dorothy on the virtues of seclusion. He may even have felt somewhat isolated himself, for when Pat Rooney, Jr., phoned, Mitchum urged him to come for a visit. Rooney didn't make it, but Charles Laughton and others did. Laughton later told Helen Lawrenson that during his visit Mitchum "put on a bewildering performance for me; he can talk in about twenty different Irish accents, and they were all perfect. You would have thought he had spent his life in the streets and pubs of Ireland. Then I started telling him that I was about to make *Advise and Consent* and complaining that I would have to play the role of the Senator with a Southern accent. 'Bob, it's as if you had to play Cockney,' I said. He answered me with, 'You bullnecked son-of-a-bitch, what makes you think I can't play a Cockney?' . . . He has great talent. . . . All his tough talk is a blind, you know. He's a literate, gracious, kind man, with wonderful manners, and he speaks beautifully—when he wants to. He's a very tender man and a very great gentleman. You know, he's really terribly shy." Laughton then warned Lawrenson that Mitchum wouldn't be pleased to have her demolish the roughneck image he had carefully built up in her *Esquire* profile.

Years later, his sister Julie expressed a similar thought. "I think he promotes the ruffian image because that front is supposed to keep people from tromping all over his very, very, very sensitive insides," she says.

That first year—and all the years they lived in Maryland—when the winter months made life dreary, Mitchum, who has an aversion to the cold, drove his family across the bridge to the Baltimore airport. There they caught a plane for the Bahamas or some other sunny spot. "This is living," he commented with some satisfaction.

Similarly, after being exposed to Maryland's summer heat, he also vowed that hereafter he was going to make every effort to be committed to a picture which was being filmed in a Scandinavian country during the "dog days of summer."

From his point of view, he had life both ways now. When he wanted to be a star, live like a star, call in the perks of stardom including the big money, he had only to hop a plane to wherever his next starring vehicle was being shot. On the other hand, when he felt the need for another kind of life, it awaited him. "In Maryland I'm not an actor," he told a reporter. "I'm just another farmer. I like it that way."

In the first year on the farm, he managed to avoid the cold months in Maryland and the expense of a trip to the Bahamas by making Metro-Goldwyn-Mayer's *Home From the Hill* in balmy Southern California. For his portrayal of the randy Southern rancher, he won the National Board of Review's nod for the best performance by an actor that year. Director Vincente Minnelli gave him full credit for his contribution not only to his own performance, but also to the performances of the other actors. But Minnelli discounted Mitchum's protestations that he never bothered to see his own films. "I personally believe that when the truth comes out after his death, his shameful vice will be revealed," he predicted. "In some dark cellar, a celluloid cache will be discovered. It will be revealed as belonging to the late Robert Mitchum, and it won't be a year's supply of blue films. They'll be pictures he made, which he would sneak in to see time and again."

Upon finishing *Home From the Hill*, Mitchum went to Dublin where his DRM Productions coproduced *The Night Fighters* (also known as *A Terrible Beauty*) with Britisher Raymond Stross. Stross took Mitchum's hijinks more seriously than Minnelli and developed an ulcer during the filming. Informed of this, Mitchum responded with a twinkle in his eye, "I can't imagine what caused it unless it was the time I slipped a noose over his ankles and hoisted him over a lamppost and let him hang head down for a few minutes. I do that to all my producers. It's kind of playful. I think a playful set makes a good picture."

This proved a false assumption on Mitchum's part. *The Night Fighters* met with a disastrous critical reception.

Almost immediately upon finishing work in Ireland, Mitchum did a strange thing for a man who claimed to yearn for the seclusion of his Maryland farm. He boarded a plane for Sydney, Australia, his explanation being that director Fred Zinneman had offered him a part opposite Deborah Kerr and that he would go anywhere at any time for the privilege of "feeding lines" to this gifted actress. Once he made the extravagant claim that such an affinity existed between the two of them that she could play her part three thousand miles away in Switzerland and he could do his in Maryland and the result would be perfection.

In this project, *The Sundowners*, Kerr, Mitchum and Michael Anderson, Jr., were a family unit of itinerant sheep drovers who in the course of their travels acquire a racehorse, Sundowner, which the son races. He wins a number of purses. This starts the Carmody family on the way to accumulating enough money to buy a farm, but the father gambles the savings away and with them the opportunity to purchase a farm and settle down. Contrite, he offers to sell the horse if it wins the upcoming big race, as it seems certain to do. His wife refuses to consider such a sacrifice on his part. In the end neither has to make a noble gesture, since Sundowner is disqualified for interference. Once more the nomadic family who come to rest wherever they happen to be at sundown—hence their nickname and the name of the film—sets off on their endless trek, herding sheep.

Never has Mitchum been better. The ensemble playing of Kerr, Mitchum and Anderson captures a family feeling superbly and the range of emotion displayed by Mitchum equals Kerr's. Critics found much to praise. *Variety* announced: ". . . This may be the finest work he [Mitchum] has done in films." *The New Yorker*'s Roger Angell noted: "Mr. Mitchum, by the way, manages the down-under nasal patois with considerable consistency." The *New York Times* considered this to be a portrait of "as sweet and nice a fellow as Robert Mitchum has ever put

on the screen." *Films in Review* embraced the portrayal with
enthusiasm: ". . . He projects a surprising variety of emotions,
effortlessly. Mitchum deserves more critical attention than he
has received. His forte is an ability to reveal how intellectually
acute the merely instinctual intelligence can be." Director
Zinneman said, "Bob is one of the finest instinctive actors in
the business, almost in the same class with Spencer Tracy."

Under the circumstances, Mitchum, although he claimed to
regard the role as nothing special, rightfully expected that he
would be among the nominees for an Academy Award in the
Best Actor in a Leading Role category. But when the list of
nominees in various categories was released Kerr was among
the actresses, and he was missing among the males. Friends
say he was disheartened at this rejection by his peers and vowed
to continue giving the back of his hand to the establishment.
When Hedda Hopper bitchily needled him by asking how many
Oscars he had won, he told her bitterly, "None, and that's
enough. You walk up there and you say, 'Thank you very
much,' and everybody looks at you. There's no way out. I'm
already in enough trouble."

Following *The Sundowners*, Mitchum completed two more
films—the lamentable *The Grass Is Greener* with Deborah
Kerr, Jean Simmons and Cary Grant, and Jack Webb's *The
Last Time I Saw Archie*—before heading back to Belmont
Farms. It was his intention to make up for his absence by taking
the restless and unhappy Dorothy on a trip to Hong Kong.
Instead he entered into a deal with Gregory Peck's Melville
Productions to coproduce *Cape Fear*. Mitchum's role was that
of a former convict intent upon avenging himself against the
lawyer (Peck) whose testimony had convicted him. His plan
was to stalk and rape the lawyer's wife and teenage daughter.*

Filming this chilling tale took Mitchum to Savannah, Georgia. Arriving on the set the first day, he kept singing, "How
dear to my heart are the scenes of my childhood; when fond
recollection presents them to view." No one could figure out

---

*Columnist Army Archerd reported in a 1961 column, "The spoken word rape has
been entirely removed from *Cape Fear*, and Greg Peck and cohorts have substituted
'attack' at all points in the film which could be one of the year's controversial
epics."

what he was up to. When director J. Lee Thompson inquired, Mitchum explained that it was in Savannah where he had been thrown in jail and sentenced to a term on the chain gang. "These are the scenes of my childhood, man, and they are very dear, very dear indeed, to my heart." Although he claimed to still owe the county time no one took it seriously, and he was lionized as much as he would allow.

After an interview with him appeared in the local newspaper, one of the residents inquired whether he didn't feel he'd come a long way from the police news to the society page. Mitchum thought over the question and then replied, "Not necessarily."

Not completely satisfied with the shooting script even though he was coproducing the film, Mitchum told a UPI reporter: "I show up at 9 and punch out at 6. That's all I do. The pictures belong to other guys, and I don't care too much. . . .

"I do some good pictures and some lousy ones—some for good pay, some for not so good. I don't know why anybody gets excited about us."

However irritating his badmouthing of a picture might be, it seldom affected his performance or his consideration for coworkers. Barrie Chase, the dancer who was making her dramatic debut playing a call girl in *Cape Fear*, became so uptight about the challenge of creating the character she secretly considered quitting the cast. Sensing her anxiety, Mitchum tactfully gave her the support and encouragement which she later said enabled her to give what the director called "an extraordinary performance."

Polly Bergen, who played one of Mitchum's potential victims in the film, felt that wonderful as he was, he was not reaching his full potential as an actor. Asked whether he could do so, she replied, "That would require a lot more exposure of himself. And he's not sure that he likes what's inside him, which is a shame."

After completing *Cape Fear*, Mitchum again postponed the Hong Kong trip he had promised Dorothy. Instead he signed for a cameo role in Darryl Zanuck's star-studded *The Longest Day*, and the Mitchums headed for France. While filming a re-creation of the D-day landings in Normandy amidst rain and heavy seas, Mitchum began griping about the decision to load him and other actors on the landing craft before 250 U.S. soldiers and French extras dressed in military garb were in place. In a UPI correspondent's dispatch Mitchum was quoted as saying at a luncheon allegedly attended by Dorothy Mitchum and Zanuck, "I had to hop aboard first myself with some other actors and stunt men before they [the soldiers] gave in.... It was raining, the wind was blowing and the sea was rough and these troops were afraid to board the landing craft to go to sea." UPI's man said the last straw for Mitchum had been when a man following him fired his blank cartridge rifle into his back. "And when I needed him to give me a boost up this steep cliff, I discovered the guy had decided to get himself 'killed' and was lying on the beach," Mitchum supposedly said.

The U.S. Army denied the star's allegations. At first Zanuck remained silent, avoiding committing himself one way or the other. Then on November 15, 1961, after the Mitchums hopped a plane headed for California (to reach the side of his mother and stepfather who had been injured in an automobile accident), Zanuck called columnist Art Buchwald. "Bob Mitchum got a bum rap," he protested. "He couldn't have said what United Press International quoted him as saying.... Bob might knock a general but he would never knock a G.I. I'm plenty sore about it." He later pointed out that Mitchum supposedly made the remark at a luncheon at which he was present. Since he had never attended such a luncheon nor heard Mitchum utter any such statements, he dismissed the story.

Bob and Dorothy, Julie and her husband, Eliot, John, Carol, and various other family members gathered at the Palmdale Hospital where Ann and the Major had been taken. As details emerged, they learned that Ann had been driving their station wagon when it collided with a farm truck four miles south of Palmdale. Ann had barely been thrown clear of the vehicle, but her 83-year-old husband had been flung a hundred feet onto the gravel siding. Both were still unconscious when the family arrived. The doctors' prognosis was good for Ann, but dim for the Major. "The old fellow's fading fast," one doctor informed John and Bob as they stood at the Major's bedside, only to have the old fellow open his eyes and inquire, "How did you boys find out?"

John explained that the news had been on the radio and, naturally, all of them had come running. The Major expressed his approval. Encouraged, John told him that he must promise to come to his house upon release from the hospital. Through the bloody bandages, the Major croaked, "It's a promise. But only one!" At this point both Bob and John began to feel confident that both of their parents would pull through.

Mitchum and Dorothy remained until after the crises had passed. Then, having made arrangements to take care of expenses not covered by insurance, they boarded a plane for France in order not to delay further shooting.

"Bob has always been generous in taking care of Mother," Julie says. "He can be counted on to assume any out-of-the-ordinary expenses and he's helped other members of the family, too. But he's never given anything to Eliot or me, because we've never needed or wanted it. As Sophie Tucker's mother said in her will, she left such and such to so and so, but to her daughter Sophie she didn't leave nothin', because her daughter Sophie didn't need nothin'."

One of Bob's nieces throws a somewhat different light on the subject. "As a member of the poorer side of the family, I arrived at the hospital in a car with very slick tires," she says. "I remember when Uncle Bob saw them, he was horrified. 'You can't go driving about with those,' he told me. 'It's dangerous.' I mumbled something about getting by okay. 'No way,' he said. 'I'm going to get you a set of new tires.' Well, you can imagine how thrilled I was at the prospect, but I didn't want him to feel he had to do it, so I made another feeble protest. But he insisted. Then Dorothy spoke up. 'Robert, you heard what she said. She doesn't want new tires.' And he just folded. I thought, shit, Dorothy's not going to let a penny go. And I was right. I didn't get any tires.

"In fact, I'm surprised she let him pick up the other expenses. She's the one I'll never understand. Uncle Bob's a very warm and generous person. Dorothy's cold. People have said I shouldn't be so hard on her. They say maybe she is shy or insecure. That may be. It also may be true she just doesn't care about most of his family."

CHAPTER 14

The original plan was to costar Elizabeth Taylor and Paul Newman in the screen version of *Two for the Seesaw*, but when an agreement could not be reached producer Walter Mirisch immediately went after Shirley MacLaine and Mitchum. Mitchum read the script and turned it down, but Mirisch persisted in calling him and his representatives in an attempt to get him to reconsider. As the producer pointed out, this was a presold vehicle based on a long-running Broadway play. It would be an opportunity to demonstrate his versatility.

Mitchum was dubious that he could play the part. Mirisch could think of no better choice. Mitchum could. He instantly reeled off such names as Henry Fonda,* Gregory Peck, Dana Andrews, William Holden and others. Then Shirley MacLaine signed and Mirisch offered Mitchum financial participation. He wavered, but it was not until Mirisch snared director Robert Wise, fresh from his triumph with *West Side Story*, that Mitchum agreed to talk.

At a meeting with the star, Wise expressed his conviction that Mitchum could effectively portray the diffident, down-

---

*Fonda had originated the role on Broadway, but was considered too old for the screen version.

trodden Nebraska lawyer who falls in love with the volatile Bronx ballet dancer. With that, Mitchum said, "I'm not the kind of guy who thinks he knows it all. I can be talked into things." Shortly thereafter, he informed Mirisch and Wise he would accept the role.

Even after signing, he continued to voice doubts about his suitability. The only person who seemed to openly agree with him was his friend George Fargo. Fargo was a marijuana smoker of such proportions that Mitchum had nicknamed him "Gray Cloud" because of the fumes that so often enveloped his head. Fargo warned Mitchum he ought never to consider doing a picture opposite Shirley MacLaine. "That dame will eat you alive," he predicted. "The audience will never know you're there. You're going to end up a blank wall against her." But Mitchum was intrigued by the actress's free-spirited, elfin quality. She was, he heard, easy to work with. She seemed to him to have everything. As he later wrote, "So much talent it was embarrassing. Quick. Responsive. Open and honest. Best of all, she had a weird sense of humor. What more could anyone ask?"

Nevertheless he took Fargo's comments to heart. Although he always claimed he never worried about anyone overshadowing him, because he felt pictures were a collaborative effort and the better his coworkers were the better he looked, he allegedly took steps to see Fargo wasn't proved correct.

"What he did was to begin a subtle campaign to win her affections—and Bob can be very, very compelling," his brother John claims. "So he led Shirley to believe that they were going to have the most torrid romance of all time. He was very attentive and thoughtful—the whole thing. And he talked about when the picture was over and they had the freedom they would go away together to Mexico or someplace and just have a storybook romance.

"Now Shirley is such a professional that she believed all of this, but she didn't let it throw her off stride," John continues. "She still put on one hell of a performance which galled the hell out of Brother Robert. But I can prove to you that nothing transpired from all this in spite of gossip to the contrary.

"I was getting ready to go to a party with my wife Nancy one night and the doorbell rang. I went and there was Shirley.

Dressed fit to kill she was, and she had a half-gallon of vodka slung over her back. Now Brother Robert happened to be on television as she came in. She took off her shoe and threw it at the TV set. 'That son-of-a-bitch,' she said. I asked what was the matter. She said, 'What's this? Explain this to me!' and she handed me this note.

"I read it. And it said something like, 'Dear Shirley, This afternoon I walked down the Pacific shores and I heard the pounding of the surf on the white sand and the breezes brought with them the smells of faraway places. They also brought nostalgia and the deep longing need. The loneliness that I've always had as an inner part of me stirred and I became so removed, so distant, so cut off that I knew it wouldn't be fair to ask you to share this loneliness. So, Shirley, goodbye.'

"She said, 'What does that mean?'

"'It's the kiss off, that's what it means. I've read that note or ones like it forty times.' Well, she was sore as hell that night, but she asked where we were going. I said, 'To a party.' She asked if she could come, too. So she joined Nancy and me and everybody had a hell of a good time.

"That is what actually happened—you're not getting this from someone off the street corner. See, he goes into this deep, expansive, profound reasoning why he can't see them anymore, because he doesn't really want to get involved. And it's always some inner mystique, some power-driven thing that he can't control. The faraway places, the sounds, the loneliness—'I can't ask you to share my loneliness.' When it comes down to the decision, Dorothy always wins hands down. Talk about a con artist."

Apparently Bob is not the only con artist in the Mitchum family. Out of loyalty to his brother, John has spun a tale that lets everyone off fairly easily. For the romance that existed between the two stars was self-evident to some of those working on the production of *Two for the Seesaw*. They nuzzled and openly displayed affection for one another on the sound stages. She made no secret of her possessiveness. That there may be some truth to John's contention that Mitchum experienced conflict about the escalating seriousness of the affair might be deduced from the fact that while he is famed for his ability to pull himself together and perform no matter how severe his hangover, it is sometimes necessary to shoot around him on this production.

When the reviews appeared Fargo proved himself an astute prognosticator. Most critics agreed with *Newsweek*'s assessment although they didn't phrase their opinions as colorfully: "Mitchum, rigid to begin with, plays the movie as if he were wearing tight shoes."

Dorothy, who had long ago learned to overlook her husband's fleeting indiscretions, secure in the knowledge that he would wander only temporarily, was apparently stunned to find him deeply involved with anyone else. Verifiable details are sketchy, but those that exist present at least some picture of what was transpiring.

For example, Dorothy spent New Year's Eve with a small party at Romanoff's. Intermittently, she excused herself and after a time returned to the table with red eyes. Rumor has it that MacLaine allegedly precipitated a crisis wherein she gave Mitchum the ultimatum to choose between her and his wife.

Despite Mitchum's refusal to make any such move, he and MacLaine continued seeing one another. Then in October 1963, when he was working on *Rampage* with Elsa Martinelli, Jack Hawkins and Sabu, Dorothy and he appeared on the verge of a reconciliation. But it was short-lived. When the company returned to California from its location shooting in Hawaii, trouble surfaced.

"The Mitchums were definitely at odds over Shirley," says the wife of a member of the company. "The only time I ever met Dorothy was at a cast dinner party thrown by the producer. Neither Bob nor Dorothy showed up for predrinks at the producer's home. At the restaurant, she arrived with three young male friends. They sat at the far end of the table so I didn't do much more than acknowledge the introduction. But from what I could see she seemed like an exceptionally nice person. But when Bob arrived, she stood up. Her three friends also arose and all of them departed. That was my only contact with her although we were very friendly with him and knew Shirley as well."

Commitment to make a cameo appearance in *The List of Adrian Messinger* and, more importantly, *Man in the Middle* took him to England and India for several months. While in

England, Mitchum, Dorothy, Chris and Trina lived in a small house only five minutes' drive from Elstree Studios where the picture was being shot. A semblance of amiable domesticity seemed to have been restored—so much so that, disturbed by the way the picture was turning out, he began talking of retiring to his farm and devoting himself to his quarter horses.

In Hollywood, meanwhile, Liz Taylor and Frank Sinatra's joint appearance in *What a Way to Go!* hit a snag. With Miss Taylor's withdrawal, the producers decided to give pixie-ish Shirley MacLaine the glamour treatment in this broad farce about a young woman who yearns for simple middle-class domesticity but grows increasingly wealthy with the demise of each of her six husbands and ends up the richest woman in the world. For the six spouses, the producers signed Paul Newman, Dean Martin, Gene Kelly, Bob Cummings and Dick Van Dyke. Sinatra reportedly demanded $200,000 for his two-weeks' work, but Darryl Zanuck, for reasons best known to himself, didn't want the charismatic singer-actor at any price. This left the producers with a starting date and no one to play the world's richest man, a combination of J. Paul Getty and Howard Hughes.

Shirley MacLaine inquired what would be wrong with Bob Mitchum. Everyone practically leaped up and shouted *Eureka*! A call was placed to Belmont Farms, and a day and a half after arriving home from Europe, Mitchum boarded a plane headed for Hollywood.

Reminded that he had talked of retiring or at least taking a long break, Mitchum admitted to Hedda Hopper, "I'm actually working for nothing as I've made too many films this year (taxwise), but I worked with Lee Thompson on *Cape Fear* and I couldn't turn down a chance to work with him and Shirley again."

Once more the Mitchum-MacLaine friendship blossomed. While the sequence which depicted the heroine's fantasy of what life would be like if she married a trillionaire was disappointing to audiences, the participants had a wonderful time working together.

As in *Two for the Seesaw*, the pairing failed to produce on-screen fireworks. But in those pre-black-comedy days, not much worked in a film whose comic plot was propelled from sequence to sequence by one death after another.

With his work completed, Mitchum returned for a couple of months to Maryland. Relations between him and Dorothy were cool, but calm. In January 1964 he took off for Africa alone. His new project, which Talbot Productions was co-producing with Frank Ross for United Artists release, was called *Mister Moses*.

This was the first full-length feature to be filmed in Kenya, and it took full advantage of the scenic beauty as well as the use of an elephant of which Mitchum grew so fond that he was tempted to buy it and ship it back to Maryland.

Initially, Mitchum, leading lady Carroll Baker and most of the company were put up at a hotel in Nairobi, which entailed a round-trip drive of sixty miles to and from their location. The story cast Mitchum as Joe Moses, a diamond smuggler on the lam, who meets a missionary's daughter. "I'm strictly a bum, an itinerant con man, a lusty guy who is forced by circumstances to become a modern-day Moses and lead an African tribe to a promised land when their ancestral diggings are about to be flooded by a newly erected dam," Mitchum said.

The rugged shooting schedule and the daily sixty-mile trip soon began to bore Mitchum and he settled in a trailer in the native village, but not before word seeped back to the United States that a romance had sprung up between him and Carroll Baker. This seems to have alarmed her husband who announced that because of political unrest in the area he had decided to join his wife. Contacted by Earl Wilson, he assured the columnist that his marriage was stable. It was nonsense to think he was concerned because Baker had told an interviewer that "an actress must be attracted to her leading man to be able to play love scenes with him."

Shirley MacLaine had earlier left Hollywood for Japan to spend the holidays and several months after with her husband, Steve Parker. Gossip columns, however, carried news that she had been seen in New York with Mitchum before departing. She brushed that news aside, contending that the meeting was accidental. Gossips also reported that her stay with Parker had been "fleeting . . . and stormy." Almost immediately after the holidays, she left Japan bound for Rome. From there, she flew to Kenya.

Parker almost simultaneously paid a visit to Hollywood where he confirmed to the press that his wife was in Kenya, visiting "our pal Bob Mitchum." Did he approve of the trip? Of course, and all the rumors that he didn't were "poppycock." But when reporters discovered that he had already booked passage to Kenya, he explained that it was necessary for him to confer with his wife on business problems related to their production *John Goldfarb, Please Come Home*.

A fan magazine writer got to Jim Mitchum and inquired about his reaction to the gossip about his father. He responded that he was "proud," and countered by asking how many Hollywood men were virile enough to cause two husbands to fly to Africa just because their wives were reported dining with an actor there. "But," he added, "if two husbands went to Africa because their wives were there with Robert Mitchum—that's different. And it's great for my father's image. He's an invincible man. People don't think my father will ever die. He'll never get old. He's Superman. . . . Anything my father does is all right because of his image. He's a star. . . . To be one, you have to be able to do more—to have no fear because you're public property."

News reports mistakenly conveyed the information that Dorothy had also flown to Kenya. Earl Wilson, who was familiar with the unusual amount of freedom she had granted her husband in order to make their 24-year marriage work, called her to find out just what she knew of the apparent marital upheavals taking place around her spouse. He decided that the most tactful way to ascertain whether or not she was aware of or concerned about them would be to ask if she planned to join her husband abroad. She said she had no such plans and before he was able to formulate his next question, she volunteered, "I've been through this a good many times before, you know." Wilson says he concluded then and there that she was fully aware of what was going on and she was confident that she would prevail.

She was correct. The Carroll Baker rumor apparently was little more than that; later, when an interviewer inquired whether Mitchum agreed with those who were hailing the young star as the new sex goddess, he exhibited an unexpected streak of cruelty by answering, "There's got to be someone for everyone. How should I know?"

For her part, Baker claimed, "I was afraid of Mitchum before I met him. And I never quite got over my apprehension. I was always waiting for him to sock someone in the nose but he didn't. It's strange how a reputation for violence precedes him."

Although Shirley MacLaine is reputed to have confided that Mitchum is the one man with whom she has had an affair that she wanted to marry, they have for many years simply been old friends. A few weeks after returning from Africa, he and Dorothy belatedly celebrated their silver wedding anniversary. And as this is written, their 44-year marriage appears for the most part a solid and happy one.

Even though the marriage crisis had passed, Mitchum was restless. Upon finishing *Mister Moses*, he couldn't wait to get back to his farm. Yet he had hardly settled in when the press department of United Artists put in a perfunctory request for him to do a promotional tour for the film. The man who generally balked at doing a single interview responded, "Set it up. I'll do whatever you think is necessary."

At the beginning of April, he and Dorothy set out on the first lap of the tour. Ensconced at their first stop, the Sherry-Netherland Hotel in Manhattan, he grumbled that he was no damn good at interviews and then proceeded to tailor his material for each writer. He came up with a couple of jokes and a dash of sex for Earl Wilson. For a reporter whose column concentrated on industry news, he trotted out anecdotes about location shooting problems. Interviewed by a politically oriented critic-feature writer, he spoke of President Jomo Kenyatta's taking a liking to him and insisting that he was going to request that the star be appointed American ambassador to Kenya, assuring him, "We'll have some good times."

In addition to New York, the Mitchums traveled to Boston, Pittsburgh, Cleveland, Chicago, Denver, San Francisco, Los Angeles and other major cities, capping the tour in Houston where *Mister Moses* premiered in three new twin theaters simultaneously. The resulting space in newspapers was so impressive that the press agents suggested that if he were as tired of acting as he said, he could become a flack.

The Mitchums' arrival in Los Angeles coincided with the Academy Awards ceremonies, but when columnist Vernon Scott inquired whether they were attending, Mitchum confessed he had been unaware of the event. "I don't pay much attention to that stuff," he claimed.

Scott reported that the new Mitchum *was* paying attention to his sartorial appearance. Gone were the customary jeans, western shirts and cowboy boots. When they met, Mitchum was wearing a shirt with special cuffs which he himself had designed. "Twenty years ago, the ex-hobo would have belted any guy for wearing such fancy cuffs," Scott commented. "But the muscular star has mellowed."

In truth, he was merely emphasizing one aspect of his many-faceted personality to give Scott a fresh story. Twelve days later, he was extolling the easy living in Maryland to NEA's Dick Kleiner and telling him, "I'm as happy as a henpecked man can be." Boasting that he now totally lacked ambition (disregarding the fact he was in the midst of a self-promotion tour), he said he could do nothing forever except "just sit on the warm side of the house."

Whatever her husband had to say about Belmont Farms, Dorothy surprised California friends by asking them to alert her if they heard of a suitable house that could accommodate Trina, Bob and her. They were, she said, definitely interested in returning to Southern California. Naturally someone leaked the news to the press and Mitchum was asked about it. He shrugged in response. "Why not? I don't care where I live as long as the roof doesn't leak. Dottie complains everytime one of those Maryland bees stings her. I guess she's looking around Laguna now so we soon may be living there. It's immaterial to me. No matter where I live, whatever I do will get in the papers. I have to face the fact that I lost my precious privacy years ago."

With his publicity chores completed, instead of heading back for the farm, the family took a place at Malibu. He said that he just wanted to sit on the beach and look at the ocean. He didn't want anyone sending him scripts or making him any offers over the phone. Nevertheless, he quickly accepted a costarring role in Andrew McLaglen's *The Way West* with Kirk Douglas and Richard Widmark. When the company went on location in Oregon, he did make one gesture toward retaining his simple lifestyle. While Widmark and Douglas rented private houses in a nearby village, Mitchum bunked with the wranglers.

The Way West was hardly finished when Howard Hawks approached him about costarring with John Wayne in *El Dorado*, an offer Mitchum had no intention of refusing, though he inquired what the story was. "Story? There's no story," he later claimed Hawks replied. "You and Duke play two old cowboys." Intrigued, Mitchum accepted. "He was right. There was no story. It was all character development. Hawks would stand there and stand there just before a shot. The crew would say, 'Shhhhh! He's writing.' Once he stood there for so long I thought he was going to fall asleep on his feet. Finally he said, 'That's all for today!' He had a mystique about him."

That neither movie was critically well-received seemed not to bother Mitchum in the least.

In March 1966 Mitchum traveled to Vietnam and Thailand. The trip had grown out of his offer to tour for the USO Overseas Committee to entertain American soldiers. His appearances there were good for both his and the troops' morale. He sang, told his tales and, by his own account, consumed fourteen cans of beer and a bottle of whiskey in one morning in a show of congeniality toward everyone from the lowliest private to top brass.

When he arrived back in the States, wearing an Australian cowboy hat and carrying a crossbow that had been presented to him, he headed directly for a telephone. Even though it was ten p.m. PST, he dug out a list of telephone numbers in towns scattered across the country and began calling parents to tell them he had talked and shared a beer with their sons during the preceding two weeks and that Jack or Tom or Charlie was doing just fine.

He emerged from the experience with deep respect for the troops. "Sure they are over there to fight a war which is wrong in principle maybe, but that isn't their doing," he said.

A surprise awaited him at home: Dorothy had found a buyer for Belmont Farms. He acquiesced to the move—as long as a place could be found for his twenty-three quarter horses. Reva and assorted friends helped him search and soon a small ranch was found near Atascadero.

A house for the family was not so easy to come by, so they

rented a place in Brentwood which Cole Porter had leased for twenty-three years preceding his death. But Mitchum was not interested in rejoining the film world. His thoughts and conversation centered on Vietnam even though his doctor told him it would be a year before he was in shape for a return visit. In an interview with Tim Tyler, Mitchum said of the war, "That's what people are for; to be pushed this way and that. Ignorance is just to be made money of, by the smart guys.

"If there were no more pestilence and war, everybody would be out of work. . . . There's no more happy cobbler. Today he has to own the factory. . . . When you think you've arrived, nothing has happened. The realization comes too late, when you realize life is the purpose of life."

Approximately six weeks before the year prescribed by the doctor was up, on February 16, 1967, to be exact, Mitchum made his second morale boosting trip to Vietnam. He later said that his own belief in humanity was restored by some of the behavior he had observed, citing soldiers returning from search or battle missions and going directly to the village school to see how classes in hygiene and other simple subjects that would make the quality of life among the Vietnamese better were progressing. A suggestion that these visits might have been staged for his benefit brought the response, "No way. No way for my benefit. I came in hot. They didn't know I was coming in." Discussing the subject with a writer from *Rolling Stone* later, he observed, "There are always the advantagists [sic], the opportunists who make a lot of money out of other people's misery. . . . Same way on both sides. . . . The single thing I'm grateful for that's come out of the whole war mess has been some recognition of the need for communication. . . . One thing I've learned is the greatest fuckin' slavery is ignorance, and the biggest commodity is ignorance—the dissemination of ignorance, the sale and burgeoning marketing of ignorance."

Mitchum was popular not only with American servicemen, but with the South Vietnamese. As he was about to leave for home, a group gathered near his plane and a child came forward and handed him a bag. He thanked her and the crowd and opened the sack. Inside were scores of live crickets. Nonplussed, he asked a sergeant what he was supposed to do with them.

"Eat 'em."

"Not me," Mitchum replied.

"Look at all those happy, little brown faces," the sergeant said. "You don't want to disappoint them, do you?"

"Okay." Mitchum sighed. "How do I do it?"

"Watch me." The sergeant reached into the bag and took a cricket. "First bite the head off. Then you pull the legs so they won't twitch inside your mouth." His actions matched his words. Then he popped the cricket into his mouth and chewed it up. Mitchum followed suit, feeling as if he were about to die as he swallowed the insect. But he thanked the people for the hours they had spent gathering this great delicacy. However, he said to show how much he appreciated their generosity, he wanted to reciprocate by having them share the gift with him. In that way, he managed to get away with eating only one of the creatures.

Back in Los Angeles, Mitchum took a strong dislike to the gloomy house on Rockingham in Brentwood. And when his daughter saw a rat in an upstairs bedroom, he urged Dorothy to find another place for them to live. She leased Ruth Roman's home and while he was in Italy playing a war correspondent in Dino De Laurentiis's *Anzio*, the move was accomplished.

After the reality of Vietnam, the theatrics of *Anzio* seemed all the more hollow to him. This proved to be an accurate assessment. Both he and the picture were indifferently received, with Vincent Canby of the *New York Times* castigating him as "the most unlikely war correspondent since Lana Turner covered the Japanese invasion of the Philippines in *Somewhere I'll Find You.*"

From Italy, Mitchum went directly to Spain to play a gun-smuggling aviator to Yul Brynner's Pancho Villa in the controversial *Villa Rides!* Dorothy and Trina briefly joined him there and then flew back to Los Angeles in time for Trina to register at Westlake School for Girls. Of Mitchum's performance, the always-witty Judith Crist commented: ". . . He's reached the point of seemingly counting to ten before talking, but considering the lines allotted him, a hundred would be a wiser figure."

After spending the Christmas holidays in their new residence, Mitchum and Dorothy decided that she ought to look for a house to buy while he was in Durango, Mexico, filming the mystery-western *Five Card Stud* with Dean Martin and Roddy McDowall. Once more he played a murderous preacher—though less effectively than in *Night of the Hunter*.

One day in Durango, Mitchum received a call from director Joseph Losey in London. Losey explained that he was looking for someone with an "indifferent British accent" to appear opposite Elizabeth Taylor and Mia Farrow in *Secret Ceremony*. Taylor had suggested calling Mitchum, a master dialectician. Mitchum demonstrated a variety of "indifferent English accents" and Losey offered him the part. A problem developed because Mitchum was not yet finished in Mexico and was committed to shoot a western in Tucson, Arizona, during the summer. For once he appreciated the advantages of stardom, since Losey offered him a special contract which grouped all of his scenes within a ten-day period. He accepted with alacrity.

He and Dorothy arrived in London to find the film was already in trouble and Mitchum later said he didn't feel he did anything to help matters. They shot for ten days in England and Holland. Then his previous commitment demanded that he leave even though some material involving him had not been filmed. By his account, Losey solved the problem by changing the screenplay so that Taylor played scenes he was to have done with Farrow. "Originally I was in the bathtub with Mia—the scene where she rubs Elizabeth's back. In the script it was my back. The changes confused things a bit. Just the same, *Secret Ceremony* did well at the box office. Just after we made it lesbianism came in. Maybe that's why they reworked the bathtub scene. I'm no damned good as a lesbian."

Back in the United States, he continued his marathon movie-making by going to Tucson for the western originally titled *Who Rides With Kane?* but which was released as *Young Billy Young*. In the cast were Angie Dickinson, Robert Walker, Jr., David Carradine, Deana Martin and Chris Mitchum—all offspring of established stars. Mitchum sang the title song. The film did not fare well with critics. Kevin Thomas in the *Los Angeles Times* rapped Mitchum for giving "a rather mechanical performance."

While shooting the picture, Mitchum griped to *Time* magazine's Tim Tyler that once again he was stuck with the same role. "I'm wearing the same damn hat and the same damn boots I wore in *Five Card Stud*," he groused. It must have slipped his mind that the blame rested on his own shoulders, for his company was coproducing with Max Youngstein, who was married to his highly influential executive secretary, Reva Frederick. What he had not overlooked, his protests to the contrary, was that he was receiving $200,000 plus twenty-seven percent of the gross for appearing in the picture.

The final film of this clutch was *The Good Guys and the Bad Guys*, another western directed by Burt Kennedy, who had done *Young Billy Young*. Of this tale of two survivors of the Old West whose code of behavior time has rendered passé, audiences finally seemed ready to agree that Mitchum had made basically the same story once too often. Only in foreign markets which were not saturated with television westerns did the picture fare well. It was his final western.

After a string of fourteen pictures in which he could not be said to have had a solid hit, he again began to talk of retirement. Explaining but not apologizing for the run of bad pictures, he said that throughout his career he had appeared in four clinkers to every good film. "I'm not a person," he said sardonically. "I'm a paragraph in a contract. And I never see the money. Somebody else takes care of that. Every once in a while, he comes around and nudges me and says, 'You just bought a hotel'—or something."

At one time, he observed, he had naively supposed there was the possibility of achievement, that if he did well he would get better opportunities. Not so. "You just get to do more," he said bitterly. "I am disenchanted."

CHAPTER 15

Nothing helped. Julie, Carol and his mother believed conversion to the Baháí faith would rescue him. If only he would embrace the tenets of Baha Ullah and follow the footsteps of Sir Abdul Baha, who trod the mystical path with practical feet, they felt certain Bob would share the richness that had pervaded their lives since they had embraced the prophet's teachings.

Julie reasoned that if she, who had been so belligerent against Christ, Moses and Mohammed could find solace in the manifestations of the Baháís, then so could her brother who up until then had simply not been interested in organized religion of any kind. She held an unshakable conviction that beneath the macho movie image there remained undamaged the reverent, sensitive human being with whom she had enjoyed since childhood such total rapport that verbal communication was all but unnecessary.

When he seemed not to respond to the women's overtures, they read and reread the Christmas card he had created for his mother one year. True, the painting was crude because he was not a painter, but, they asked, who could doubt the true character of the man who wrote *Trumpet in the Dark?*

We turned to blow the music of the earth in embryo
And all throughout time's corridors is an echo
on the future's waiting doors . . .

Elsewhere in the poem he spoke of the golden note blending with all hearts, standing as one, yet standing apart and searching for one, brighter than all the rest, to give others objectives.

For all his family's efforts, they were unable to persuade him to embrace the faith.

Temporarily, he helped himself by hiding out on his ranch with his quarter horses. The horses and the evanescent euphoria produced by the consumption of Chivas Regal, tequila, brandy— or whatever he happened to be drinking that day—provided fleeting solace. But it was not enough.

He had no greater interest in politics than in religion. "Philosophically, I'm an anarchist," he often said. He had none of his peers' interest in golf, tennis or bowling. He refused to watch television or to go to the movies. On impulse, he once had bought ten thousand dollars' worth of camera equipment, but several years had passed and he had never seen anything of sufficient interest to cause him to remove the camera from its case.

In 1968, while he was suffering this profound disenchantment, Dorothy found a four-bedroom, California colonial house at 268 Saint Pierre Road in Bel-Air for $265,000. The Mitchums purchased it and hired Mel Lashley to decorate it. On moving day, Lashley looked over the furniture that had been transported from one house to another and fixed Dorothy with a baleful glance before announcing, "It won't work. The Steinway's nice but that's it." Dorothy protested that it would be too expensive to replace the other pieces, but Lashley bullied her by saying, "It's cheaper to get new than spend money having this redone."

The relationship between Dorothy and Lashley was a stormy one. "It was the same thing over and over," he says. "I'd tell her the bill was, say, fourteen hundred dollars and she'd begin complaining how low her bank account was getting, as if Robert Mitchum were some struggling actor. Did she think he was still making a thousand a week at RKO? I still have a stack of letters from her. 'Cute letters'—she was playing little miss precious from another time.

"She told me how furious Robert was. I never saw him pay the slightest attention. Usually he had Orson Welles or somebody up there and these 'great geniuses' were solving the problems of the world. If there was nobody else around he'd talk to me. It didn't mean he cared what I thought, he just wanted somebody to talk to. If you interrupted, he'd give you a look as if he'd cheerfully kill you. I think that's the reason he and Reva [Frederick] got along so well. She took care of business. She was capable. She wasn't demanding and she'd sit and listen. If you'll just sit quietly with him, he'll happily drink and expound for hours."

Nevertheless, the house was finished to everyone's satisfaction. To celebrate, the Mitchums gave a party. "You'd never think of them as great party givers," says Henny Backus. "Jim and I go everyplace and we've been to maybe ten brilliant parties out here. Two of the best ones were given by the Mitchums. The first one was several years before they moved to Bel-Air. For one of their wedding anniversaries. They held it in the great big, gorgeous dining room at Romanoff's, with a red carpet leading clear out to the curb. It was one of the finest, best organized, most exciting evenings I've ever spent.

"The second great do," Henny says, "was at their home on Saint Pierre Road. Most people give no more than maybe half of one good party. Glamorous, beautiful, warm. This was a formal party with an orchestra, place cards, the whole thing. When they do it, they do it. And you ask yourself which one is responsible. Jim and I concluded they collaborate, but that Bobby is probably more inclined to be social. Because Dorothy is terribly shy until she's had a cocktail or two. Then she loosens up and is absolutely wonderful. I adore her."

Adore her she may, but Henny will not venture to explain Dorothy. "I think probably her main interest is really Bobby and the kids and their families," she says. "She's not a luncheon girl. I'd say she has maybe four close girlfriends. But I doubt whether they can figure her out. She's a shadowy figure no one really knows."

Another unexpected friend, Phyllis Diller, concurs. "Imagine lasting all those years with Bob. I mean most women would have gone years ago. He's a wonderful, charming person. Never dull. But, my God, living with him must be something else.

"He claims he doesn't associate with actors, but he does. Once he and Dorothy came to one of my parties for about one hundred fifty people. The party favor was a brandy snifter, half full of water with a goldfish swimming in it. One at each place. Bob drank everything in sight—including the goldfish. Isn't that precious!

"Also when I have the Mitchums, I always serve chili. *Northern* chili which has nothing in common with cowboys, or Spain, or Mexico. On the buffet will be roast beef, shrimp, smoked oysters—all this expensive stuff—but Bob always gorges on my chili. Well, he kept saying, 'You've got to open a chain of chili parlors. I promise you it will make you rich beyond your dreams. Forget about show business. This stuff is gold.' Well, I thought, if Bob Mitchum thinks my chili is so great he'll lick the bowl—how can I miss? So I sunk a bundle in a place I called Philli Dilli Chilli—and I lost my shirt!

"What an incredible man! I love him. But as a business adviser—forget it!"

While Mitchum, disenchanted with himself and his career, was telling everyone that he was ready to retire, scripts poured in. Among the offers was one from director David Lean and writer Robert Bolt, who had previously collaborated on *Lawrence of Arabia* and *Dr. Zhivago*. The screenplay they submitted, *Ryan's Daughter*, was set in Ireland around 1915 during the time of "the troubles" and told of the love between a middle-aged schoolteacher and a bright-eyed pupil many years his junior. The two fall in love and marry, he proves to be impotent and she begins a passionate affair with a crippled but handsome English officer who commands the hated local garrison. Their relationship is not only looked upon as scandalous but also treasonable by the patriotic villagers. After a devastating storm in which the guns and ammunition being smuggled in are endangered, the villagers sneak down to the beach to rescue them, only to be met by the English officer and his men. The girl falls under suspicion of having tipped him off. She is shorn, stripped and beaten. She returns to her husband, and the young officer kills himself. The two outcasts—the cuckolded schoolteacher and his disgraced wife—leave the village together, perhaps, it is suggested, to find a new life together in Dublin.

Upon reading the script, Mitchum excitedly informed Reva that it was the best ever submitted to him. Then he riffled through the pages and announced in horrified tones, "My God, the schoolteacher works every day. No way am I going to do that."

When Lean called from England to inquire about his availability, Mitchum informed him that he never would consider undertaking such a taxing role and demanding schedule. He hung up.

Upon arriving home, he was told by Dorothy that Bolt had telephoned and she had promised that he would return the call. Mitchum informed her she was wrong. He had nothing more to say about the project. Subsequently the phone rang. It was Bolt. He said it was his understanding the extended tenure of the project—six months' shooting—disturbed the actor. "We've worked through the schedule and found several spots that allow you ten days vacation."

"Sorry," Mitchum replied. "I had planned to commit suicide."

Bolt thought their connection was bad.

Mitchum repeated his statement. Bolt spluttered incoherently and then recovered, saying, "I say, if you'd do us the favor and appear in the picture, I'll take on the expense of burial."

Bolt's sense of humor won over Mitchum. Grumbling that Lean's long shooting schedules would undoubtedly do him in, he signed the $750,000 contract prepared by Metro-Goldwyn-Mayer. Others in the company included Sarah Miles, John Mills, Trevor Howard and Christopher Jones.

Mitchum and Dorothy set out for Ireland in January 1969 with some trepidation on his part. They stopped briefly at the Dorchester Hotel in London where he submitted to interviews, receiving reporters in white kimono pajamas, dark glasses and black socks.

His views were as unorthodox as his clothing. He confided that his biggest fault was lack of virtues. What those virtues were he didn't have a clue, but he was certain he lacked them. He said that when he died he would like it said that he was a whore with a heart of gold. He came out against legalizing marijuana, but said that if he had a son who asked about trying it he would hand him a roach and warn him to be careful of the company he kept while using it. He quoted his favorite line from Joseph Conrad: "Loneliness is the hard and absolute condition of existence."

Surprise. Perverse observations. Shock tactics. These equaled newspaper lineage and increased interest in the film. Purpose accomplished, he met with Lean, Bolt and Sarah Miles, submitted to costume fittings and, almost as an afterthought, appeared on a TV talk show before setting out for Dingle, County Kerry, Ireland.

Upon arrival on February 3, 1969, for what turned out to be a grueling wait, he and Dorothy took over an entire building which he claimed bore the name Hotel Milltown. Miles says it was "more of a boarding house really." Unsuspecting tourists frequently received a shock when Mitchum answered the calls for reservations by informing them, "Oh, you wouldn't be liking it here anymore. Americans are running it now. Nudists, you know."

According to Miles, the entire company stayed there and on evenings when shooting ran late and all restaurants had closed, Mitchum would invite everyone to dine and then would roll up his sleeves and make a late supper for them. "He was awfully good at cooking," she says. "I remember what I think was the day he went off me. It was never the same after this moment. He got some lobsters which were not that abundant at that time of year. He obtained two lobsters and he was going to cook them. For some obscure reason I went into the kitchen and saw these little fellows looking up at me and I removed them. He was having a very big dinner party that night and I took them and put them back into Dingle Bay. He just went bananas. And quite rightly so. I mean it was a dreadful thing for me to do. But it seemed I had no choice once I looked into their eyes. I'm a vegetarian now. Perhaps that's why. But he's actually never been the same about me since."

Dorothy also admires her husband's expertise in the culinary department—*except* in doing steaks. According to her, he has never grasped that medium and well-done ones should be put on first. He invariably puts all of them on together and removes the rare ones first. Thus those who prefer their meat rare also get it cold.

During the first ten days of shooting, by the actor's count, Lean fell seven days behind schedule in filming. Studying the dailies, Lean decided that Mitchum's makeup made him look like a giant Charlie Chaplin. As a result, Mitchum received a new wardrobe and makeup; and when Lean complained that the star "seemed so large," other members of the company were padded and outfitted with elevator shoes.

Mitchum's casual attitude toward acting unnerved Lean, who had invested two years' preproduction work in the project before the first camera rolled. Mitchum believed that the director shot a sequence, examined the results and then reshot it until it coincided with the image in his head. This, the star thought, accounted for the slow progress.

These delays tended to dissipate the actors' energies, but Lean cajoled, ridiculed, pleaded, flattered and did whatever was necessary to create dramatic tension. Sometimes this was more difficult than others. For example, on one occasion, Mitchum and Miles spent six hours in the middle of a field waiting, according to her, for gulls. "David had a passion for sea gulls," she says, "and was determined to get one crapping for the camera."

On the other hand, during a scene on the beach, Lean employed a wind machine to blow a gale of saltwater at the actors at seventy-five miles per hour and was angry when they failed to register the proper degree of "anxiety and anguish." "But one couldn't complain about the demands," Miles says. "When we signed for the picture, we knew what we were in for, that's for sure."

Frequently, Mitchum rose to the challenge of being able to deliver the required emotion in one take. "I think it would really canker him when I did because he didn't have time to instill his own vision," Mitchum says. The actor also suspected that in spite of their mutual respect he sometimes tried Lean's patience. "Basically that's because he speaks English and I speak American," he observed. "And I understand English, but he doesn't understand American." Mitchum also surmised that it upset Lean to have him laughing and joking with the crew until the director called "Action!" and then to have him step into the scene and do it perfectly the first time. "Lean would be almost tearful, and he'd say, 'Bob, that was spot-on! I can't tell you how lovely it was . . . that was simply marvelous.' And instead of saying, 'Thank you,' I'd ask, 'You don't think it was a little too Jewish?' It would just drive him crazy the way I kept putting him on."

Underneath the put-on, Mitchum has admitted he was grateful to meticulous directors in general and Lean in particular for having frequently saved him from himself by curbing his inclination to take the easiest way to get a scene finished.

Mitchum, who is inclined to project a don't-give-a-damn attitude, is nevertheless a conservative craftsman. During one take, he realized he had reversed hands. He called Lean's attention to his error and began again. Not to have done so would have ruined the continuity of the scene. When someone complimented him on it later, he shrugged it away. "Acting is a matter of cadence," he said. "You have to remember what you are doing in the scene and pick up the exact same physical movements."

Having learned his craft in little theater and B movies, Mitchum has never held acting schools in high regard. "Today every fruit figures he must be an actor, so he gets a diploma from Lee Strasberg's school. But how many of them do you ever see on the screen?" he has often asked. "Do you go to school to be tall? Do you go to school to be blond? Talent is like having an ear for pitch. You can't develop it."

As he adjusted to conditions on *Ryan's Daughter*, the incessant talk of retirement temporarily ceased. "You know, each morning when I get up I think about quitting the business," he said. "But actually I enjoy working. It's exciting to develop scenes and make people believe them. Creating another identity on the screen is fun. I guess I'll stay around until I get a medical discharge."

In addition to Lean's methodical pace, the production moved slowly because of numerous accidents. Christopher Jones miraculously emerged shaken up but unhurt when he demolished his new Ferrari on a narrow, winding road. Two Land Rovers were lost in a peat bog. John Mills, who played the grotesque village idiot, and Trevor Howard, the parish priest, barely escaped drowning when their boat capsized. Mills suffered a concussion and Howard, a broken collarbone and bruised ribs.

Mitchum's promised series of ten-day vacations shrunk to one sixteen-hour trip to Los Angeles. Summoned back at once, he then moped around for days waiting for his services to be utilized. As the months passed, his grousing became incessant. Once when he and Sarah Miles were having tea in her trailer with an American journalist, Mitchum's obsessive complaints about Vietnam, the weather and being stuck in Dingle ruffled the volatile actress, who snapped at him, "Shut up! I'm sick to death of your complaints. You knew when you signed on for a David Lean picture that it would take a long time and no one can help the fucking weather." Taken aback by her vehemence, an amused Mitchum bowed deeply in mock apology.

Nevertheless, her outburst did not deter him from the litany of complaints about being trapped by a whim of nature as they awaited the big storm which was to serve as the dramatic centerpiece for the film. Day after day, Mitchum led revelers from the company at a pub run by Tom Ashe, who turned out to be Gregory Peck's cousin.

By the time the film neared completion, Mitchum and Miles had developed deep admiration for each other, despite her belief that he had "gone off" her because of the lobster incident. He rated her along with Deborah Kerr and Jane Greer as his favorite costars. Shaking his head in wonder, he commented, "She's wild, that Sarah. Sometimes she has come to my room and wakened me at three in the morning and in those refined English accents asked, 'Bob, can I procure a woman for you?' That's some girl, I'll tell you."

When a journalist later asked whether he had had an affair with her, Mitchum evaded a direct answer by responding, "I think you should always make out with your leading lady if you have a chance. I've discussed the subject several times with Dorothy. Unfortunately, my old lady doesn't agree."

In the summer of 1983, Miles wrote about him: "Mitchum claims not to give a damn about acting and cries all the way to the bank. I believe he wants desperately to be a good actor and as long as he had his dope he wouldn't need money at all. The reason he never became the actor he should have become is because he finally is too shrewd to over-believe in himself which after all is what an actor has to do. He's really not an actor, you see. He's more of a human being.

"When I say that he's not really an actor he's more of a human being, I mean that as the deepest compliment, you know. He's more than just an actor, he's a 'one of a'—he doesn't fit into any category at all. This, of course, is what makes it so hard for him to really do what he ought to have done, but I think he is a person who will go down as being one of the 'one of a's.'"

After almost ten months on *Ryan's Daughter*, Mitchum's obligations were fulfilled and he returned to Bel-Air while Lean cut, helped choose the music and supervised the scoring of the picture. "He's the complete director," Mitchum said admiringly. "There is nothing else. He lives for nothing else as long as he's involved." Then fleetingly Mitchum drew aside the curtain and admitted that while acting, he committed himself fully. "If I'm actually in operation, the wall could fall down— I wouldn't notice," he said. "They ask, 'Would you like us to clear the eye line? There are people standing there!' Not at all. I don't care, I don't see them."

Then as if he had revealed too much of himself, he hopped in his car and drove a hundred miles north to Atascadero where he spent the greater portion of his time with his herd of quarter horses which had grown in number to thirty-five.

With no professional activity in the offing until he journeyed east for the Manhattan premiere of *Ryan's Daughter*, he again began talking about devoting himself completely to developing superior horses, doing some long-postponed writing and making the rounds of all the best parties.

MITCHUM RETIRES AT 52

His official announcement garnered the hoped-for attention even though Dorothy candidly informed reporters that she was alarmed at the prospect he might be serious. She said she felt he was too young to give up acting and expressed the hope that he would find a role that interested him. Mitchum's younger son, Chris, told columnist Jim Bacon that he had tried to talk his dad into quietly taking a year off. "If he still doesn't want to act, he can write and produce," Chris said. Bullets Durgom, Mitchum's new representative, at least pretended to take him seriously. But when columnist Marilyn Beck asked John Wayne his reaction to his friend's announcement, Wayne replied, "Heck, Bob says that everytime he's not working! I don't think it would be too hard to get him back in the harness."

A former studio press agent took a more cynical view. "At RKO I always said if Mitch ever wanted to give up acting, he could always become a press agent." He laughed. "He knew an announcement like that would be a space grabber. Once— after he left RKO—all hell broke loose when some broad from the SPCA asked him for a donation for 'doomed doggies' and he leered at her: 'Don't you think all dogs should be shot?' He's a master at stirring up controversy. And he's never given a damn how he did it."

Four months later talk of retirement was forgotten. Mitchum acquiesced to MGM's request to do special publicity to hype the opening of *Ryan's Daughter* and to plant the notion that he would be receptive to an Academy Award nomination. Replying to a newsman's startled response to his frank campaigning, he asked, "Why not? I've never said anything against it."

In the latter part of October he and Dorothy flew to New York and checked into the Plaza Hotel. Explaining his previous scorn for ad-taking and log-rolling, he observed, "I've never liked all the patting yourself on the back and I've doubted there's any intrinsic value in it. Suppose another industry took a day off to give itself a lot of awards. Wouldn't everybody say they were nuts? The validity lies—as Cary Grant said last year—in the fact you get recognition from your peers. . . . The fact that people you respect vote their respect for you."

Outside the Ziegfeld Theater at the New York premiere on November 9, 1970, the compulsion to be controversial led Mitchum to tell a Canadian telecaster that *Ryan's Daughter* was too long and gave him cramps in the butt. He volunteered the opinion that he was not very good in it, then altered that to "well, pretty good." And what did he plan to do next? Always alert to the value of the unexpected, he assured the telecaster, "Oh, I plan to join the Gay Liberationists as a sympathizer."

At the post-opening party at the Museum of Modern Art, he consumed quantities of Chivas Regal which put him in the mood to join the orchestra where he proceeded to sing such old-time rousers as "Waitin' for the Robert E. Lee," "Bill Bailey, Won't You Please Come Home?" and "I Wonder What's Become of Sally"—which he changed to Sarah.

Ironically, the film and Mitchum both enjoy far greater acceptance in the 1980s than at the time of the picture's release. "Poor David Lean," Sarah Miles sighs. *"Lawrence of Arabia* came out and they called it the Four Pillars of Boredom. They wee-wee'd all over it. Then *Dr. Zhivago* comes out and they say, 'Oh what a shame! *Dr. Zhivago* isn't as good as *Lawrence of Arabia*. David Lean has lost his touch.' Then he does *Ryan's Daughter*. They wee wee all over it and say he'll never do another *Zhivago*!"

In spite of mixed reviews, one person who never wavered in his appreciation of Mitchum's work was Lean, who said, "After twenty years of playing a comic-strip character called Superstud, Mitchum at last is being recognized as the gifted actor he has always been. He is a master of stillness. Other actors act. Mitchum is. He has true delicacy and expressiveness, but his forte is indelible identity. Simply by being there, Mitchum can make almost any other actor look like a hole in the screen."

Business was brisk enough to encourage MGM's publicity department to persuade Mitchum to undertake a fourteen-city tour, beginning in January 1971. The purpose was to hype box-office receipts and reinforce Mitchum's chances of being nominated for an Oscar. It proved an exercise in futility on the latter count. Not only did Mitchum lose to George C. Scott in *Patton*, he failed to qualify as one of the five nominees. Friends claim that he was visibly disappointed. Neither he nor they mentioned this defeat—much less indulged in the customary ridicule that attended such a situation. For some time after the announcement of the nominations, he seemed to walk about surrounded by a sense of loss.

* * *

Response to *Ryan's Daughter* may not have won Mitchum an
Oscar, but it reinforced his reputation and paved the way for
a series of memorable screen portrayals. Before this occurred,
however, he had rushed into what turned out to be two dismal
films, *Going Home* with Brenda Vacarro and Jan-Michael Vincent, and *The Wrath of God* with Rita Hayworth and Frank
Langella. *Going Home* dealt with the attempt at accommodation
and reconciliation between an ex-convict and his son. Years
before the boy had seen his father murder his mother and he
had helped convict his dad by testifying. Off-beat material
which required sensitive handling, the picture was mutilated in
the cutting room at the direction of MGM president James T.
(Smiling Cobra) Aubrey. Then Mitchum and director Herbert
B. Leonard, who had worked for deferred salaries, saw the
studio show it to the press on November 16, open it in four
major cities the following day and close it as a dead flop a
week later.

For *The Wrath of God*, Mitchum went to Mexico to play a
defrocked priest who toted a gun inside his hollowed-out Bible.
The picture—written, directed and produced by Ralph Nelson—confused audiences and critics alike. Asked why he had
agreed to appear in it, Mitchum avoided answering by giving
one of his flip responses, such as "I'll do anything to get out
of the house."

His fortunes improved with *The Friends of Eddie Coyle*, a
crime film with Pinteresque dialogue. Mitchum initially had
been approached to play the police informer, but when he read
and admired the novel, Paramount producer Paul Monash suggested he play the small-time hood who through economic
pressure finds himself inexorably transformed into the very
thing he hates—"a permanent fink." Although one contingent
who apparently had not seen *Ryan's Daughter* worried that he
was too strong to play such a weak character, Mitchum responded by turning in a masterful performance. Perhaps by
calling upon the contradictions in his own personality, he created a multifaceted character which served once more to remind
viewers what a skillful actor he had become.

"I have to say I really don't understand how Mitchum acts,

what his techniques and resources are. It just happens. It's kind of an event," Paul Monash said at the time. "It's up there on the screen before you know it. He simply does it. It's like Willie Mays, you know—running back to the wall and catching the ball over his shoulder. Mitchum's a natural."

In *Time*, Richard Schickel commented: "At 56, when many of his contemporaries are hiding out behind the remnants of their youthful images, he has summoned up the skill, the courage to demonstrate a remarkable range of talents." Of the same performance, *Playboy*'s critic enthused: "Mitchum lurches through the title role with a curse on his lips for every occasion, in total command of the meatiest role he has had in years. . . . Director Peter Yates . . . filmed *Eddie Coyle* on location in Boston and he keeps unflinchingly in focus that particular urban jungle, a district where the decline and fall of a petty crook whose luck has run out is ugly, tragic and part of the daily routine." *Variety*'s critic viewed the film and dubbed Mitchum "one of the more underrated actors in films."

Although no one probably could have persuaded Mitchum to admit it, at the beginning of 1974 he seemed to be attempting to stretch himself as an actor in an ambitious Japanese-American film. *The Yakuza* (strictly translated *gambler* but popularly connoting *gangster*) was an adventurous attempt by film critic Paul Schrader to wed his brother's tales of the strict code of honor and duty by which the Japanese underworld operated with the conventions of *film noir*. When Schrader's script proved too melodramatic, Robert Towne was brought in to polish it, but it remained somewhat inaccessible for mass audiences. In the plot Mitchum plays a former detective who returns to Japan to rescue the kidnapped daughter of an Army buddy. He enlists his ex-mistress's brother, played by Takakura Ken, an ex-Yakuza, to help undertake the rescue. Their scheme fails and a number of the kidnapper's men are killed. The Japanese code requires that the kidnapper seek revenge against Mitchum's cohort. Mitchum pitches in to help Ken. The girl is rescued, only to have her father agree that the kidnappers can murder Mitchum. Mitchum shoots his former buddy. After discovering that his ex-mistress is Ken's wife and not his sister as he has always thought, Mitchum enlists Ken's aid in killing all the kidnapper's guards, the kidnapper and his son. For this last death, which had been prohibited, Ken is honor-bound to slice off his little finger as penance. Mitchum follows suit to demonstrate his remorse over his unintentional relationship with Ken's wife.

Melodramatic as the script sounds, it attracted such first-rate talent as director Sydney Pollack and Takakura Ken, the Japanese Robert Mitchum. Redeemed by exquisite photography and universally good performances under Pollack's sure-handed direction, it proved too special for commercial success. Almost immediately, however, it achieved cult status. Among its earliest admirers were Rex Reed, Judith Crist, Pauline Kael, and Derek Elley. In his *Films and Filming* review Elley wrote: "As Kilmer, Robert Mitchum turns in his finest performance in years, marshalling all his power of under-statement and knowing acceptance into a convincing portrait of a 'special stranger,' an American with rare empathy for Japanese mores." Kael commented in her review: [Mitchum] "seems to be the only movie star who is becoming a more commanding figure as he ages," while Reed observed: "Robert Mitchum looks as ravaged as a bomb site in Hiroshima, as sleepy as a wombat, and as gloriously bigger than life as the Imperial Hotel."

In what emerged more and more clearly as a pattern in Mitchum's life, he followed an underappreciated piece of excellent work with something of an outrage.

In mid-1974, it was announced that he would costar with Richard Burton and Charlotte Rampling in *Jackpot*. The producers later insisted he had given his word, but Mitchum was even more insistent that their inability or unwillingness to place his salary in an American bank before he left the country put the kibosh on the deal.

Instead, he was reunited with Otto Preminger with whom he had previously worked in *Angel Face* and *River of No Return*. The film was *Rosebud*, a tale of extortion, blackmail, terrorism, kidnapping and murder. When Mitchum had read the script during the shooting of *The Wrath of God* in Mexico, he had felt little enthusiasm. But instead of turning Preminger down flat, he made monetary demands he felt the producer couldn't afford to accept. To his surprise, Preminger met his terms.

After arrival in Juan-les-Pins with Dorothy, Mitchum worked only two days during the first three weeks. Then another twelve days elapsed before he again appeared before the cameras, this time in Corsica. Even so the demands were mild. He spent his free time sharing drinks with the crew and grumbling about getting on with the work. Late in the afternoon Preminger announced that he was needed in town and was entrusting the assistant director to film a simple scene on a bus. Mitchum took violent exception to such cavalier treatment and began insisting at the top of his voice that the bus driver be replaced by a stunt man to avoid endangering the actors' lives. After prolonged hassling between him and the assistant director, he agreed to let the bus driver drive and the scene was wrapped up.

Next morning his wake-up call was for four a.m. Two hours later he arrived ready to film a scene in which he, as the CIA agent, came over a wall and repelled an Arab assassin. He was nursing a gigantic hangover from the *pastiche* he had guzzled the night before, and his surly mood had been exacerbated by the hot, dusty ride to three wrong locations before the driver succeeded in finding the correct one.

As Mitchum emerged from the car, the sound of carpenters' hammering assaulted his ears. He saw that the track being laid along the wall was only half finished. At the top of his voice he demanded explanations for his early call, the inability of the driver to find the company and the indignity of finding the track uncompleted. Receiving no satisfaction, he strode over to the tent where others were trying to cure *their* hangovers with breakfast, grabbed the center pole and shook it like King Kong, all the while shouting threats that this lack of consideration was going to cost Preminger plenty.

Spotting the director near the uncompleted track, Mitchum descended on him, roaring his displeasure at having been rousted out of bed at four in the morning, being driven all over the country only to arrive to find he was expected to stand around watching a lousy track shot being set up.

Preminger bristled, "You are drunk. You ver drunk last night and you are drunk now."

The carpenters' hammers froze in midair. The actors and

crew fell silent. Only the roosters continued to crow.

"All right, Dad. Let's say goodbye. *Now!*" Mitchum proposed, extending his hand which the seething Preminger refused to shake. Nonchalantly Mitchum turned, ambled back to his car and ordered himself driven back to the hotel.

He and Dorothy started packing and arranging for their exit, but before this could be accomplished, another confrontation between Mitchum and Preminger took place. Afterward Preminger insisted that Mitchum had walked off the picture, and Mitchum was vehement about the hot-tempered director firing him. Subsequently both threatened legal action, but after headlines and sensational news stories around the world, the controversy died down and was seemingly forgotten.

A few months later when Mitchum was asked about the contretemps, he claimed that he had been "more than half joking" and that Preminger had lost his temper and could not keep him in the role without losing face. "It's funny, Preminger objects to drinking actors," he mused. "But he replaced me with Peter O'Toole. Hell, that's like replacing Ray Charles with Helen Keller."

After marching to the sound of his own drummer regarding *Jackpot* and *Rosebud*, Mitchum agreed to face the challenge of playing Raymond Chandler's Philip Marlowe, a character which had been portrayed with resounding success by Humphrey Bogart and Dick Powell and with widely divergent approaches by such dissimilar actors as George Sanders, Elliot Gould, James Garner and Robert Montgomery.

The vehicle was *Farewell, My Lovely*, arguably the most admired of the Marlowe mysteries; Mitchum, with his lazy-lidded eyes, scarred face and slightly over-the-hill body clad in a double-breasted, pin-stripe suit, trench coat and snap-brim hat seemed perfectly cast. Other elements were more questionable. Los Angeles in the 1970s was not the Los Angeles of the 1940s; billboards, TV antennas, skyscrapers and even traffic lights and lanes had to be avoided. There had to be acceptable substitutes for the seedy establishments of Chandler's mean streets. Luckily, director Dick Richards and cohorts found Myron's Ballroom in downtown Los Angeles still operating, and Echo Park could be shot to suggest the period. A vacant house on Vermont Avenue was furnished to approximate Mrs. Florian's rundown home and, given the freedom of a relaxed censorship code, a deteriorating mansion was turned into a whorehouse instead of the mysterious clinic of the Powell film. Streets were repainted, stoplights temporarily removed and scenes were shot on the pier and aboard the now-stationary *Queen Mary* in Long Beach.

The production got off to a rocky start, however, when the Screen Extras Guild manned a picket line and the question arose whether other unions would honor it and shut down filming. But after five days a compromise was reached in which half SEG and half nonunion people were employed.

Mitchum was skittish about working with Richards. He tended to regard the director, a former still photographer, maker of TV commercials and two mildly received movies, as a novice. Understandably nervous, Richards annoyed the veteran star by constant rewrites until he said, "Listen, Richards, you've got to get your act together. I didn't sign my name on the dotted line to have you change the script every five minutes. I have twelve lawyers outside in the parking lot and they're ready to leap on you if you make me do anything I didn't sign for. Stick to the script." The other actors and the crew privately thanked him for his stand. Years later Mitchum said of Richards, "He was a fine still photographer. I think, though, that moving objects confused him a little. Once when he meant to say 'Action!' he said, 'Cut.'"

Nevertheless, Mitchum found pleasure working with such friends as John Ireland and Harry Dean Stanton. He also delighted in the adulation of two actresses. Charlotte Rampling, who plays the sensuous, dangerous saloon singer turned judge's wife, told anyone who would listen that she had signed for the picture because it provided an opportunity to get to know and work with him. She confessed she only had agreed to appear in *Jackpot* because she had believed he was going to be in it. "He really *is* a legend," she bubbled, "and oh so cool. He's been at this forever. It's nice to see somebody who's absolutely straight and direct. No flies on him."

The other actress, Sylvia Miles, had had one nude scene

with Jan-Michael Vincent in *Going Home*. "It was a mad, wild sequence with Jan, who played Bob's son," Miles says. "But I never really actually got to meet Bob. Worse still, the scene was cut out because the film was released on television before theaters.

"Then I got this hurry-up call for Mrs. Florian. When I got to the Coast, I was in for a surprise. He'd always been a favorite actor of mine, but I didn't realize that he's a very, very sensitive man and a very professional guy. I'd heard—obviously, you hear—all kinds of wild stories. Now I'm not that much of a a rara avis, but I found him to be so helpful. He saw I had a godawful trailer. He insisted I use his big trailer to change and dress in. Now don't make that in such a way that it will be misunderstood. He just made sure that I was well taken care of in my role. When I first got there we ran dialogue for about five minutes and he said, 'Let's forget this. It's going to work fine.' Then when I was in front of the camera he watched. If something happened that wasn't in my favor, he'd come over and tip me off so I'd be aware of it. So I got a better camera shot, a close-up that I might not have gotten otherwise. I interjected little things into the role—the song and dance, whatever. And he most willingly agreed to do it without making a fuss about it."

As a result, reviewers pretty much echoed what Donna Lyons wrote in Andy Warhol's *Interview*: "Sylvia Miles . . . evokes the whole history of a has-been dame in five minutes." Miles also received an Academy Award nomination. "It was a fun shoot," she says. "And I really do believe it was because he saw to it that I was well taken care of that I received my nomination."

Even many of those, such as Molly Haskell, who were not entirely pursuaded of the validity of Richards's interpretation of Chandler's novel, found Mitchum impressive. She wrote: "Mitchum's age and iconographic wrinkles that he brings to any role are, in a sense, the keys in which the film has been composed. Aware of the resonance built into an older movie star's mere presence, today's writers and directors are learning how to exploit this gift from the medium. By simply rack-focusing on Mitchum in an occasional close-up, his face filling half the screen, Richards evokes an entire biography, a sense of the past, of weariness and reflection. The film adds another meaning to the 'farewell' of the title by becoming a twilight movie, a Trent's Last Case, into which the voice-over monologue, so familiar a device in the '40s, will fit as a kind of meditation on the genre. We are persuaded by Mitchum that this is the way Marlowe would look and think and feel if he were grown old, and if the funny, haunting saga of the lovesick gorilla and his two-faced woman were his last assignment. We sense that those eyes—a perennial 'cover,' suggesting the sophistication and concealing the true innocence that is also Marlowe's—are about to shut all the way for the big sleep."

On the other hand, those who liked the film were ecstatic. In *Glamour*, Michael Korda found Richards's film came close to rivaling *Chinatown*. ". . . But the important thing remains. Mitchum," he wrote. "He was, quite simply, an inspired choice, and like Marlowe himself, he is a rumpled skeptic who has seen it all."

Rex Reed found Mitchum's portrayal "so sardonic and lazily convincing" that he almost began questioning the presence of a camera. "Mitchum has been steadily growing as an actor, giving beautifully modulated performances, in *The Friends of Eddie Coyle* and *The Yakuza*, and *Farewell, My Lovely* is a tailor-made showcase for him." Reed ventured that this was the kind of movie Bogart would have stood in line to see.

Once again there were predictions that Mitchum would be nominated for an Oscar. Once again he was overlooked.

"Anyway you look at it, it's demeaning for a man of my age to work," Mitchum said. When Walter Mirisch approached him to play Admiral Chester W. Nimitz in his star-studded production *Midway*, a restaging of the epic World War II naval battle, Mitchum turned him down flat. He suggested instead Henry Fonda for the role. Mirisch then offered Mitchum the part of Rear Admiral Raymond A. Spruance and Mitchum proposed Glenn Ford. Again, Mirisch took his suggestion. Then Mitchum astonished Mirisch by suggesting that he play Admiral William F. (Bull) Halsey, who missed participating in the battle because he was bedridden with a skin ailment. He worked one day and donated his salary to charity.

His next move was less altruistic, but equally unorthodox. He played Pat Brady to Robert DeNiro's Monroe Stahr in the film version of F. Scott Fitzgerald's *The Last Tycoon*. In so doing, he violated a long-standing Hollywood tenet against a Hollywood star voluntarily demoting himself from leading man to supporting player. There followed predictions that he would never play another starring role. People began to take seriously his claim that he evaluated offers by how long it would take him to complete the assignment. Worse still, it seemed he might have misjudged the value of working under the direction of Elia Kazan in a Harold Pinter scenario. Upon release of the picture, he received the citation "extremely effective" from the *New York Times*, but he himself was more inclined to agree with the *Los Angeles Times*'s Charles Champlin, who found his performance dull. "I did see that [*The Last Tycoon*]" Mitchum confessed after saying he seldom attended films. "It's good, but dull. Still I got ten days' work and to wear a suit and to speak with some authority. So what the hell."

As the actor who had passed up *Dirty Harry* as "a piece of junk," the opportunity to appear in such a distinguished work as *Patton* because he didn't want to "spend all that time in a tank," and *Cat on a Hot Tin Roof* for no good reason, his judgment was open to question. Especially after he committed himself to appear as a dishonored drug agent fighting to clear his name in the misconceived *The Amsterdam Kill*. Or in a "but-why?" remake of *The Big Sleep* with Sarah Miles. "The whole thing was awful," she says. "Bob thought it could be transferred to London, but that didn't work. He was much nearer the mark in *Farewell, My Lovely* than all dressed up in *The Big Sleep*. And everyone else was miscast so I think the culprit was Michael Winner, the director, bless his heart." When the reviews came out *New York* magazine called it "The Big Snore"; *Time*, "Small Snooze"; and *Newsweek*, "The Big Yawn."

In *US* magazine, Mitchum cultist and Pulitzer Prize-winning critic Roger Ebert used his space to propose that children then in the first grade would make Mitchum "the next movie cult hero, the Humphrey Bogart of, say, 1990." Citing the release of *The Big Sleep* as an appropriate reason for comparing Mitchum and Bogart, he immediately segued into a discussion of Mitchum's portrayal in *Farewell, My Lovely*. Admitting that "when most movie classics are remade, the immediate reaction is outrage," he went on, "but Mitchum, aged 60, displays such cynicism, such wry understatement, such stubborn courage cloaked in surface indifference that he makes even Bogart look like a fresh kid trying a little too hard." Ebert also managed to include Warren Beatty's opinion that Mitchum is "one of the best actors. It's just that he doesn't call attention to his performance by doing anything more than exactly what the character calls for."

The decline continued with *Matilda*, a comedy about a boxing kangaroo who becomes a contender, in which Mitchum played a sports writer in support of Elliot Gould and actor Gary Morgan, who was hidden inside a thirty-thousand-dollar costume made of kangaroo skins and a computerized kangaroo head.

Agency, a Canadian-financed psychological thriller about the nefarious world of advertising, brought him star billing and big money for playing the heavy who is secreting subliminal political propaganda into television commercials. Playing more of an extended cameo than a role, Mitchum expended little effort on the film. A flop in theaters, *Agency* became a perennial on pay TV.

Breakthrough at 14, also known as *Breakthrough* and *Sergeant Steiner*, was a war film. A sequel to *Cross of Iron*, it was filmed in West Germany but aimed at the international market with a cast headed by Richard Burton, Rod Steiger and Mitchum. Although these three as well as Curt Jurgens, Michael Parks and others were praised for their performances, war films were out of fashion and this one disappeared without a trace.

Matilda (1978), *Breakthrough at 14* (1979) and *Agency* (1979) were all delayed before achieving limited release. Even so, both the films and Mitchum fared better than the supposedly suspenseful *Nightkill* (1980) in which Mitchum received fourth billing in a special box after Jaclyn Smith, Mike Connors and James Franciscus. Instead of releasing it theatrically as originally planned, the production company sold it directly to NBC-

TV, causing *The Hollywood Reporter* to comment that the move to dump the feature was no mystery. "Yes," the critic assured readers, "it's that bad."

Contributing something of a melancholy feeling of a career winding down and the desire on the part of reviewers to make up to a performer for past slights before it was too late, on October 9, 1980, the Los Angeles Film Critics Association chose Mitchum as the recipient of its Career Achievement Award. Surprisingly, he turned up to accept it and allowed critic Robert Osborne to introduce him as "living proof that without ever becoming a conformist you can still swim in the Hollywood waters." In an archetypical acceptance response, Mitchum wondered what had led the critics to pick him up from "the astral firmament." He said he had as a youngster enjoyed imagining himself as invisible and had held on to that illusion after becoming a working actor. It had taken a trip to the tank in the County Jail to disabuse him of his invisibility. Long after accepting the fact of his stardom, he said, he had persisted in turning down parts if he believed someone else could give a better performance. "I got to rest a lot that way," the confirmed insomniac confided, "but by my calculation I'm still nine years behind on my sleep." If those who assessed his work were curious about his reasons for choosing certain roles, he could only answer that it was because he liked the people making those pictures or he liked the places the movies were being shot. "A free lunch in Paris is better than a free lunch in Opeleika," he assured his listeners.

He closed by observing that there remained some question in his mind as to just how famous he had become. "No star on Hollywood Boulevard," he said with a distinctive shrug. "Hell, I'm like Lionel Barrymore, they'll wheel me out to play Scrooge when I'm eighty. I'm really a character actor, a mime, a dialectician."

CHAPTER 16

In 1978, the Mitchums surprised their friends by selling their home and moving ninety-five miles north of Los Angeles to Montecito where they bought a two-bedroom, ranch-style house with a pool overlooking the Pacific Ocean. Asked why, Mitchum explained, "It all got to be too much. Our house in Bel-Air seemed to be a halfway point between any two points. I spent most of my time dispensing flagons of expensive white wine to thirsty travelers." Surprisingly, he also sold his Atascadero ranch and most of his quarter horses. More surprisingly still, in the latter part of 1980, this man who had always maintained that he would only consider television if tragedy suddenly overtook him reversed himself. Forgotten was the contention that television would force him to work too hard. He agreed to play the pivotal role in a sixteen-hour mini series, the second longest ever produced by American television. It was Paramount Pictures' production of Herman Wouk's best-seller, *The Winds of War*, which was to cost $35,000,000 and to be shot in six countries. Mitchum was to play the central character, Navy captain Pug Henry, who hopscotches from one trouble spot to another in wartorn Europe from the time of

245

Hitler's invasion of Poland on September 1, 1939. Although Mitchum was older and considerably taller than Wouk's character, producer-director Dan Curtis said that after meeting the actor nobody else was even under consideration. Gary Nardino, then president of Paramount's television division said, "I put it like this. Name any other actor in the world at any price who would be better than Mitchum. He's the only Gary Cooper still alive."

Filming began in Long Beach around the *Queen Mary* in December of 1980. There Victoria Tennant, a neophyte who was playing the young woman with whom Pug Henry is tempted to have an affair, met the star for the first time. "I had the world's worst case of virus," she told *TV Guide* writer Bill O'Halloran. "When wake-up call came I had to crawl on my hands and knees to the bathroom. A driver took me to the set, the *Queen Mary*, and Mitchum turned out to be even bigger than I expected and he looked terribly fierce. I thought he would send me home. He said, 'Why don't we just walk up and down the deck and smile at each other?' Everything was fine from then on."

With Tennant and Polly Bergen, who played his wife, he showed his gentler side. Although reputedly Bergen was lured out of retirement from acting at his request, he pretended to be surprised to see her. Admitting that Mitchum can be intimidating, she says he is never "rough and tough with those who can't take care of themselves."

From Long Beach to Los Angeles to Zagreb, Yugoslavia, to Vienna and London—the filming ran to 267 locations requiring in excess of 4000 camera setups, 285 English-speaking actors and who knows how many anonymous extras. Mitchum's wardrobe consisted of ninety-seven changes which may have caused him more concern than interpreting the role. Early on, a makeup artist noticed that Mitchum had gone through his script and coded certain pages with a mysterious NAR. After pondering the meaning for a time, he inquired what the letters stood for. Mitchum shrugged and explained, "No acting required."

As for the physical hardships, Mitchum claimed the filming was uninterrupted agony. An old leg injury suffered during the making of *The Yakuza* flared up. He fell on the ice going to an outhouse and broke his shoulder on the right side, making the frequent salute exercises in pain. During the winter shoot in Yugoslavia, he developed pleural pneumonia. Talking about it later, he claimed to have coughed up blood one morning, causing everyone to ask how he had done that—as if it were a parlor trick. With customary exaggeration, he insisted that even the doctors avoided him in fear of contracting what he had.

James Butler, the ABC-TV publicist, recorded his impressions on the making of *The Winds of War* so vividly that ABC Television published the diary from which the following excerpts are drawn.

"Robert Mitchum will insist that it was 10° or 20° below every day. It wasn't—Mitchum I will discover never lets absolute accuracy interfere with a good story."

"Feb. 8: A gigantic party with a guest list of 450, including Robert and Dorothy Mitchum. . . . Dorothy, who has been Mrs. Mitchum for 40 years, is an attractive woman who travels with her husband whenever possible; she has been here for this rugged phase of the filming and now they will vacation together until he is called back in the spring. The company still has a few days filming left at Zagreb, but the Mitchums are well-liked by the cast and crew, so their departure seems reason enough to have the wrap party a little early."

"Vienna: His humor tends to be dry to a point that can confuse the literal minded, though. When he was introduced to a very serious young man from the Austrian Tourist Board his comment was: 'That's nice. Know your way around yet?'"

In a section titled: "Close Up: Robert Mitchum," some of Butler's random observations: "All things conspire against Robert Mitchum. . . . Shooting schedules are arranged to bedevil him. Producers plot together to assure he gets no more than two or three hours sleep a week. . . . On the other hand, Robert Mitchum gets more mileage out of those hard-times-everybody's-down-on-me stories than Rodney Dangerfield gets from a lifetime of disrespect. . . . Robert Mitchum has a good time with his hard times. . . . If Job had been gifted with a sense of humor hidden behind those hooded eyes, Job would have been Robert Mitchum. . . . Summing up his 'method' as an actor he told a Yugoslavian writer: 'I'm from the school of naughty boys.'"

Elsewhere Butler notes: "A key to Mitchum: It can be astonishing to discover how often that phrase—'I've read the book'—shows up in his conversation. And equally surprising to discover that he really has."

According to Butler, Mitchum not only read the novel but also the 967-page script as well.

Elsewhere, Butler ventured the opinion: "Mitchum represents something free and untamed in the American nature; something incorruptible, and that understated determination and honor are key elements in Pug Henry as well.

"Play the vulgarian, the bad boy, the been-down-so-long-it-looks-like-up-to-me cynic. That's the best way to hide vulnerability. And, above all, keep a ready sneer and the back of your hand for anything smacking of pretentiousness, of taking yourself seriously.

"On location he is singing softly to himself much of the endless time between scenes. Country songs, usually. His voice is warm, low, spirited. He sounds good. . . . Mitchum singing is the other Mitchum. The one the outsized complaints and stories of violence and obscenity are designed to shield. It's Mitchum wide-open, bare-faced for the world to see, and it makes him enormously human and enormously likeable. Listening to him sing blew the hell out of my objectivity, I like him."

On December 7, 1981, the fortieth anniversary of the bombing of Pearl Harbor, the event was recreated at Port Heuneme, California. One year and one week after the filming began, *The Winds of War* was completed.

Now Paramount was faced with the problem of editing the vast amount of footage down to the projected sixteen hours. By October of 1982, the conclusion was reached that to do so meant discarding effective scenes and diminishing the overall impact. The studio and ABC-TV announced that the forty-million-dollar production would run eighteen hours beginning February 6, 1983—making it, at that time, the second-longest mini-series telecast. The first three-hour segment drew a larger audience than the blockbusting premier episode of *Roots* had, and ratings held up well throughout the week.

*   *   *

During the editing of *The Winds of War*, Mitchum's resurgence as a major star got another boost. On July 7, 1982, he began filming *That Championship Season*. A decade earlier Jason Miller had won the triple crown with the stage version—a Pulitzer Prize, the New York Drama Critics Award and a Tony. Almost immediately, Playboy Productions had acquired the film rights; when they failed to get the screen version into production within seven years, Miller exercised his option to buy back those rights, paying approximately fifty percent of what he had received for them originally. Ironically, he was also forced to purchase his own screenplay from Playboy.

After a lengthy delay, Miller teamed with director William Friedkin. Together they attempted to produce the screenplay by persuading actors to help finance the film by accepting small salaries in return for percentages of anticipated profits. Initially, George C. Scott, Martin Sheen, Nick Nolte, Paul Sorvino and Miller himself were to head the cast. Conflicts between Scott and Friedkin led to Scott's withdrawing from the production. Then William Holden agreed to undertake the part of the coach which Scott had given up. But Holden's untimely, accidental death once again brought the project to a halt. Finally Menahem Golan and Yoram Globus agreed to produce the screenplay as written and to allow Miller to direct. Bruce Dern, Stacy Keach and, most importantly, Mitchum joined the cast.

Projections about what Mitchum would do with the role of the coach were so strong that before filming was finished rumors circulated that his was an interpretation of Academy Award caliber. In anticipation of his nomination as Best Actor of the Year, Mitchum's credits and biographies were extensively updated. The feeling was that at last the man and the perfect role had finally come together. Alas, early previews soon dispelled any such illusion.

At the beginning of the film, Miller attempted to "open up" the play. He introduced a political rally where one of the members of that championship season team is campaigning for mayor, then a bus station where a slightly seedy member of that golden team is arriving.

Four of the five champions—the fifth has never attended a

reunion for good and sufficient reason—assemble at the coach's house, from which they head for the site of their youthful triumph—the high school gymnasium. There, in a bittersweet scene, they toast one another and recall their glory days.

From that point on the going got tough. The struggle to hold the audience's attention mounted as the successive revelations that worked so well on the stage became little more than exposition in the film. Mitchum received good notices from such respected critics as Arthur Knight ("one of his strongest appearances in years"); Vincent Canby ("best of all is Mr. Mitchum, his laid-back authority works very well"); Judith Crist ("Robert Mitchum at his most subtle and satiric"); and Gene Shalit ("an all-star cast led by Robert Mitchum as you've never seen him before"). Equally respected critics held very contrary opinions, however; witness Sheila Benson of the *Los Angeles Times*. She wrote: "The film's most unsettling revelation is Robert Mitchum's performance as the coach. In addition to looking wrong for the part . . . Mitchum seems completely unsure of his man. There is no power, no snap in his delivery of the coach's aphorisms—the cornerstones of thinking that crippled his 'boys.'"

The release of *That Championship Season*, the telecasting of a movie-of-the-week, *One Shoe Makes It Murder*, in which Mitchum starred with Angie Dickinson, and especially the upcoming showing of *The Winds of War* resulted in a cornucopia of personal appearances on television and newspaper interviews. There were major stories in *Time, TV Guide, Newsweek* and *People*. *Time* and *TV Guide* gave him full-cover treatment and *Newsweek* squeezed a postage-stamp-size head shot between the sell-lines "Mitchum stars in 'Winds of War'" and "The split in Opec: Cheaper Oil Ahead." Everywhere there was a genuine outpouring of affection for the old rebel who had not only survived but triumphed. He was warmly welcomed on the *Tonight* show by Johnny Carson, and in one of his two appearances on *Today*, Gene Shalit described him as "one of the most popular of all film actors." Columns were filled with his comings, goings and witticisms. It was as if the prodigal son had at last rejoined the family.

On many occasions, he oozed charm; when he didn't, so

great was his personal magnetism the victim often forgave him. An observer at a press conference in Hollywood says, "He was curt and unresponsive to Kay Gardella of the *New York Daily News*. She came away steaming.* Then, at the subsequent group lunch she sat at a table with him . . . and he was witty, charming, professional, and provided her with more than enough material for a column." The person who reported this said, "I've seen him do that often: start by rejecting anything with the formality of a *question* . . . and then tale-telling for an hour."

On other occasions when the tequila or Scotch has been at hand, he has exploded the image of the sensitive nice guy who has always protected his true nature by gross behavior. He has simply become gross. For example, during the afternoon before the Manhattan premiere of *That Championship Season*, Cheryl Lavin of the *Chicago Tribune* attempted to interview him. She later told her readers that he was sucking on a Scotch and had been "living it up steadily since he arrived several days earlier." The interview, it seems, went badly. Speaking of it eight months later, there was still frost in Lavin's voice when she was questioned about it. From her manner, it was clearly an experience she would prefer not to think about.

In the story that appeared in the *Tribune*, Lavin portrayed Mitchum as a grumbling injustice collector, quoting him as complaining, "Everybody is pushing me. Grabbing me. Sticking their fingers in my face. Turn this way or this way. Everybody wants something." Her physical description of him was laced with venom. She called him "a wreck" with "thin mean lips," "dimples turned to wrinkles," and observed that he had a "healthy gut." Even so, she conceded that he retained his sex appeal.

The evening of the premiere she described the ordeal of a "woman reporter" who made an innocuous remark only to have the star "shove his hand down the V-opening of her blouse," grab her and ask whether this was what she wanted. Trying to "play it light," she said the woman reporter replied, "Well, I've got the lead to my story." This, she claimed, caused Mitchum to remove his hand from the woman's blouse, but he seized

---

*When contacted, Gardella denied being angry. She said she had not considered Mitchum's remarks rude, although she was aware others had.

the woman by the arm and bent it backward, demanding whether she would like him to humiliate her. In response to the woman's complaint that he was hurting her and her question about what she had done, Cheryl Lavin quoted him as answering that if she wanted ambulances he would gladly give them to her. He growled that he would give the reporter a real story to write.

Although the victim was described as a "woman reporter," it seemed likely that Lavin was writing about herself. Contacted and asked whether she was that woman, she replied, "That's right. He was twisting arms all evening. At first I thought it was a joke—until it happened to me. I don't really have a great deal more to say than what's in the story." Then she added, "Of course, I got off easy compared to the girl with the camera."

The incident also allegedly occurred at the party following the Manhattan premiere. Sometime during the evening, Mitchum and Martin Sheen arrived and were photographed—Sheen smiling, Mitchum sticking out his tongue.

Shortly after, Mitchum, who claimed his eyes had been blinded by the strobe lights, was approached by Yvonne Hemsey, a free-lance photographer, on assignment for *Time*, who had taken pictures of him during location filming in Scranton, Pennsylvania. "I'd requested a setup with his costars Martin Sheen, Stacy Keach, Bruce Dern and the director," Hemsey later said. "Someone threw a basketball to the guys as a prop. Mitchum threw it in my face. Directly at me. I was stunned. I didn't say anything at all. All I remember is getting hit." She said Mitchum had been in a bad mood even before the premiere and that the film's press agents had warned her and others to stay away from him, but since he had been affable to her during the shooting in Scranton, she had approached him anyway. The ball hit with such impact that it broke her camera, set off the flash equipment, knocked her eyeglasses to the floor and raised a bump on the side of her head.

Producer Menahem Golan, who witnessed the incident, immediately rushed to Hemsey's side and took her to Mitchum's. She said that the star refused to apologize or even discuss his actions. "He looked me right in the eye and said, 'Tough shit!' Then he mumbled something about fuck and said, 'This comes with the territory.'"

Two days later, not having received an apology for the alleged attack, Hemsey engaged attorney Joseh Ettinger to file a thirty-million-dollar lawsuit. Eventually the suit was dropped, as it was settled out of court.

As Mitchum was leaving New York, a few days after this incident, his erratic behavior again surfaced, although not a word about it appeared in the press until mid-February. This incident, which might be tagged "The Winds of Mitchum," occurred when he, Dorothy, Martin Sheen, Paul Sorvino, Bruce Dern and Stacy Keach entered the first-class, no-smoking section of TWA's Flight 7 at Kennedy Airport bound for Los Angeles. Already seated was Janet Sartin, operator of several New York beauty salons and manufacturer of a line of skin-care products. Sartin had been transferred to this smaller plane when the one upon which she had been booked malfunctioned. Since the plane was not equipped with individual air ducts, she had taken the front-most seat in the section because of her allergy to cigarette smoke.

During the flight she detected the smell of cigarette smoke and, although she had taken two antihistamines, she felt her throat begin to close. When she turned around in her seat, she saw that Mitchum, Dorothy and some of the others in his party were puffing away on cigarettes. She pointed out that they were in the no-smoking section and suggested they go to the area designated for smokers in the rear of the plane. With that, she says, Mitchum snuffed out his cigarette on the arm rest of his seat and said, "Next thing they'll have a no-farting area."

Later, according to her, Mitchum rose "like an old man," walked toward her seat, turned his back toward her, bent over and "let out a rolling burst of wind such as you've never heard in your life. Then he stood up proudly and looked around. Apparently he had discussed what he intended to do because he said to someone, 'I told you I could.'"

Sartin says she informed him that she had always been an admirer of his art, but what he had just done was rude and uncalled for. He ignored her and returned to his seat. There was no further contact between the Mitchum party and Sartin.

Next day she called a Los Angeles columnist who ran an account of the incident as a blind item. Then in February, a reporter from the *New York Post*'s "Page Six" contacted her and wrote up the story. She told him that while she still chuckled a bit when she saw Mitchum on the screen, for the most part she no longer enjoyed his work. "I don't appreciate him anymore. I thought he was a nice person, but he's common and coarse," she said.

By far the most serious image-shattering incident occurred when *Esquire* magazine's February 1983 issue, containing an interview with Mitchum, appeared on newsstands. It was written by Barry Rehfeld, a *Time* employee, and began with an account of Mitchum on the set of *That Championship Season* in the grip of his Sherwood Anderson syndrome, spinning fantastic tales, motivated by a desire, as Rehfeld interpreted it, to divert any curious intruders.

Next day, the interview continued in Montecito, where Mitchum began trotting out such staples as his oft-made contention that six-foot-four John Wayne wore four-inch lifts in his boots and a ten-gallon hat to make the world Wayne conscious.

Mitchum dismissed his own career, saying, "I was unclassifiable. I am not a leading man. I am not a heavy. I enjoy playing heavies, and I can be a most convincing heavy, but really I have a baritone voice, that's all." Adding, "I don't care what I play. I'll play Polish faggots, midgets, women, anything."

He recalled that he was offered the part of Stanley in *A Streetcar Named Desire* and went to the studio with it. According to him, he was given the explanation that every studio had a drawer full of scripts whose artistic merit was comparable to horseshit. And every studio had its horseshit salesman. At Paramount, he was Alan Ladd; at Warners, Humphrey Bogart; at RKO, salesman Mitchum. He didn't take exception to that often. He wanted to do the lead in *From Here to Eternity*, but Howard Hughes refused to let him do it. Mitchum told Rehfeld, "I had met Harry Cohn after a dinner and I had said to him, 'You don't seem like such a prick to me.' Cohn said, 'Wait till you work for me.' So then when Columbia came buzzing around about *Eternity*, we had secret meetings, and I put in a petition at RKO. I called Howard [Hughes] and he said, 'Jesus Christ, Bob, that's being done by those people up the street, isn't it?

All those Jews. You don't want to be associated with *those* people, Bob. They're terrible people.' So later I walk into Romanoff's for lunch and Harry Cohn is sitting there. He calls me chicken shit. I said, 'I tried.' He says, 'Bullshit, you tried.'"

When Rehfeld and Mitchum broke for lunch, there came more of Mitchum's standard routine about his approach to acting, flacks, as he calls press agents, how he offered to demonstrate what he did in the Army on the David Frost television show, his marijuana bust and its consequences, his confrontation with the old sensationalist rag *Confidential* and his explanation that he's sitting still for the interview only because it means publicity for *That Championship Season* and *The Winds of War*.

Then, in a sudden switch of mood, perhaps brought on by the double tequilas he'd been drinking, he says he's actually doing it for the film's publicist. "Like Eichmann said, 'Ees my job.'"

Rehfeld attempts to change the subject, but Mitchum persists, saying a bunch of his cronies were going to go to Israel wearing buttons saying, "I Like Ike" to see how that fared.

Eliciting no response from the interviewer, who happens to be Jewish, he asks, "How do you say 'Trust me' in Jewish?" Mitchum's answer: "Fuck you."

After a disagreement over Vietnam, the situation deteriorates. Mitchum tells of a colonel who said the war could be stopped in three days by blowing up a dam and sweeping everything out to sea. Rehfeld's mention of moral principles and Hitler leads Mitchum to observe, "Hitler needed *lebensraum* [elbow room]." When Rehfeld asks about the slaughter of six million Jews, Mitchum replies, "So the Jews say." Responding to Rehfeld's astonished "So the Jews *say*?" Mitchum answers, "I don't know. People dispute that."

From there the exchange ricochets off to implied approval of Adolf Eichmann and Idi Amin. Then, according to Rehfeld, seeming to sense he has gone too far, Mitchum calms down and tells how as a boy he used to light sabbath candles for friends in Philadelphia. Rehfeld asks about the blacks and Mitchum becomes indignant. "My family, being part Indian, were niggers," he says. "I grew up with bl——" He almost says blacks, but corrects himself. ". . . niggers all my life."

Rehfeld observes that the slip is interesting and brings up such past activities as writing the oratorio for Jewish relief presented by Orson Welles at Hollywood Bowl during the war. He also mentions Mitchum's narration of documentaries on drug abuse and alcoholism. Mitchum brushes it aside, saying, "I choose not to say why I act the way I do. It is all a matter of momentary instinct. Sometimes I piss on myself a little, but I do as well as I can most of the time. I think if I die of anything, it will be of embarrassment."

From that he segues into the futility of voting, claiming an international cartel controls who is elected President of the United States. He advises Rehfeld to get the story on the international conspiracy and warns that if he does, the banks that own the publications Rehfeld writes for will pull him up short. He asks if Rehfeld knows who Ralph Beaver Strassburger is and is appalled to receive a negative answer. Strassburger, he says, is a wealthy Pennsylvania newspaper publisher who married a Singer sewing machine heiress and ended up owning everything of importance in Pennsylvania as well as thousands of acres of land in Bavaria. Mitchum claims to have been his guest for the summer over there. He says he inquired where Strassburger's wealth came from and when Strassburger said he inherited it, Mitchum quotes himself as saying, "Don't give me my-inheritance crap, you sneaky hebe. All the mines, all the cities, you raped for them." Later, he claims he read *A Man Called Intrepid* which revealed the two greatest contributors to Hitler were Henry Ford and Ralph Beaver Strassburger. And it was Strassburger, so Mitchum claims, who told him who would be the next President of the United States.

Later, Rehfeld checks. Strassburger's land holdings are in France rather than Bavaria, Strassburger is not Jewish, and he made no direct contributions to Hitler.

Six hours have passed. Mitchum has consumed at least six tequilas. His conversation has rambled, from the CIA to Southeast Asia to the late Shah and the late villainous Strassburger. When Mitchum's wife enters and interrupts, he explodes. He threatens to have the publicity woman on *That Championship Season* dismissed. Sensing, perhaps, that he has been foolhardy, he demands to know what Rehfeld will write and predicts it will be something sensational, concluding, "I'm not the best interview in the world."

As Rehfeld is about to leave, he shakes Mitchum's hand. He has entered his car and is about to pull away when suddenly the door is pulled open. Rehfeld reports that there stood Mitchum with a gleam in his eye. Love? Hate? It could be either. Then the writer sees Mitchum extending a handful of paper towels and a diet Sunkist. Thrusting them at Rehfeld, he says, "It's a long way back. You might want a drink."

The publication of the article was greeted with consternation on all sides. Mitchum had widely been regarded as pro-Israel and pro-Jewish. Those who had been amused by his rebellious antics over the past forty years were mystified. Loyal friends speculated on the possibility that he had had a stroke or was losing his mind. Others thought he had been drunk, but took little consolation in that possibility, since, as one said, *"In vino veritas."* Those who had previously been indifferent shrugged the article off as the ravings of a lightweight, over-the-hill movie star seeking attention or simply marked him down as a bigot. Why take him seriously?

The Jewish Defense League answered that question. Having read Rehfeld's piece, the JDL executive chairman held a press conference against the background of a Nazi flag with Mitchum's photograph superimposed over a swastika. The JDL head called Mitchum "a Jew hater" and demanded an apology. Otherwise, he swore that the JDL would hire a private detective to locate the Mitchum residence. "This organization has in its ranks the best street fighters in the city of Los Angeles," he said. "If he doesn't apologize, we have to do everything in our power—legally, of course—to get him to. We don't want to do anything violent to him. But I can't be responsible for everything that happens in Mitchum's life. You know the JDL's eleventh commandment—'Thou Shalt Not Mess With God's Chosen People!'"

The *Los Angeles Herald-Examiner* ran a headline asking: "Is Pug Henry Really a Nazi?"

Mitchum, in face of a rising tide of criticism, uncharacteristically did not attempt to tough this one out. He claimed to have been joking, but nevertheless agreed to apologize. "It was just sort of an academic debate with me playing the coach and him [Rehfeld] playing the wounded journalist. I was just putting him on. I couldn't believe he didn't understand."

Although he resolutely refused to cooperate on this book and told a sister that I worked for *The National Enquirer* only to have her reply, "If so, it's the nicest thing I've heard about the *Enquirer*," I sent him the following letter:

Dear Mr. Mitchum:
I know that you do not want to cooperate with me in any way on my biography of you. However, in the interest of fairness, I want to tell you that a number of people have inquired whether or not I have read the interview with you in *Esquire*. All have been surprised or indignant at many of the statements allegedly made by you.

I, of course, have read it and am troubled by what comes across as anti-Semitic and anti-black attitudes. I have no way of knowing whether or not you have been correctly quoted. I would welcome any explanation that you may care to offer. In conducting my interviews, I have found that you are a well-loved figure and I don't want to include anything in the book that distorts your true position. On the other hand, the issue is one which cannot be ignored.

Sincerely,

A couple of weeks later, he answered in what appears to be a form letter:

Dear Mr. Eells:
In retrospect it appears unseemly that I took a holiday out of the country in February to return to a desk of letters such as yours. I actually had to borrow a copy of *Esquire* to learn what was going down.

For several months a young lady employed as a publicist by my employers had repeatedly suggested a meeting with a writer from *Esquire* magazine, which I steadily declined. Finally, under pressure, I reluctantly agreed, on the condition she be present. The writer arrived alone and, under the circumstances, not entirely welcome. I am quite sure that after the long procrastination he was aware of my lack of warmth in receiving him.

Early on in our meeting, I recited a speech by Coach Delaney of "That Championship Season" which he mistakenly believed to be my own. From that point on, he approached me as the character in the script, and in playing the devil's advocate, in a prankish attempt to string him along, we compounded a tragedy of errors.

I am truly sorry that this misunderstanding has upset so many people, especially since it is so foreign to my own principle. The attendant misfortune is that it has brought me a spate of mail from people and organizations who are encouraged to believe that I share their bigotry and discrimination.

In the future I shall either fairly represent myself, or assume a less abrasive character than Coach Delaney, and leave the realm of acid jest to the comedic talents of professionals like Richard Pryor or Don Rickles.

Sincerely,

Syndicated columnist Liz Smith phoned Mitchum at his home in Montecito and reported he was "perplexed and upset." He said the *Esquire* story "appalled" him. "In fact," he joked with the former Texan, "I am shocked. I think I have a general reputation for fairness and tolerance. Actually, I am not 'anti' anything—except maybe Texans.

"Unfortunately, what he printed was very selective to say the least. At one point, I quoted a speech right out of Jason Miller's 'That Championship Season.' It was so obviously old Coach Delaney's racist speech, but this reporter thought it was my own idea. So I kept putting him on because it kind of amused me and also, since he seemed intelligent, I figured he'd catch on. Also, maybe I was sort of showing off that I still remembered this long, extraordinary speech from the movie. It begins, 'Yea, Israel, I'm all for Israel. . . .'

"I didn't think anyone in his right mind would be fooled by

this. But he never asked, 'Do you really feel that way? How can you?' And he edited out a lot of the answers I gave him. So it seems that assuming the mantle of Coach Delaney was a tragic mistake. What else can I say? This is difficult; something like answering to, 'Have you stopped beating your wife?' It sounds absurd to say that I am not an anti-Semite. And also I have no platform unless someone like you calls me to ask. I have no press agent, and the whole thing makes me sad and angry."

Rehfeld's response to Mitchum's explanation was temperate. "It's really a ridiculous story that he was quoting dialogue—that's malarkey. It upsets me he would try such a lame tactic. He said it and that's it. You'd have to be coldly sophisticated to pass off the interview as a 100% snowjob. But I wouldn't take his remarks at face value. They're a mixture. I wouldn't discount any part. I wouldn't attribute them all to drunkenness. I wouldn't attribute them all to anti-Semitism. I wouldn't attribute it all to a put-on or contrariness. I would say there was some mixture of it, but I couldn't say to what degree it was any one thing.

"It's hard to say what state of inebriation he was in. I, for one, would have been drunk, had I drunk as much as he had drunk through the afternoon.

"There are some factual things which are disturbing about the man even before this. In interviews gone past he would brag of his friendship with the Shah. Now five or ten years ago, perhaps that was fine. But he still talks about him admiringly.

"There is no question the man is a conservative. I sort of challenged him on Vietnam and later the anti-Semitic remarks I thought were directed at my confronting him on that issue. I think he was quite honest in his feelings on Vietnam. He was going to see Goldwater the next day after I left. But again, even his friends, Goldwater and Sinatra, they're extremely pro-Israel and pro-Jewish. I said at the time and I say now I don't think too much should be made of it. The man is predictable only in that he will say anything to try to get a rise out of you.

"This time he went too far and he lost control. He gained nothing. Not even being outrageous. There are other ways to be outrageous. If not to shock me, at least to shock readers. I mean he's a complex man. There's good and bad in him, but there was no call for a lot of things he said."

Having apologized, Mitchum hunkered down to ride out the storm. The JDL faded into silence. Mitchum was signed for two or three movies of the week. Then another lawsuit was filed, one that may contain the key to the sudden, mysterious outbreak of boorish behavior.

The plaintiff was Reva Frederick Youngstein, Mitchum's "office manager, controller, script reader, personal finance manager and editor" of 34 years. Her suit stated that she had been felled by a disabling stroke and had been forced to take a temporary leave of absence in November, 1981. What it did not say was that Dorothy, who had always felt that she could perform the services rendered by Frederick, had gone into the office and begun examining records. Some of these already had been removed, but Dorothy was dissatisfied with what she found. Charges and counter charges flew back and forth, culminating in the firing of Frederick. On March 29, 1983, she filed an $1.85 million suit in Los Angeles Superior Court charging Mitchum with breaching an oral agreement, reached in 1977, promising Frederick $150,000 retirement benefits. (The case was settled out of court.)

Since then Mitchum's life has calmed down and the Hollywood community appears to have forgotten these last incidents in the checkered career of the film colony's self-proclaimed bad boy. Yet on August 4, a signal was given that he was not to escape without a reprimand. As star of the longest, most-highly publicized mini-series of the year it had seemed a foregone conclusion that he would be nominated for an Emmy as outstanding leading actor in a limited series or special. On that day, his name was missing from the list of nominees. The only plausible interpretation seemed to be that he was being served notice that he had finally gone too far.

Yet given his resilience, only a fool would predict what the future holds for this complicated, lovable, rebellious, infuriating, totally original man. For on October 7, 1983, little more than two months after his Emmy rebuff, Mitchum was the recipient of the third annual Life Achievement Award of the

American Theatre Arts. At a black-tie, $150-a-plate dinner, held at the Century Plaza, he received a framed letter from President Ronald Reagan commending him on a career, "spanning some 40 years and 130 films . . . and includes some of the classic performances in movies." Mayor Tom Bradley proclaimed October 5 Robert Mitchum Day in Los Angeles. The Secretary of the Army, the Secretary of the Navy, the Governor of California, Bette Davis, Ralph Bellamy, Frank Sinatra, John Huston, and Hal Linden sent messages or paid him compliments from the stage. And the president of the Hollywood Chamber of Commerce revealed that at last Mitchum was to receive his star on Hollywood Boulevard's Walk of Fame.

How did Mitchum behave? He remained sober, behaved well, accepted the accolades with wit and humility and completely charmed the assembled guests. Clearly, he is a man about whom one could say almost anything—and at some point be correct.

ROBERT MITCHUM
FILMOGRAPHY

Compiled by
Phil Boroff

Films are listed in the order of their release. Titles are followed by: alternate titles, if any; the producer and/or distributor; the year of release; the director; and the cast—starring and featured as well as selected bit players. The names of the characters that Mitchum played are indicated in parenthesis and quote marks after the initials, BM (for Bob Mitchum) or RM (for Robert Mitchum).

1. BORDER PATROL (Working Title: MISSING MEN), Harry Sherman/United Artists, '43. Dir: Lesley Selander. William Boyd, Andy Clyde, Jay Kirby, Russell Simpson, Claudia Drake, Duncan Renaldo, Cliff Parkinson, BM (as "Henchman"), Herman Hack, Pierce Lyden

2. HOPPY SERVES A WRIT, Harry Sherman/United Artists, '43. Dir: George Archainbaud. William Boyd, Andy Clyde, Jay Kirby, Victor Jory, George Reeves, Jan Christy, Hal Taliaferro, Forbes Murray, BM (as "Rigney"), Byron Foulger, Earle Hodgins, Roy Barcroft, Ben Corbett

3. THE LEATHER BURNERS, Harry Sherman/United Artists, '43. Dir: Joseph E. Henabery. William Boyd, Andy Clyde, Jay Kirby, Victor Jory, George Givot, Shelley Spencer, Bobby Larson, BM (as "Randall"), George Reeves, Hal Taliaferro, Forbes Murray

4. THE HUMAN COMEDY, MGM, '43. Prod-Dir: Clarence Brown. Mickey Rooney, James Craig, Frank Morgan, Fay Bainter, Marsha Hunt, Van Johnson, Donna Reed, John Craven, Dorothy Morris, Jackie "Butch" Jenkins, Mary Nash, Katharine Alexander, Ray Collins, Henry O'Neill, Darryl Hickman, S. Z. Sakall, Alan Baxter, Barry Nelson, Don DeFore, BM (as "Horse"), Ann Ayars, Ernest Whitman, Mark Daniels, William Roberts, Rita Quigley, David Holt, Byron Foulger, Wallis Clark, Wally Cassell, Mary Servoss, Morris Ankrum, Lynne Carver, Carl "Alfalfa" Switzer, Clem Bevans, Adeline de Walt Reynolds, Hobart Cavanaugh, Emory Parnell, Connie Gilchrist, Howard J. Stevenson, Frank Jenks, Howard Freeman, Robert Emmet O'Connor, Jay Ward, James Craven, Gibson Gowland, Sarah Padden, Don Taylor

5. AERIAL GUNNER, Pine-Thomas/Paramount, '43. Dir: William H. Pine. Chester Morris, Richard Arlen, Jimmy Lydon, Lita Ward, Dick Purcell, Keith Richards, Billy Benedict, Ralph Sanford, BM (as "Sergeant")

6. FOLLOW THE BAND, Universal, '43. Dir: Jean Yarbrough. Eddie Quillan, Mary Beth Hughes, Leon Errol, Anne Rooney, Samuel S. Hinds, BM (as "Tate Winters"), Russell Hicks, Bennie Bartlett, Frank Coghlan, Jr., Jean Ames, Frances Langford, Leo Carrillo, Ray Eberle, Alvino Rey and His Orchestra, The King Sisters, The King Men, Skinnay Ennis and The Groove Boys, Hilo Hattie, The Bombardiers, Irving Bacon, Isabel Randolph, Frank Faylen, Robert Dudley, Paul Dubov, Frank Mitchell, Joe Bernard, Charles Sherlock

7. COLT COMRADES, Harry Sherman/United Artists, '43. Dir: Lesley Selander. William Boyd, Andy Clyde, Jay Kirby, George Reeves, Gayle Lord, Earle Hodgins, Victor Jory, Douglas Fowley, BM (as "Bart"), Herbert Rawlinson

8. BAR 20, Harry Sherman/United Artists, '43. Dir: Lesley Selander. William Boyd, Andy Clyde, George Reeves, Dustin Farnum, Victor Jory, Douglas Fowley, Betty Blythe, BM (as "Richard Adams"), Francis McDonald, Earle Hodgins

9. WE'VE NEVER BEEN LICKED (aka FIGHTING COMMAND; British Title: TEXAS TO TOKYO), Walter Wanger/Universal, '43. Dir: John Rawlins. Richard Quine, Anne Gwynne, Martha O'Driscoll, Noah Beery, Jr., William Frawley, William Blees, Harry Davenport, Edgar Barrier, Samuel S. Hinds, Moroni Olsen, Roland Got, Allen Jung, BM (as "Panhandle Mitchell"), Alfredo DeSa, Bill Stern, George Putnam, Malcolm McTaggart, Paul Dubov, David Street, Dick Chandlee, Michael Moore, Danny Jackson, John Forrest, Ward Wood, Kenneth MacDonald, Mantan Moreland, John Hames, Don McGill, Paul Langton

10. CORVETTE K-225 (British Title: THE NELSON TOUCH), Howard Hawks/Universal, '43. Dir: Richard Rosson. Randolph Scott, James Brown, Ella Raines, Barry Fitzgerald, Andy Devine, Fuzzy Knight, Noah Berry, Jr., Richard Lane, Thomas Gomez, David Bruce, Murray Alper, James Flavin, Walter Sande, Oscar O'Shea, RM (as "Shephard"), John Frederick, Holmes Herbert, Gene O'Donnell, John Diggs, Edmund MacDonald, Matt Willis, Charles McGraw, Addison Richards, Jack Wegman, James Todd, Milburn Stone, Ian Wolfe, Lester Matthews, Frank Faylen, Guy Kingsford, George O'Hanlon, Oliver Prickett, William Forrest, Morton Lowry, Peter Lawford, Richard Crane

11. THE LONE STAR TRAIL, Universal, '43. Dir: Ray Taylor. Johnny Mack Brown, Tex Ritter, Fuzzy Knight, Jennifer Holt, George Eldredge, Harry Strang, Jack Ingram, BM (as "Ben Slocum"), Ethan Laidlow, James "Jimmy" Wakely Trio, Earle Hodgins, Henry Rocquemore, Michael Vallon, Eddie Parker, Reed Howes

12. CRY HAVOC, Edwin Knopf/MGM, '43. Dir: Richard Thorpe. Margaret Sullavan, Ann Sothern, Joan Blondell, Fay Bainter, Marsha Hunt, Ella Raines, Connie Gilchrist, Heather

Angel, Dorothy Morris, Gloria Grafton, Frances Gifford, Fely Franquelli, Diana Lewis, Billy Cruz, Allan Byron, William Bishop, James Warren, Richard Crane, Morris Ankrum, Richard Derr, Anna Q. Nilsson, Roque Espiritu, BM (as "Groaning Man"), Bob Lowell, Russ Clark

13. FALSE COLORS, Harry Sherman/United Artists, '43. Dir: George Archainbaud. William Boyd, Andy Clyde, Jimmy Rogers, Tom Seidel, Claudia Drake, Douglas Dumbrille, BM (as "Rip Austin"), Glenn Strange, Pierce Lyden, Roy Barcroft, Sam Flint, Earle Hodgins, Elmer Jerome, Tom Landon, Dan White, George Morrell

14. MINESWEEPER, Pine-Thomas/Paramount, '43. Dir: William Berke. Richard Arlen, Jean Parker, Russell Hayden, Guinn "Big Boy" Williams, Emma Dunn, Charles D. Brown, Frank Fenton, Chick Chandler, Douglas Fowley, Ralph Sanford, Billy Nelson, BM (as "Chuck")

15. BEYOND THE LAST FRONTIER, Republic, '43. Dir: Howard Bretherton. Eddie Dew, Smiley Burnette, Lorraine Miller, Ernie Adams, Richard Clarke, BM (as "Trigger Dolan"), Harry Woods, Charles Miller, Kermit Maynard, Jack Kirk, Wheaton Chambers

16. THE DANCING MASTERS, Lee Marcus/20th Century–Fox, '43. Dir: Malcolm St. Clair. Stan Laurel, Oliver Hardy, Trudy Marshall, Robert Bailey, Matt Briggs, Margaret Dumont, Allan Lane, BM (as "Mickey"), Nestor Paiva, George Lloyd, Edward Earle, Charles Rogers, Sherry Hall, Sam Ash, William Haade, Arthur Space, Daphne Pollard, Emory Parnell, Hank Mann, Buddy Yarus, Chick Collins, Robert Emmett Keane, Harry Tyler, George Tyne, Hallam Cooley, Jay Wilsey (Buffalo Bill, Jr.)

17. DOUGHBOYS IN IRELAND, Jack Fier/Columbia, '43. Dir: Lew Landers. Kenny Baker, Jeff Donnell, Lynn Merrick, Guy Bonham, Red Latham, Wamp Carlson, BM (as "Ernie Jones"), Buddy Yarus, Harry Shannon, Dorothy Vaughan, Larry Thompson, Syd Saylor, Herbert Rawlinson, Neil Reagan,

Constance Wood, Harry Anderson, James Carpenter, Craig Woods, Muni Seroff

18. RIDERS OF THE DEADLINE, Harry Sherman/United Artists, '43. Dir: Lesley Selander. William Boyd, Andy Clyde, Jimmy Rogers, Richard Crane, Frances Woodward, William Halligan, Tony Ward, BM (as "Drago"), Jim Bannon, Hugh Prosser, Herbert Rawlinson, Montie Montana, Earle Hodgins, Bill Beckford, Pierce Lyden, Herman Hack

19. GUNG HO!, Walter Wanger/Universal, '43. Dir: Ray Enright. Randolph Scott, Grace MacDonald, Alan Curtis, Noah Beery, Jr., J. Carroll Naish, David Bruce, Peter Coe, BM (as "Pigiron Mathews"), Rod Cameron, Louis Jean Heydt, Richard Lane, Milburn Stone, Sam Levene, Harold London, John James, Walter Sande, Harry Strang, Irving Bacon, Joe Hayworth, Carl Varnell, Robert Kent, Eddie Coke, Don McGill, Chet Huntley (Narrator)

20. MR. WINKLE GOES TO WAR (British Title: ARMS AND THE WOMAN), Jack Moss/Columbia, '44. Dir: Alfred E. Green. Edward G. Robinson, Ruth Warrick, Ted Donaldson, Bob Haymes, Richard Lane, Robert Armstrong, Richard Gaines, Walter Baldwin, Art Smith, Ann Shoemaker, Paul Stanton, Buddy Yarus, William Forrest, Bernadene Hayes, Jeff Donnell, Howard Freeman, Nancy Evans, Ann Loos, Larry Thompson, Early Cantrell, Warren Ashe, James Flavin, BM (as "Corporal"), Herbert Hayes, Fred Kohler, Jr., Fred Lord, Cecil Ballerino, Ted Holley, Ben Taggart, Sam Flint, Nelson Leigh, Forbes Murray, Hugh Beaumont, Emmett Vogan, Tommy Cook, Bobby Larson, Harry McKim

21. GIRL RUSH, John Auer/RKO Radio, '44. Dir: Gordon Douglas. Wally Brown, Alan Carney, Frances Langford, Vera Vague (Barbara Jo Allen), RM (as "Jimmy Smith"), Paul Hurst, Patti Brill, Sarah Padden, Cy Kendall, John Merton, Diana King, Michael Vallon, Sherry Hall, Kernan Cripps, Wheaton Chambers, Ernie Adams, Lee Phelps, Byron Foulger, Chili Williams, Rita Corday, Dale Van Sickle, Bud Osborne.

22. JOHNNY DOESN'T LIVE HERE ANYMORE (aka AND SO THEY WERE MARRIED), King (Maurice and Frank) Brothers/Monogram, '44. Dir: Joe May. Simone Simon, James Ellison, William Terry, Minna Gombell, Chick Chandler, Alan Dinehart, Gladys Blake, RM (as "CPO Jeff Daniels"), Dorothy Granger, Grady Sutton, Chester Clute, Fern Emmett, Jerry Maren, Joe Devlin, Janet Shaw, Charles Williams, Douglas Fowley, Harry Depp, Duke York, Emmett Lynn, Pat Gleason, Milton Kibbee, Sid Melton, George Chandler, Dick Rich, Frank Scannell, Rondo Hatton, Mike Vallon, Mary Field, George Humbert

23. NEVADA, Sid Rogell and Herman Scholm/RKO Radio, '44. Dir: Edward Killy. RM (as "Jim 'Nevada' Lacy"), Anne Jeffreys, Guinn "Big Boy" Williams, Nancy Gates, Richard Martin, Craig Reynolds, Harry Woods, Edmund Glover, Alan Ward, Harry McKim, Larry Wheat, Jack Overman, Emmett Lynn, Wheaton Chambers, Philip Morris, Mary Halsey, Patti Brill, Russell Hopton, Bryant Washburn, Sammy Blum

24. WHEN STRANGERS MARRY (aka BETRAYED), King (Maurice and Frank) Brothers/Monogram, '44. Dir: William Castle, Dean Jagger, Kim Hunter, RM (as "Fred"), Neil Hamilton, Lou Lubin, Milt Kibbee, Dewey Robinson, Claire Whitney, Edward Keane, Virginia Sale, Dick Elliott, Lee "Lasses" White, Minerva Urecal, Marta Mitrovitch, Rhonda Fleming, George Lloyd, Billy Nelson, Weldon Heyburn, Sam McDaniel

25. THIRTY SECONDS OVER TOKYO, Sam Zimbalist/MGM, '44. Dir: Mervyn LeRoy. Spencer Tracy, Van Johnson, Robert Walker, Sr., Phyllis Thaxter, Tim Murdock, Scott McKay, Gordon McDonald, Don DeFore, RM (as "Bob Gray"), John R. Reilly, Horace (Stephen) McNally, Donald Curtis, Louis Jean Heydt, William "Bill" Phillips, Douglas Cowan, Paul Langton, Leon Ames, Moroni Olsen, Morris Ankrum, Selena Royle, Benson Fong, Dr. Hsin Kung Chan Chi, Myrna Dell, Peggy Maley, Hazel Brooks, Elaine Shepard, Kay Williams, Dorothy Ruth Morris, Ann Shoemaker, Alan Napier, Wah Lee, Chin Wah Lee, Jacqueline White, Jack McClendon,

John Kellogg, Peter Varney, Steve Brodie, Harry Hayden, Blake Edwards, Will Walls, Jay Norris, Robert Bice, Bill Williams, Wally Cassell, Carlyle Blackwell, Jr., Walter Sande, Arthur Space, John Dehner

26. WEST OF THE PECOS, Sid Rogell and Herman Schlom/ RKO Radio, '45. Dir: Edward Killy. RM (as "Pecos Smith"), Barbara Hale, Richard Martin, Thurston Hall, Rita Corday, Russell Hopton, Bill Williams, Harry Woods, Bruce Edwards, Perc Landers, Bryant Washburn, Philip Morris, Martin Garralaga, Sammy Blum, Italia DeNubila, Ethan Laidlaw, Jack Gargan, Larry Wheat

27. THE STORY OF G.I. JOE (aka G.I. JOE and ERNIE PYLE'S THE STORY OF G.I. JOE), Lester Cowan/United Artists, '45. Dir: William A. Wellman. Burgess Meredith, RM (as "Lt. Walker"), Freddie Steele, Wally Cassell, Jimmy Lloyd, Jack Reilly, Bill Murphy, William Self, Dick Rich, Billy Benedict, Tito Renaldo, Dorothy Coonan Wellman, and the Combat Veterans of the African, Sicilian and Italian Campaigns

28. TILL THE END OF TIME, Dore Schary/RKO Radio, '46. Dir: Edward Dmytryk. Dorothy McGuire, Guy Madison, RM (as "William Tabeshaw"), Bill Williams, Tom Tully, William Gargan, Jean Porter, Johnny Sands, Loren Tindall, Ruth Nelson, Selena Royle, Harry Von Zell, Richard Benedict, Dickie Tyler, Stan Johnson, Billy Newell, Lee Slater, Robert Lowell, Peter Varney, Richard Slattery, Harry Hayden, Mary Worth, Tim Ryan, Ellen Corby, Teddy Infuhr, Blake Edwards, William Forrest, Arthur Loft, Tito Renaldo, Dick Elliott, Eddie Craven

29. UNDERCURRENT, Pandro S. Berman/MGM, '46. Dir: Vincente Minnelli. Katharine Hepburn, Robert Taylor, RM (as "Michael Garroway"), Edmund Gwenn, Marjorie Main, Jayne Meadows, Clinton Sundberg, Dan Tobin, Kathryn Card, Leigh Whipper, Charles Trowbridge, James Westerfield, Billy McLain, Bess Flowers, Sarah Edwards, Betty Blythe, Milton Kibbee, Forbes Murray, Wheaton Chambers, Barbara Billingsley, Hank Worden, Gordon Richards, Robert Emmet O'Connor

30. THE LOCKET, Jack L. Gross and Bert Granet/RKO Radio, '46. Dir: John Brahm. Laraine Day, Brian Aherne, RM (as "Norman Clyde"), Gene Raymond, Sharyn Moffett, Ricardo Cortez, Henry Stephenson, Katherine Emery, Reginald Denny, Fay Helm, Helene Thimig, Nella Walker, Queenie Leonard, Lilian Fontaine, Myrna Dell, Johnny Clark, Vivien Oakland, George Humbert, Connie Leon, Sam Flint, Wyndham Standing, Ellen Corby, Martha Hyer, Mari Aldon, Fred Worlock, Leonard Mudie

31. CROSSFIRE, Dore Schary and Adrian Scott, RKO Radio, '47. Dir: Edward Dmytryk. Robert Young, RM (as "Sgt. Peter Kelley"), Robert Ryan, Gloria Grahame, Paul Kelly, Sam Levene, Jacqueline White, Steve Brodie, George Cooper, Richard Benedict, Richard Powers (Tom Keene), William Phipps, Lex Barker, Marlo Dwyer, Harry Harvey, Carl Faulkner, Jay Norris, Robert Bray, George Turner, Philip Morris, Kenneth MacDonald, Allen Ray, Don Cadell, Bill Nind, George Meader

32. PURSUED, A United States Picture–Milton Sperling/ Warner Brothers, '47. Dir: Raoul Walsh. Teresa Wright, RM (as "Jeb Rand"), Judith Anderson, Dean Jagger, Alan Hale, Harry Carey, Jr., John Rodney, Clifton Young, Ernest Severn, Charles Bates, Peggy Miller, Norman Jolley, Lane Chandler, Elmer Ellingwood, Jack Montgomery, Ian MacDonald, Ray Teal, Ian Wolfe, Virginia Brissac, Eddy Waller, Russ Clark, Crane Whitley, Lester Dorr, Erville Alderson, Charles Miller, Tom Fadden

33. DESIRE ME (Working Title: SACRED AND PROFANE), Arthur Hornblow, Jr./MGM, '47. Dir: No official credit, although done by George Cukor, Jack Conway and Mervyn LeRoy. Greer Garson, RM (as "Paul Aubert"), Richard Hart, Morris Ankrum, George Zucco, Cecil Humphreys, David Hoffman, Max Williams (Willenz), Clinton Sundberg, Mitchell Lewis, Hans Schumm, Jean Del Val, Stanley Andrews, Harry Wood, Sam Ash, Earle Hodgins, Gil Perkins, Albert Petit

34. OUT OF THE PAST (British Title: BUILD MY GALLOWS HIGH), Robert Sparks and Warren Duff/RKO Radio,

'47. Dir. Jacques Tourneur. RM (as "Jeff Bailey"), Jane Greer, Kirk Douglas, Rhonda Fleming, Richard Webb, Steve Brodie, Virginia Huston, Paul Valentine, Dickie Moore, Ken Miles, Frank Wilcox, Mary Field, Harry Hayden, Brooks Benedict, Theresa Harris, Michael Branden, John Kellogg, Oliver Blake, Philip Morris

35. RACHEL AND THE STRANGER, Jack L. Gross and Richard H. Berger/RKO Radio, '48, Dir: Norman Foster. Loretta Young, William Holden, RM (as "Jim Fairways"), Gary Gray, Tom Tully, Sara Haden, Frank Ferguson, Walter Baldwin, Regina Wallace, Frank Conlan

36. BLOOD ON THE MOON, Sid Rogell and Theron Warth/ RKO Radio, '48. Dir: Robert Wise. RM (as "Jimmy Garry"), Barbara Bel Geddes, Robert Preston, Walter Brennan, Phyllis Thaxter, Frank Faylen, Tom Tully, Charles McGraw, Clifton Young, Tom Tyler, George Cooper, Richard Powers (Tom Keene), Bud Osborne, Zon Murray, Robert Bray, Al Ferguson, Ben Corbett, Joe Devlin, Erville Alderson, Chris-Pin Martin, Harry Carey, Jr., Hal Taliaferro, Iron Eyes Cody

37. THE RED PONY, Lewis Milestone/Charles K. Feldman Group Production/Republic, '49. Prod/Dir: Lewis Milestone. Myrna Loy, RM (as "Billy Buck"), Louis Calhern, Sheppard Strudwick, Peter Miles, Margaret Hamilton, Patty King, Jackie Jackson, Beau Bridges, Nino Tempo, Tommy Sheridan, Little Brown Jug, Wee Willie Davis, George Tyne, Max Wagner

38. THE BIG STEAL, Sid Rogell and Jack L. Gross/RKO Radio, '49. Dir: Don Siegel. RM (as "Lt. Duke Halliday"), Jane Greer, William Bendix, Patrick Knowles, Ramon Novarro, Don Alvarado, John Qualen, Pasqual Garcia Pena, Frank Hagney, Virginia Farmer, Don Dillaway, Pat O'Malley, Rodolfo Hoyos, Salvador Baquez, Alfredo Soto

39. HOLIDAY AFFAIR, RKO Radio, '49. Prod/Dir: Don Hartman. RM (as "Steve Mason"), Janet Leigh, Wendell Corey, Gordon Gebert, Griff Barnett, Esther Dale, Henry O'Neill, Henry (Harry) Morgan, Larry J. Blake, Helen Brown, James

Griffith, Don Dillaway, George Eldredge, Frank Mills, Chick Chandler, Philip Morris

40. WHERE DANGER LIVES, A John Farrow Production–Irving Cummings, Jr./RKO Radio, '50. Dir: John Farrow. RM (as "Jeff Cameron"), Faith Domergue, Claude Rains, Maureen O'Sullivan, Charles Kemper, Ralph Dumke, Billy House, Harry Shannon, Philip Van Zandt, Jack Kelly, Lillian West, Julia Faye, Dorothy Abbott, Elaine Riley, Stanley Andrews, Jack Kruschen, Gaylord (Steve) Pendleton, Tol Avery, Sherry Jackson, Ray Teal, Lester Dorr, Herschel Daugherty, Geraldine Wall, Jim Dundee, Ethan Laidlaw, Earle Hodgins, Julian Rivero, Stuart Holmes, Erno Verebes

41. MY FORBIDDEN PAST (Working Title: CARRIAGE ENTRANCE), Robert Sparks and Polan Banks/RKO Radio, '51. Dir: Robert Stevenson. RM (as "Dr. Mark Lucas"), Ava Gardner, Melvyn Douglas, Lucile Watson, Janis Carter, Gordon Oliver, Basil Ruysdael, Clarence Muse, Walter Kingsford, Jack Briggs, Will Wright, Cliff Clark, Ken MacDonald, Everett Glass, Daniel de Laurentis

42. HIS KIND OF WOMAN, Howard Hughes and Robert Sparks/RKO Radio, '51. Dir: John Farrow. RM (as "Dan Miller"), Jane Russell, Vincent Price, Tim Holt, Charles McGraw, Marjorie Reynolds, Raymond Burr, Leslye Banning, Jim Backus, Carlton Young, Philip Van Zandt, John Mylong, Erno Verebes, Dan White, Richard Berggren, Stacy Harris, Robert Cornthwaite, Paul Frees, Daniel de Laurentis, John Sheehan, Anthony Caruso, Tol Avery, Mickey Simpson, Joan Olander (Mamie Van Doren), Joel Fluellen, Don House, Stuart Holmes, Dan Borzage, Dorothy Abbott, Mike Lally, Peter Brocco, Henry Guttman, Alberto Morin

43. THE RACKET, A Howard Hughes Production–Edmund Grainger/RKO Radio, '51. Dir: John Cromwell. RM (as "Capt. Thomas McQuigg"), Lizabeth Scott, Robert Ryan, William Talman, Ray Collins, Joyce MacKenzie, Robert Hutton, Virginia Huston, William Conrad, Walter Sande, Les Tremayne, Don Porter, Walter Baldwin, Howland Chamberlain, Brett King,

Richard Karlan, Tito Vuolo, William Forrest, Howard Petrie, Max Wagner, Ralph Peters, Iris Adrian, Mike Lally, Pat Flaherty, Milburn Stone, Don Beddoe, Richard Reeves, Don Dillaway, Matthew Boulton, George Sherwood, Herb Vigran, Harry Lauter, Gregg Barton

44. MACAO, A Howard Hughes Presentation–Samuel Bischoff and Alex Gottlieb/RKO Radio, '52. Dir: Josef von Sternberg (and uncredited Nicholas Ray). RM (as "Nick Cochran"), Jane Russell, William Bendix, Thomas Gomez, Gloria Grahame, Brad Dexter, Edward Ashley, Philip Ahn, Valdimir Sokoloff, Don Zelaya, Emory Parnell, Philip Van Zandt, Alex Montoya, Everett Glass, Trevor Bardette, Michael Visaroff

45. ONE MINUTE TO ZERO, A Howard Hughes Presentation –Edward Grainger/RKO Radio, '52. Dir: Tay Garnett. RM (as "Col. Steve Janowski"), Ann Blyth, William Talman, Charles McGraw, Margaret Sheridan, Richard Egan, Eduard Franz, Robert Osterloh, Robert Gist, Eddie Firestone, Roy Roberts, Tom Irish, Lalo Rios, Wally Cassell, Ted Ryan, Hal Baylor, Buddy Swan, Maurice Marsac, William Forrest, Tyler McVey, Dorothy Granger, Robert Bray, Stuart Whitman, Roque Espiritu

46. THE LUSTY MEN, A Wald/Krasna Production–Jerry Wald and Norman Krasna/RKO Radio, '52. Dir: Nicholas Ray. Susan Hayward, RM (as "Jeff McCloud"), Arthur Kennedy, Arthur Hunnicutt, Frank Faylen, Walter Coy, Carol Nugent, Maria Hart, Lorna Thayer, Burt Mustin, Karen King, Jimmy Dodd, Eleanor Todd, Sam Flint, Robert Bray, Sheb Wooley, Paul E. Burns, George Wallace, John McKee, Mike Lally, Dick Crockett, Chili Williams, Richard Reeves, Roy Glenn, Emmett Lynn, Glenn Strange, Denver Pyle, George Sherwood, Lane Chandler

47. ANGEL FACE, Howard Hughes/RKO Radio, '52.Dir: Otto Preminger. RM (as "Frank Jessup"), Jean Simmons, Mona Freeman, Herbert Marshall, Leon Ames, Barbara O'Neil, Kenneth Tobey, Raymond Greenleaf, Gritt Barnett, Robert Gist, Jim Backus, Morgan Farley, Alex Gerry, Bess Flowers, Mike

Lally, Gertrude Astor, Grandon Rhodes, Theresa Harris, Larry Blake, George Sherwood, Charles Tannen

48. WHITE WITCH DOCTOR, Otto Lang/20th Century–Fox, '53. Dir: Henry Hathaway. Susan Hayward, RM (as "Lonni Douglas"), Walter Slezak, Mashood Ajala, Joseph C. Narcisse, Elzie Emanuel, Timothy Carey, Everett Brown, Otis Greene, Paul Thompson, Naaman Brown, Myrtle Anderson, Dorothy Harris, Michael Ansara, Michael Granger, Floyd Shackleford, Charles Gemora

49. SECOND CHANCE, A Howard Hughes Presentation– Edmund Grainger and Sam Wiesenthal/RKO Radio, '53. Dir: Rudolph Mate. RM (as "Russ Lambert"), Linda Darnell, Jack Palance, Sandro Giglio, Rodolfo Hoyos, Jr., Reginald Sheffield, Margaret Brewster, Roy Roberts, Salvador Baquez, Maurice Jara, Jody Walsh, Dan Seymour, Fortunio Bonanova, Milburn Stone, Abel Fernandez, Michael Tolan, Martin Garralaga, Luis Alvares, Max Wagner, Eddie LeBaron, Tony Roux

50. SHE COULDN'T SAY NO (aka SHE HAD TO SAY YES; British Title: BEAUTIFUL BUT DANGEROUS), A Howard Hughes Production–Robert Sparks/RKO Radio, '54. Dir: Lloyd Bacon. Jean Simmons, RM (as "Doc"), Arthur Hunnicutt, Edgar Buchanan, Wallace Ford, Raymond Walburn, Jimmy Hunt, Ralph Dumke, Hope Landin, Gus Schilling, Eleanor Todd, Pinky Tomlin, Burt Mustin, Martha Wentworth, Goria Winters, Wallis Clark, Florence Lake, Jonathan Hale, James Craven, Tol Avery, Mike Lally, Leo Sulky, Clarence Muse, Dabbs Greer, Dan White, Charles Watts, Charles Cane

51. RIVER OF NO RETURN, Stanley Rubin/20th Century– Fox, '54. Dir: Otto Preminger. RM (as "Matt Calder"), Marilyn Monroe, Rory Calhoun, Tommy Rettig, Murvyn Vye, Douglas Spencer, Ed Hinton, Don Beddoe, Claire Andre, Jack Mather, Edmund Cobb, Will Wright, Jarma Lewis, Hal Baylor, Arthur Shields, John Doucette, Barbara Nichols, Paul Newlan, Ralph Sanford, Mitchell Lawrence, Harry Seymour

52. TRACK OF THE CAT, A Wayne/Fellows Production/ Warner Brothers, '54. Dir: William A. Wellman. RM (as "Curt Bridges"), Teresa Wright, Diana Lynn, Tab Hunter, Beulah Bondi, Philip Tonge, William Hopper, Carl "Alfalfa" Switzer

53. NOT AS A STRANGER, United Artists, '55. Prod-Dir: Stanley Kramer. Olivia de Havilland, RM (as "Lucas Marsh"), Frank Sinatra, Gloria Grahame, Broderick Crawford, Charles Bickford, Myron McCormick, Lon Chaney, Jr., Jesse White, Harry Morgan, Lee Marvin, Virginia Christine, Whit Bissell, Jack Raine

54. THE NIGHT OF THE HUNTER, Paul Gregory/United Artists, '55. Dir: Charles Laughton. RM (as "Preacher Harry Powell"), Shelley Winters, Lillian Gish, James Gleason, Evelyn Varden, Peter Graves, Billy Chapin, Sally Jane Bruce, Don Beddoe, Gloria Castillo, Mary Ellen Clemons, Cheryl Callaway

55. MAN WITH THE GUN (British Title: THE TROUBLE SHOOTER), Samuel Goldwyn, Jr./United Artists, '55. Dir: Richard Wilson. RM (as "Clint Tollinger"), Jan Sterling, Karen Sharpe, Henry Hull, Emile Meyer, John Lupton, Barbara Lawrence, Joe Barry, Ted De Corsia, Leo Gordon, James Westerfield, Florenz Ames, Robert Osterloh, Jay Adler, Amzie Strickland, Stafford Repp, Thom Conroy, Maudie Prickett, Mara McAfee, Angie Dickinson, Norma Calderon

56. FOREGIN INTRIGUE, A Sheldon Reynolds Production/ United Artists, '56. Prod-Dir: Sheldon Reynolds. RM (as "Dave Bishop"), Genevieve Page, Ingrid Tulean (Thulin), Frederick O'Brady, Eugene Deckers, Inga Tidblad, John Padovano, Frederick Schrecker, Lauritz Falk, Peter Copley, Ralph Brown, George Hubert, Nil Sperber, Jean Galland, Jim Gerald, John Starck, Gilbert Robin, Valentine Camax, Robert Le Beal, Albert Simmons

57. BANDIDO!, A Robert L. Jacks/Bandido Production— Robert L. Jacks/United Artists, '56. Dir: Richard Fleischer.

RM (as "Richard Wilson"), Ursula Thiess, Gilbert Roland, Zachary Scott, Jose I. Torvay, Henry Brandon, Douglas Fowley, Rodolfo Acosta, Victor Junco, Alfonso Sanchez Tello, Arturo Manrique, Margarita Luna, Jose A. Espinosa, Miguel Inclan, Manuel Sanchez Navarro, Albert Pedret, Antonio Sandoval

58. HEAVEN KNOWS, MR. ALLISON, Buddy Adler and Eugene Frenke/20th Century–Fox, '57. Dir: John Huston. Deborah Kerr, RM (as "Corporal Allison, USMC")

59. FIRE DOWN BELOW, Warwick Films–Irving Allen and Albert R. Broccoli/Columbia, '57. Dir: Robert Parrish. Rita Hayworth, RM (as "Felix"), Jack Lemmon, Herbert Lom, Bonar Colleano, Bernard Lee, Edric Connor, Peter Illing, Joan Miller, Anthony Newley, Eric Pohlmann, Lionel Murton, Vivian Matalon

60. THE ENEMY BELOW, 20th Century–Fox, '57. Prod-Dir: Dick Powell. RM (as "Captain Murrell"), Curt Jurgens, Al (David) Hedison, Theodore Bikel, Russell Collins, Kurt Kreuger, Frank Albertson, Biff Elliott, Alan Dexter, Doug McClure, Jeff Daley, David Blair, Joe di Reda, Ralph Manza, Ted Perritt, Jimmy Bayes, Arthur La Ral, Frank Obershall, Robert Boon, Werner Reichow, Peter Dane, Ronnie Rondell, Lee J. Winters, David Post, Ralph Reed, Maurice Donner, Jack Kramer, Robert Whiteside

61. THUNDER ROAD, A DRM Production/United Artists, '58. Dir: Arthur Ripley. RM (as "Lucas Doolin"), Gene Barry, Jacques Aubuchon, Keely Smith, Trevor Bardette, Sandra Knight, James Mitchum, Betsy Holt, Frances Koon, Randy Sparks, Mitch Ryan, Peter Breck, Peter Hornsby, Jerry Hardin, Robert Porterfield

62. THE HUNTERS, 20th Century–Fox, '58. Prod-Dir: Dick Powell. RM (as "Major Cleve Saville"), Robert Wagner, Richard Egan, May Britt, Lee Philips, John Gabriel, Stacy Harris, Victor Sen Yung, Candace Lee, Leon Lontoc, John Doucette,

Ralph Manza, Nobu McCarthy, Nina Shipman, Jay Jostyn, Robert Reed

63. THE ANGRY HILLS, A Raymond Stross Production—Raymond Stross/MGM, '59. Dir: Robert Aldrich. RM (as "Mike Morrison"), Elisabeth Mueller, Stanley Baker, Gia Scala, Theodore Bikel, Sebastian Cabot, Peter Illing, Leslie Phillips, Donald Wolfit, Marius Goring, Jackie Lane, Kieron Moore, George Pastell, Patrick Jordan, Martita Constantiou, Alec Mango, Stanley Van Beers

64. THE WONDERFUL COUNTRY, A DRM Production—Robert Mitchum and Chester Erskine/United Artists, '59. Dir: Robert Parrish. RM (as "Martin Brady"), Julie London, Gary Merrill, Pedro Armendariz, Jack Oakie, Albert Dekker, Charles McGraw, Leroy "Satchel" Paige, Victor Mendoza, Mike Kellin, John Banner, Anthony Caruso, Tom Lea

65. HOME FROM THE HILL, A Sol C. Siegel Production—Edmund Grainger, MGM, '60. Dir: Vincente Minnelli. RM (as "Capt. Wade Hunnicutt"), Eleanor Parker, George Peppard, George Hamilton, Luana Patten, Everett Sloane, Anne Seymour, Constance Ford, Ken Renard, Ray Teal, Hilda Haynes, Charlie Briggs, Guinn "Big Boy" Williams, Dan Sheridan, Orville Sherman, Dub Taylor, Stuart Randall, Tom Gilson, Joe Ed Russell, Burt Mustin, Rev. Duncan Gray, Jr.

66. THE SUNDOWNERS, Gerry Blattner/Warner Brothers, '60. Dir: Fred Zinnemann. Deborah Kerr, RM (as "Paddy Carmody"), Peter Ustinov, Glynis Johns, Dina Merrill, Chips Rafferty, Michael Anderson, Jr., Lola Brooks, Wylie Watson, John Meillon, Ronald Fraser, Mervyn Johns, Molly Urquart, Ewen Solon

67. THE NIGHT FIGHTERS (British Title: A TERRIBLE BEAUTY), A DRM/Raymond Stross Production—Raymond Stross/United Artists, '60. Dir: Tay Garnett. RM (as "Dermot O'Neill"), Anne Heywood, Dan O'Herlihy, Cyril Cusack, Richard Harris, Marianne Benet, Niall MacGinnis, Harry Bro-

gan, Eileen Crowe, Geoffrey Golden, Hilton Edwards, Wilfrid
Downing, Christopher Rhodes, Eddie Golden, Joe Lynch, Jim
Neylan, T. R. McKenna

68. THE GRASS IS GREENER, Universal, '60. Pro-Dir:
Stanley Donen. Cary Grant, Deborah Kerr, Jean Simmons, RM
(as "Charles Delacro"), Moray Watson

69. THE LAST TIME I SAW ARCHIE, A Mark VII Ltd./
Talbot Production/United Artists, '61. Prod-Dir: Jack Webb.
RM (as "Archie Hall"), Jack Webb, Martha Hyer, France Nuyen,
Joe Flynn, James Lydon, Del Moore, Louis Nye, Richard Ar-
len, Don Knotts, Robert Strauss, Harvey Lembeck, Claudia
Barrett, Theona Bryant, Elaine Davis, Marilyn Burtis, James
Mitchum, Gene McCarthy, Howard McNear, John Nolan, Mar-
tin Dean, Robert Clarke, Nancy Kulp, Bill Kilmer, Phil Gor-
don, Dick Cathcart

70. CAPE FEAR, A Melville/Talbot Production—Sy Bartlett/
Universal, '62. Dir: J. Lee Thompson. Gregory Peck, RM (as
"Max Cady"), Polly Bergen, Lori Martin, Martin Balsam, Jack
Kruschen, Telly Savalas, Barrie Chase, Paul Comi, Edward
Platt, John McKee, Page Slattery, Ward Ramsey, Will Wright,
Joan Staley, Mack Williams, Thomas Newman, Bunny Rhea,
Carol Sydes, Alan Reynolds, Herb Armstrong, Al Silvani, Paul
Levitt, Norma Yost, Allan Ray, Jack Richardson

71. THE LONGEST DAY, Darryl F. Zanuck/20th Century—
Fox, '62. Dirs: Andrew Marton, Ken Annakin and Bernhard
Wicki (and uncredited Darryl F. Zanuck). John Wayne, RM
(as "Brig. Gen. James M. Gavin"), Henry Fonda, Robert Ryan,
Rod Steiger, Robert Wagner, Richard Beymer, Mel Ferrer,
Jeffrey Hunter, Paul Anka, Sal Mineo, Roddy McDowall, Stuart
Whitman, Steve Forrest, Eddie Albert, Edmond O'Brien,
Fabian, Red Buttons, Tom Tryon, Alexander Knox, Tommy
Sands, Ray Danton, Henry Grace, Mark Damon, Dewey Mar-
tin, George Segal, John Crawford, Ron Randall, Nicholas Stuart,
John Meillon, Fred Dur, Peter Helm, Richard Burton, Kenneth
More, Peter Lawford, Richard Todd, Leo Genn, John Gregson,
Sean Connery, Jack Hedley, Michael Medwin, Norman Ros-

sington, John Robinson, Patrick Barr, Leslie Phillips, Donald Houston, Frank Finlay, Bryan Coleman, Neil Callum, Trevor Reid, Simon Lack, Louis Mounier, Sian Phillips, Richard Wattis, Christopher Lee, Irina Demich, Bourvil, Jean-Louis Barrault, Christian Marquand, Arletty, Madeleine Renaud, Georges Riviere, Jean Servais, Georges Wilson, Fernand Ledoux, Maurice Poli, Alice Tissot, Jo D'Avray, Curt Jurgens, Werner Hinz, Paul Hartmann, Gert Frobe (Gerd Froebe), Hans Christian Blech, Wolfgang Preiss, Peter Van Eyck, Heinz Reincke, Richard Munch, Ernest Schroeder, Karl Meisel, Heinz Spitzner, Robert Freytag, Til Kiew, Wolfgang Luckschy, Eugene Deckers

72. TWO FOR THE SEESAW, A Mirisch Company/Argyle Enterprises/Talbot Productions–Seven Arts Production–Walter Mirisch/United Artists, '62. Dir: Robert Wise. RM (as "Jerry Ryan"), Shirley MacLaine, Edmond Ryan, Elisabeth Fraser, Eddie Firestone, Billy Gray

73. THE LIST OF ADRIAN MESSENGER, A Joel Productions–Edward Lewis/Universal-International, '63. Dir: John Huston. George C. Scott, Dana Wynter, Clive Brook, Gladys Cooper, Herbert Marshall, Jacques Roux, John Merivale, Marcel Dalio, Bernard Archard, Walter Anthony "Tony" Huston, Roland DeLong, Anita Sharp-Bolster, Alan Caillou, John Huston, Noel Purcell, Richard Peel, Bernard Fox, Delphi Lawrence, Tony Curtis, Kirk Douglas, Burt Lancaster, RM (Cameo Role in Disguise, as "Jim Slattery"), Frank Sinatra

74. RAMPAGE, A Talbot Production–William Fadiman/Warner Brothers, '63. Dir: Phil Karlson. RM (as "Harry Stanton"), Elsa Martinelli, Jack Hawkins, Sabu, Cely Carrillo, Emile Genest, Stefan Schnabel, David Cadiente, Paul Busch, Teru Shimada, James Gavin, Charles Radilac, Michael Lally Greening, Sig Rumann, Marelyn Darrow, Ralph Helfer

75. MAN IN THE MIDDLE, A Talbot/Pennebaker Production–Max E. Youngstein and Walter Seltzer, 20th Century–Fox, '64. Dir: Guy Hamilton. RM (as "Lt. Col. Barney Adams"), France Nuyen, Barry Sullivan, Trevor Howard, Kennan Wynn,

Sam Wanamaker, Alexander Knox, Gary Cockrell, Robert Nicholls, Michael Goodliffe, Errol John, Paul Maxwell, Lionel Murton, Russell Napier, Jared Allen, David Bauer, Edward Underdown

76. WHAT A WAY TO GO!, An Apjac Production—Arthur P. Jacobs/20th Century—Fox, '64. Dir: J. Lee Thompson. Shirley MacLaine, Paul Newman, RM (as "Rod Anderson"), Dean Martin, Gene Kelly, Bob Cummings, Dick Van Dyke, Reginald Gardiner, Margaret Dumont, Lou Nova, Fifi D'Orsay, Maurice Marsac, Wally Vernon, Jane Wald, Lenny Kent, Marjorie Bennett, Christopher Connelly, Barbara Bouchet, Tom Conway, Queenie Leonard, Anthony Eustrel, Phil Arnold, Richard Wilson, Sid Gould, Paula Lane, Armand "Army" Archerd, Roy Gordon, Burt Mustin, Billy Corcoran, Jeff Fithian, Pamelyn Ferdin, Maurice Dellimore, Jean Del Val, Jacques Roux, Eugene Borden, Milton Frome

77. MISTER MOSES, A Frank Ross/Talbot Production—Frank Ross/United Artists, '65. Dir: Ronald Neame. RM (as "Joe Moses"), Carroll Baker, Ian Bannen, Alexander Knox, Raymond St. Jacques, Orlando Martins, Reginald Beckwith

78. THE WAY WEST, A Harold Hecht Production—Harold Hecht/United Artists, '67. Dir: Andrew V. McLaglen. Kirk Douglas, RM (as "Dick Summers"), Richard Widmark, Lola Albright, Michael Witney, Stubby Kaye, Sally Field, Katherine Justice, Michael McGreevey, Harry Carey, Jr., Connie Sawyer, Elisabeth Fraser, William Lundigan, Paul Lukather, Roy Barcroft, Patric Knowles, Ken Murray, John Mitchum, Nick Cravat, Roy Glenn, Anne Barton, Eve McVeagh, Peggy Stewart, Stefan Angrim, Michael Lane, Michael Heep, Jack Elam, Eddie Little Sky, Paul Wexler

79. EL DORADO, A Howard Hawks Production/Paramount, '67. Prod-Dir: Howard Hawks. John Wayne, RM (as "Sheriff J. B. Hurrah"), James Caan, Charlene Holt, Michele Carey, Arthur Hunnicutt, Edward Asner, R. G. Armstrong, Paul Fix, Christopher George, Johnny Crawford, Robert Rothwell, Adam Roarke, Chuck Courtney, Robert Donner, John Gabriel, Jim

Davis, Mariana Ghane, Anne Newman, Diane Strom, Victoria George, Olaf Wieghorst, Buzz Henry, John Mitchum, Rodolfo Hoyos, Don Collier

80. ANZIO (Original Italian Title: LOS BARCO DI ANZIO [THE ANZIO LANDING] British Title: THE BATTLE FOR ANZIO), A Dino De Laurentiis Production–Dino De Laurentiis/ Columbia, '68. Dir: Edward Dmytryk. RM (as "Dick Ennis"), Peter Falk, Arthur Kennedy, Robert Ryan, Earl Holliman, Mark Damon, Reni Santoni, Joseph Walsh, Thomas Hunter, Giancarlo Giannini, Anthony Steel, Patrick Magee, Arthur Franz, Tonio Selwart, Elsa Albani, Wayde Preston, Venantino Venantini, Annabella Andreoli, Wolfgang Preiss, Stefanella Giovannini, Marcella Valeri, Enzo Turco, Wolf Hollinger

81. FIVE CARD STUD, A Hal Wallis Production–Hal B. Wallis/Paramount, '68. Dir: Henry Hathaway. Dean Martin, RM (as "Rev. Jonathan Rudd"), Inger Stevens, Roddy McDowall, Katherine Justice, John Anderson, Ruth Springford, Yaphet Kotto, Denver Pyle, Whit Bissell, Ted De Corsia, Don Collier, Roy Jenson, Bill Fletcher, Jerry Gatlin, Hope Summers, Louise Lorimer

82. VILLA RIDES!, Ted Richmond/Paramount, '68. Dir: Buzz Kulik. Yul Brynner, RM (as "Lee Arnold"), Charles Bronson, Grazia Buccella, Robert Viharo, Frank Wolff, Herbert Lom, Alexander Knox, Diana Lorys, Robert Carricart, Fernando Rey, John Ireland

83. SECRET CEREMONY, A Paul M. Heller Production– John Heyman and Norman Priggen, '68. Dir: Joseph Losey. Elizabeth Taylor, Mia Farrow, RM (as "Albert"), Pamela Brown, Peggy Ashcroft, Michael Strong, Robert Douglas

84. YOUNG BILLY YOUNG, A Talbot/Youngstein Production–Max E. Youngstein/United Artists, '69. Dir: Burt Kennedy. RM (as "Ben Kane"), Angie Dickinson, Robert Walker, Jr., David Carradine, Jack Kelly, John Anderson, Paul Fix, Willis Bouchey, Parley Baer, Bob Anderson, Deana Martin, Rodolfo Acosta

85. THE GOOD GUYS AND THE BAD GUYS, Robert Goldstein, Ronald M. Cohen and Dennis Shryack/Warner Brothers–Seven Arts, '69. Dir: Burt Kennedy. RM (as "James Flagg"), George Kennedy, Martin Balsam, Tina Louise, Lois Nettleton, Douglas V. Fowley, John Carradine, John Davis Chandler, Marie Windsor, Dick Peabody, Kathleen Freeman, Jimmy Murphy, Garrett Lewis, Nick Dennis, Angela Greene, Dorothy Adams, Buddy Hackett, Governor David Cargo, Dick (Richard) Farnsworth

86. RYAN'S DAUGHTER, A Faraway Production for EMI–Anthony Havelock-Allan/MGM, '70. Dir: David Lean. RM (as "Charles Shaughnessy"), Sarah Miles, Trevor Howard, Christopher Jones, John Mills, Leo McKern, Barry Foster, Arthur "Archie" O'Sullivan, Marie Kean, Yvonne Crowley, Barry Johnson, Douglas Sheldon, Philip O'Flynn, Ed O'Callaghan, Gerald Sim, Des Keogh, Niall Toibin, Donal Meligan, Brian O'Higgins, Niall O'Brien, Owen O'Sullivan, Emmet Bergin, May Cluskey, Annie Dalton, Pat Layde

87. GOING HOME, A Herbert B. Leonard/Talbot Production/MGM, '71. Prod-Dir: Herbert B. Leonard. RM (as "Harry K. Graham"), Brenda Vaccaro, Jan-Michael Vincent, Jason Bernard, Sally Kirkland, Joe Attles, Lou Gilbert, Josh Mostel, Barbara Brownell, Carol Gustafson, Vicki Sue Robinson, George Mathews, Sylvia Miles

88. THE WRATH OF GOD, A Ralph Nelson Film for Rainbow Productions and Cineman Films–Peter Katz/MGM, '72. Prod-Dir: Ralph Nelson. RM (as "Father Van Horne"), Frank Langella, Rita Hayworth, John Colicos, Victor Buono, Ken Hutchinson, Paula Prichett, Gregory Sierra, Frank Ramirez, Enrique Lucero

89. THE FRIENDS OF EDDIE COYLE, Paul Monash/Paramount, '73. Dir: Peter Yates. RM (as "Eddie Coyle"), Peter Boyle, Richard Jordan, Steven Keats, Alex Rocco, Joe Santos, Mitchell Ryan, Helena Carroll, Peter MacLean, Kevin O'Morrison, Carolyn Pickman, Marvin Lichterman, James

Tolkan, Matthew Cowles, Margaret Ladd, Jane House, Michael McCleery, Alan Koss, Dennis McMullen, Judith Ogden Cabot, Jan Egleson, Jack Kehoe, Robert Anthony, Gus Johnson, Ted Maynard, Sheldon Feldner

90. THE YAKUZA, Shundo Koji–Michael Hamilburg/Warner Brothers, '75. Prod-Dir: Sydney Pollack. RM (as "Harry Kilmer"), Takakura Ken, Brian Keith, Herb Edelman, Richard Jordan, Kishi Keiko, Okada Eiji, James Shigeta, Kyosuke Mashida, Go Eiji, Christina Kokubo, Lee Chirillo, M. Hisaka, William Ross, Akiyama, Harada

91. FAREWELL, MY LOVELY, An E.K./ITC Production–Elliott Kastner and Jerry Bick, George Pappas and Jerry Bruckheimer/Avco Embassy, '75. Dir: Dick Richards. RM (as "Philip Marlowe"), Charlotte Rampling, John Ireland, Sylvia Miles, Anthony Zerbe, Harry Dean Stanton, Jack O'Halloran, Joe Spinell, Sylvester Stallone, Kate Murtagh, John O'Leary, Walter McGinn, Jim Thompson, Logan Ramsey, Stu Gilliam, Joan Shawlee

92. MIDWAY, A Walter Mirisch Production–Walter Mirisch/Universal, '76. Dir: Jack Smight. Charlton Heston, Henry Fonda, James Coburn, Glenn Ford, Hal Holbrook, Toshiro Mifune, RM (as "Adm. William F. Halsey"), Cliff Robertson, Robert Wagner, Robert Webber, Ed Nelson, James Shigeta, Christina Kokubo, Monte Markham, Bill McGuire, Kevin Dobson, Christopher George, Glenn Corbett, George Walcott, Edward Albert, Dabney Coleman, Conrad Yama, Dale Ishimoto, Larry Csonka, Pat Morita, Clyde Kusatsu, Erik Estrada, Kip Niven, Robert Ito, Steven Kanaly

93. THE LAST TYCOON, A Sam Spiegel/Elia Kazan Film–San Spiegel/Paramount, '76. Dir: Elia Kazan. Robert DeNiro, Tony Curtis, RM (as "Pat Brady"), Jeanne Moreau, Jack Nicholson, Donald Pleasence, Ingrid Boulting, Ray Milland, Dana Andrews, Theresa Russell, Peter Strauss, Tige Andrews, Morgan Farley, Jeff Corey, John Carradine, Diane Shalet, Seymour Cassell, Angelica Huston, Bonnie Bartlett, Sharon Mas-

ters, Eric Christmas, Leslie Curtis, Lloyd Kino, Brendan Burns, Carrie Miller, Peggy Feury, Betsey Jones-Moreland, Patricia Singer

94. THE AMSTERDAM KILL (aka QUINLAN MUST DIE!), Golden Harvest-Raymond Chow and Andre Morgan/ Columbia, '77. Dir: Robert Clouse. RM (as "Quinlan"), Bradford Dillman, Richard Egan, Leslie Nielsen, Keye Luke, George Cheung, Chan Sing, Stephen Leung

95. THE BIG SLEEP, An E.K./ITC Production–Elliott Kastner and Jerry Bick/United Artists, '78. Prod-Dir: Michael Winner, RM (as "Philip Marlowe"), Sarah Miles, Richard Boone, Candy Clark, Joan Collins, Edward Fox, John Mills, Oliver Reed, James Stewart, Harry Andrews, Colin Blakely, Richard Todd, Diana Quick, James Donald, John Justin, Simon Turner, Martin Potter, David Saville, Dudley Sutton, Don Henderson, Nik Forster, Joe Ritchie, Patrick Durkin, Derek Deadman

96. MATILDA, An Albert S. Ruddy Production–Richard R. St. Johns and Albert S. Ruddy/American-International, '78. Dir: Daniel Mann. Elliott Gould, RM (as "Duke Parkhurst"), Harry Guardino, Clive Revill, Karen Carlson, Roy Clark, Lionel Stander, Art Metrano, Larry Pennell, Roberta Collins, Lenny Montana, Frank Avianca, John Lennon, Don Dunphy, George Latka, Mike Willesee

97. BREAKTHROUGH (aka SERGEANT STEINER), Palladium (Hubert Lukowski)–Rapid Film Production, Munich–Wolf C. Hartwig, Ted Richmond, Achim Selius and Alex Winitzky/Maverick Pictures International, '79. Dir: Andrew V. McLaglen. Richard Burton, Rod Steiger, RM (as "Colonel Rogers"), Curt Jurgens, Helmuth Griem, Michael Parks, Klaus Loewitsch, Veronique Vendell, Joachim Hansen

98. AGENCY, RSL Films, Ambassador (Canada)–Robert Lantos and Stephen J. Roth/Jensen Farley, Inc., '79. Dir: George Kaczender. RM (as "Ted Quinn"), Lee Majors, Valerie Perrine, Saul Rubinek, Alexandra Stewart, Hayward Morse, Anthony Parr, Michael Kirby, Gary Reineke, George Tauliatos, Jonathan

Welsh, Hugh Webster, Franz Russell, Malcolm Nelthorpe, Marilyn Gardner, Eric Donkin, Donald Davis

99. NIGHTKILL (aka NIGHT KILL), Cine Artists–Davis Gil and Richard Hellman/Avco Embassy, '80. Dir: Ted Post. RM (as "Donner"), Jaclyn Smith, Mike Connors, James Franciscus, Fritz Weaver, Sybil Danning, Tina Menard, Belinda Mayne, Burke Rhind, Don Myers

100. ONE SHOE MAKES IT MURDER (Working Title: SO LITTLE CAUSE FOR CAROLINE) (TV Movie), The Fellows-Keegan Co., in association with Lorimar Productions, Inc.–Arthur Fellows, Terry Keegan and Mel Ferrer/CBS '82. Dir: William Hale. RM (as "Harold Shillman"), Angie Dickinson, Mel Ferrer, Jose Perez, John Harkins, Howard Hesseman, Asher Brauner, Bill Henderson, Catherine Shirriff, William Schilling, Sandy Martin, Grainger Hines, Peter Renaday, Tony Matranga, Roger Rook, Valerie C. Ribinson

101. THAT CHAMPIONSHIP SEASON. A Golan-Globus Production–Menahem Golan and Yoram Globus–Robert F. Levine/Cannon Films, '82. Dir: Jason Miller. Bruce Dern, Stacy Keach, RM (as "Coach Delaney"), Martin Sheen, Paul Sorvino, Arthur Franz, Michael Bernosky, Joseph Kelly, James M. Langan, Terry Santaniello, William G. McAndrew, Barry Weiner

102. THE WINDS OF WAR (TV Mini-Series), Paramount TV and Dan Curtis Productions/ABC, '83. Prod-Dir: Dan Curtis. RM (as "Harry 'Pug' Henry"), Ali McGraw, Jan Michael Vincent, John Houseman, Polly Bergen, Lisa Eilbacher, David Dukes, Topol, Ben Murphy, Peter Graves, Jeremy Kemp, Ralph Bellamy, Victoria Tennant, Ben Astar, Richard Barnes, William Berger, Peter Bourne, Scott Brady, Peter Brocco, Justin Buehrlen, David Cardy, Francesco Carnelutti, John Carter, Enzo Castellari, Anatoly Changuinian, Allan Cuthbertson, John Dehner, Anton Diffring, Andrew Duggan, Sky Dumont, Belle Ellig, Stefan Gierasch, Hugh Gillin, Jack Ging, Leo V. Gordon, Joseph Hacker III, Eloise Hardt, Elizabeth Hoffman, John Karlen, Mickey Knox, Rene Kolldehoff, Charles Lane, Howard Lang, Michael Logan, Art Lund, Ken Lynch, Ferdy Mayne,

Gunter Meisner, Byron Morrow, Barry Morse, George Murdock, Linwood McCarthy, Tom McFadden, Edmund Peege, Ben Piazza, Roy Poole, Wolfgang Preiss, Lawrence Pressman, Edmund Purdom, Osman Ragheb, Logan Ramsey, James Ray, Ron Rifkin, Richard X. Slattery, Barbara Steele, Deborah Winters, William Woodson (Narrator)

103. A KILLER IN THE FAMILY (Working Title: CASA GRANDE) (TV Movie), Stan Margulies Productions, in association with Sunn Classic Pictures, a Taft Entertainment Company—Stan Margulies, Paul Freeman and Robert Aller/ABC, '83. Dir: Richard Heffron. RM (as "Gary Tison"), James Spader, Lance Kerwin, Eric Stoltz, Salome Jens, Lynn Carlin, Arliss Howard, Amanda Wyss, Susan Swift, Catherine Mary Stewart, Stuart Margolin

104. MARIA'S LOVERS, A Golan-Globus Production—Menahem Golan and Yoram Globus, Lawrence Mortorff and Bosko Djordjevic/MGM/United Artists and Cannon Films, '84. Dir: Andrei Konchalovsky. Nastassia Kinski, John Savage, RM (as "Ivan's Father"), Keith Carradine, Anita Morris, Bud Cort, Karen Young, Tracy Nelson, Vincent Spano

105. THE AMBASSADOR, A Golan-Globus Production—Menahem Golan and Yoram Globus/MGM/United Artists and Canon Films, '84. Dir: J. Lee Thompson. RM (as "Peter Hacker"), Ellen Burstyn, Rock Hudson, Fabio Testi

INDEX

Bestselling Books
from Berkley